Advance

M000085512

"*Life After Lockdown* is brilliant. It is a must-needed resource for every-one who loves or supports an autistic person! Further, even though this book is structured around COVID, this book has a much broader reach. In reality, this book is essential for <u>any</u> novel situation—any situation in which guidance, support, or instruction would be helpful. Refer to this book anytime that ideas are needed for <u>any</u> situation. Essential, easy-to-read, and very accessible."

-**Brenda Smith Myles, PhD, Author and Speaker**

"Whether you're a self-advocate, parent, educator, or medical profes-sional, *Life After Lockdown: Resetting Perceptions of Autism* provides the positivity and energy needed to bring the autism community together during otherwise unpredictable times. This collection of essays written by more than 40 distinctive voices skillfully explores our new world as we attempt to return to post-pandemic daily life. From sensory issues and social struggles to anxieties and emotional health, *Life After Lockdown* uniquely presents the strategies and encouragement needed to move forward."

-**Amy KD Tobik, Editor-in-Chief, *Exceptional Needs Today*,**
CEO, Lone Heron Publishing

"As a high school autism teacher, *Life After Lockdown* has helped me tremendously to support my students as they transition back into the classroom. The book is full of strategies to help people on the autism spectrum deal with the uncertainties of COVID-19, as well as strategies to help adjust to life as the country continues to open back up. Professionals, parents of autistic children, and autistic individuals share their experiences and insights in this extraordinary masterpiece. Perfect material for teachers as children all over the country are return-ing to school."

-**Amanda Ackerman, RCOE Special Education Teacher**

"Sharing our stories, experiences, and strategies is a time-honored way to help each of us make sense of, cope with, and learn from difficult times. Given the sudden onset of the COVID-19 pandemic and its ongoing global impact on humanity, particularly on autistic individuals, the many different points of view shared in this book assure readers they'll find valuable information to inspire their own quest to understand themselves in the world as they learn to manage their feelings, emotions, actions, and reactions to meet their own goals, especially when life is unpredictable and unsettling."

-Michelle Garcia Winner, Founder of the Social Thinking Methodology, Speech-Language Pathologist, MA-CCC

"The stories of other's experiences made me feel validated. The strategies help address the anxiety that accompanies returning to work, school, and social settings. The pandemic required a lot of flexibility and taxed my family's coping mechanisms. I'm thankful to have this resource to help us ease back into the world after lockdown."

-Laura Sneden, Parent

"This book is a wonderful response to a global event that challenged and united many of us, an event that caused many to rethink and re-evaluate what we know and what we needed to know about ourselves and about autism. The book is full of useful knowledge and wisdom from an impressive collection of credible writers, thinkers, and individuals. As well as experienced and authoritative names, there are some that are new to me but in every section, there is valuable information and much to learn.

In my view, this outstanding resource will have a shelf-life way beyond the pandemic and our current experiences. I was particularly taken with how some skills and qualities, such as transitioning and resilience were highlighted and promoted. I suspect that I will find myself referring to it often and sharing it with individuals, families, and professionals. The book may be entitled *Life After Lockdown*, but it is so much more. Thank you to everyone involved. This is an essential book."

-Jim Taylor, Award-winning Speaker and Consultant, Chair of the Expert Advisory Body, Scotland, UK

Life After Lockdown: Resetting Perspectives of Autism is the go-to book we all need now! Clearly written and well-organized, *Life After Lockdown* is chock full of clear information and easy-to-follow tips. Individuals on the spectrum share their personal stories and insight on how they coped with the lockdown, and how they are now helping themselves navigate this new world after lockdown. Professionals and parents include useful advice that has helped them teach or support students or loved ones on the spectrum. Often when reading you may be reminded of a strategy you used before, long-forgotten—but definitely needed in your toolbox now. *Life After Lockdown* is a great resource you will use often.

-Chantal Sicile-Kira, Author of 5 books on autism and co-author of *A Full Life with Autism*, Founder, Autismcollege.com

"*Life After Lockdown* is an incredibly practical guide to living with COVID. While the book's title is 'Life After Lockdown' the truth is additional lockdowns may be looming on the horizon. Trying to adjust to this reality with no long-term idea of what to expect is challenging for everyone. This book offers practical advice on how to manage this new normal from top educators, therapists, and individuals on the spectrum. Each chapter explains what is working NOW to help individuals become social again, manage anxiety, manage the issues of going back to school, and more. On a personal note, I found myself identifying with several of the personal stories and have found a few strategies that I will personally be using. This is a must-have resource that I will be recommending to both families and educators."

-Bonnie Arnwine, Founder and President, National Autism Resources

"*Life After Lockdown* is such a timely resource full of practical tips as well as meaningful and inspiring stories that describe people's lived experiences both during the stay-at-home orders as well as during the periods of reopening. There is something in this book for caregivers, educators, professionals, and people with autism. So many evidence-based practices are described in very practical ways and links to additional resources where the reader can learn more. The usefulness of this resource will go far beyond this pandemic as a guide to assist with many of the things that individuals with autism, their caregivers, and professionals may find challenging."

-Patricia Schetter, MA, BCBA, Executive Coordinator, CAPTAIN

"The pandemic and its aftermath have dramatically impacted many aspects of life. For individuals on the spectrum, this has made a confusing world even more perplexing. Since there is considerable diversity within the spectrum population and significant individual variations in what will work, contributions from a large number of authors help ensure that strategies appropriate for each individual can be identified. With the overwhelm and uncertainty that so many changes experienced at the same time can readily bring about, I am pleased to see that a number of the chapters address dealing with anxiety and maintaining emotional well-being. I also appreciate the emphasis on experiences of individuals at different stages in their lifespan. Quite a treasure chest of insight, strategies, and perspective!"

-Lars Perner, PhD, Assistant Professor of Clinical Marketing, Department of Marketing, Marshall School of Business, University of Southern California

"Whether you are looking for guidance on helping someone with COVID-related anxiety, needing back-to-school tools, or seeking encouragement for teaching or parenting in a pandemic, *Life After Lockdown* will provide the support you need. This unique and timely book is filled with tips, stories, and research-based recommendations that have been collected from a wide range of experts including families, educators, and researchers. Autistic voices are also highlighted throughout and provide readers with critical reminders of the struggles and lessons of this time period and the potential power of rethinking "the norm" as we move forward."

-Paula Kluth, PhD, author of *"You're Going to Love This Kid!"*: *Teaching Students with Autism in the Inclusive Classroom*

"Many people feel queasy after being on a merry-go-round, not so much because of the continuous spin, but from the sudden interruptions in motion when others get on or off. They experience such stomach discomfort because their physical equilibrium has been askew. The prolonged COVID-19 pandemic has had the merry-go-round effect of throwing off many people's mental and emotional equilibriums—especially those on the autism spectrum who may find ordinary, granular transitions difficult to handle. Not just daily routines, but entire life structures, have been altered, interrupted and, in many cases, removed altogether and replaced with lockdown edicts, Zoom gatherings, and virtual instead of physical classroom routines.

Life After Lockdown: Resetting Perceptions of Autism provides a variety of perspectives from a slew of experts in the field whose narratives and perceptions restore much of that lost equilibrium. A thread that runs through this practical, compassionate, and timely work is a sense of unity—that we're all in this crisis together and have the power to double down on our best individual and collective wills to better prioritize our own values while reaching beyond ourselves to help others who are struggling because of the pandemic.

I feel this book is a must-read for anyone still trying to find ways to cope with the health crisis, even—or perhaps especially—as we transition to a new normal that remains a work in progress."

**-Sean Barron, Author and Journalist, The Vindicator,
Youngstown, Ohio**

Life After Lockdown

Resetting Perceptions of Autism

Edited by

Rebecca Silva, Ruth Prystash, René DeLoss, and Carol Burmeister

Foreword by Peter Vermeulen

Jennifer Cork
pg 100

Carol Burmeister

AAPC PUBLISHING
PO Box 861116
Shawnee, KS 66218
Local Phone (913) 897-1004 Fax (913) 728-6090
www.aapcautismbooks.com

Names: Silva, Rebecca, editor. | Prystash, Ruth, editor. | DeLoss, René, editor. | Burmeister, Carol Ann, editor. | Vermeulen, Peter, 1962- writer of foreword.

Title: Life after lockdown : resetting perceptions of autism / edited by Rebecca Silva, Ruth Prystash, René DeLoss, and Carol Burmeister ; foreword by Peter Vermeulen.

Description: Shawnee, KS : AAPC Publishing, [2021]

Identifiers: ISBN: 978-1-956110-03-6

Subjects: LCSH: COVID-19 Pandemic, 2020- –Psychological aspects. | Quarantine–Psychological aspects. | Autism spectrum disorders–Patients–Life skills guides–Handbooks, manuals, etc. | Autism spectrum disorders in children–Patients–Life skills guides–Handbooks, manuals, etc. | Autistic children–Life skills guides–Handbooks, manuals, etc. | Autistic youth–Patients–Life skills guides–Handbooks, manuals, etc. | Asperger's syndrome–Patients–Life skills guides–Handbooks, manuals, etc. | Sensory integration dysfunction–Patients–Life skills guides–Handbooks, manuals, etc. | Teachers of children with disabilities–Handbooks, manuals, etc. | Parents of autistic children–Handbooks, manuals, etc.

Classification: LCC: RC553.A88 L54 2021 | DDC: 616.85/882–23

Back cover image by Kevin Immel.

TABLE OF CONTENTS

Foreword xvii
Peter Vermeulen

Introduction xix
The Life After Lockdown Editorial Team

Section 1: Becoming Social Again 1

Adjusting to Life After Lockdown 3
Temple Grandin

Positive Parenting After the Pandemic 8
Elizabeth Sautter

Conquering Your Anxiety 18
Maureen Bennie

Cracking the Social Cipher 29
Vanessa Gill

Stress and Anxiety: An Echo of COVID 36
Kiti Freier-Randall

Talking Head Syndrome 45
Jeffrey Jessum

The New Normal: How I Manage Anxiety 54
Kerry Magro

Helping Your Child While Helping Yourself 63
Carol Burmeister

Moving Forward: Finding the Sunshine 70
Gail Shoffey

Section 2: Back to School..77

Leaving the COVID Zone..79
Cort Rogers

Surviving the Tsunami 85
Tracey DeMaria

Communication is Everything!
School and Home Connection...93
Christa Smith

A Successful Transition to and from School..........................100
Jennifer Cork

Back to School: We're in This Together 110
Lisa Kistler & Gaby Toledo

Addressing Challenging Behavior:
Transition Back to School 119
Robert Pennington & Monique Pinczynski

A Recipe for Student Success...127
Amy Gaffney & Cathy Pratt

It's Time to Shine, Young Adults!..137
Jennifer M. Schmidt

Section 3: Adults in Transition 145

My Trip to Cancun 147
Kelly Londenberg

Computer Gaming and COVID..152
Tony Attwood

College: Back to Campus..163
Linda Murdock

Adulting in the Time of COVID 172
Amanda Backer

Rebooting After Living Virtually (and Virtually Not Living)......180
Sandy Petrovic & David Petrovic

Our Family Was Made for Quarantine 196
  Lesley Clark

Older Autistic Adults Emerging from Quarantine 200
  Wilma Wake

Section 4: Into the Community 209

Arts and Audiences and Autism, Oh My! 211
  Sydney Edmond

Encouraging Positive Behavior Outside the Home 218
  Sheri Wilkins

Sensory Strategies for Success................................225
  Jek Barrozo

Paying for Coffee is Paying for Inclusion in Society...............236
  Larry Bissonnette

It's Finally Time to Go Out Again!...............................239
  Jill Hudson

Parents Are Experts, Too! 251
  René DeLoss

From Sea to Shining Sea: An Autism Adventure 260
  Awit & Edward Dalusong

Section 5: Reboot 267

A Professor's Pandemic Tale:
Lessons for Coping During Uncertain Times 269
  Stephen Shore

Surviving a Pandemic 279
  Lillian Vasquez

How Our Children Thrived During COVID 287
  Bea Moise

Leveling UP! After Locking Down 292
  JÂcqûelyn Fede & Amy Laurent

Reset 297
  Ruth Prystash & Rebecca Silva

About the Editors 307

CONTRIBUTORS

Tony Attwood, PhD, Clinical Psychologist, Author, Speaker, Consultant at Minds and Hearts Clinic, Brisbane, Professor, Griffith University, Queensland, Australia

Amanda Backer, MEd, Founder, California Autism Network, California

Jek Barrozo, MA, OTR/L, ATP, Pediatric Occupational Therapist and Assistive Technology Specialist, California

Maureen Bennie, Director, Autism Awareness Centre Inc., Alberta, Canada

Larry Bissonnette, Disability Rights Advocate and Artist, Vermont

Carol Burmeister, MA, Educational Consultant and Author, Idaho

Jason and Lesley Clark, Parents of Jalon, California

Jennifer Cork, LCSW, Individual and Family Therapist, Idaho

Awit Dalusong, PhD, BCBA-D and Edward Dalusong, PhD, Parents of Ethan, California

René DeLoss, Special Education Teacher, Editor, Massachusetts

Tracey DeMaria, OTD, OTR/L, Occupational Therapist, Advocate, Parent, New Jersey/Pennsylvania

Sydney Edmond, Painter, Poet, Public Speaker with Autism, and Advisor to the Autism Society Inland Empire, California

JÂcqûelyn H. Fede, PhD, Co-Director, Autism Level UP! Rhode Island

Kiti Freier-Randall, PhD, Medical Director, Inland Empire Autism Assessment Center of Excellence, Professor, Loma Linda University Health, California

Amy Gaffney, MA, CCC-SLP, Educational Consultant, Speech-Language Pathologist, Indiana Resource Center for Autism, Indiana

Vanessa Castañeda Gill, CEO and Co-founder, Social Cipher, California

Temple Grandin, PhD, Professor, Department of Animal Science, Colorado State University, Colorado

Jill Hudson, Coordinator, National and State Partnerships, OCALICON, Ohio

Jeffrey Jessum, PhD, Clinical Psychologist, Author, Speaker, and Co-founder of Social Detective Academy, California

Lisa Kistler, MA, Educational Consultant and Coach, California

Amy C. Laurent, PhD, OTR/L, Co-Director, Autism Level UP! Rhode Island

Kelly Londenberg, BS, COTA/L, Autistic Adult and Licensed Pediatric Occupational Therapy Assistant, California

Kerry Magro, EdD, Professional Speaker, Author, Autism Entertainment Consultant, and Autistic Self-Advocate, New Jersey

Bea Moise, MS, BCCS, Board-Certified Cognitive Specialist, Parenting Coach, Author, and National Speaker, North Carolina

Linda Murdock, PhD, Professor and Chair of the Communication Sciences and Disorders department, University of Montevallo, Alabama

Robert Pennington, PhD, BCBA-D, Lake & Edward J. Snyder, Jr. Distinguished Professor, Special Education and Child Development, University of North Carolina, Charlotte

David Petrovic, BA, MAT, Autistic Adult, Middle School/Junior High Teacher, Author, and National Speaker, Ohio

Sandy Petrovic, RN, BSN, Instructional Advisor/Tutor, Notre Dame College/ Thrive Learning Center, Parent of David, Ohio

Monique Pinczynski, MEd, Special Education Teacher and Doctoral Studies Student in Special Education, North Carolina

Cathy Pratt, BCBA-D, Director, Indiana Resource Center for Autism and the Indiana School Mental Health Initiative at Indiana's Institute on Disability and Community, Indiana University

Ruth Weir Prystash, Editor, Writer, Teacher, Consultant, California

Cort Rogers, Student, Newcastle Independent School District, Texas

Elizabeth Sautter, MA, CCC-SLP, Director, Communication Works, Author/Trainer, California

Jennifer M. Schmidt, MEd, Author and Speaker, High School Special Education Teacher, Beavercreek High School, Ohio

Gail Shoffey, DCSc, Autistic Adult and Advanced Education Tutor, California

Stephen Shore, EdD, Clinical Assistant Professor of Special Education, Author, Presenter, and Consultant, Adelphi University, Massachusetts and New York

Rebecca Silva, PhD, Educational Consultant and Author, California

Christa Smith, MA, Special Education Administrator, California

Gaby Toledo, MA, Director of Special Education, Beaumont Unified School District, California

Lillian Vasquez, Parent of Grant, Radio Host and Producer, Autism Advocate, California

Peter Vermeulen, MSc, PhD, Clinical Educationalist, Lecturer and Author, Autism in Context, Belgium

Wilma Wake, PhD, LCSW, Autistic Adult and Social Worker, Maine

Sheri Wilkins, PhD, President, Innovative Educational Solutions, LLC, California and France

FOREWORD

PETER VERMEULEN

 We live in a world that is VUCA: Volatile, Uncertain, Complex, and Ambiguous. This has never been more true than since the outbreak of the COVID-19 pandemic. Life before was not completely predictable and has always been a bit uncertain, but the pandemic has made our lives even more unpredictable and uncertain. People look differently because of face masks. Rules change all the time, especially the rules that have an impact on our social functioning. Many routines we had before the outbreak of the pandemic got lost or have changed. Shopping, traveling, free time . . . everything changed. And, yes, we are slowly moving forward to normal life again, but as we all know, this new normal will include many things that are unfamiliar to us.

That is why uncertainty is now probably a bigger threat to our physical and mental well-being than the virus itself. We are facing an amount of uncertainty that is much bigger than what most of us can cope with. This heightened uncertainty makes many of us anxious and stressed. But it affects people on the autism spectrum even more. They crave predictability because even without the pandemic life is pretty unpredictable for them. And for them, all the changes on the way towards the new normal can lead to increased stress and anxiety. It is therefore very important we support people on the autism spectrum in this time of transition. How can we make this changing world more predictable? How can we prepare them for a post-COVID-19 world? How can we make them feel safe and well? How can we help them to reconnect with the world?

These are the challenges we face. And this book will help you to cope with those challenges.

The pandemic had a huge impact on our lives, all of us. Many people suffered from stress because of the uncertainty and unpredictability caused by the pandemic. Neurotypicals experienced what is probably the daily experience of autistic people. I hope that this shared experience will bring the autistic and non-autistic communities closer to each other. We are all in the same boat. And together we will make the post-COVID-19 world a better place for all of us.

More about Peter . . .

o   As we enter life after lockdown, I am most concerned about . . . *the long-term effects of the pandemic on people's mental health.*
o   As we enter life after lockdown, I am most excited about . . . *traveling again and meeting all those interesting people at autism conferences.*

I have been active in the autism field for almost 35 years as an author of many books and a presenter. I am passionate about increasing awareness and knowledge about autism. In 2019, I received a Lifetime Achievement Award for my contribution to the autism world in Belgium.

INTRODUCTION

This book started out as a guidebook of sorts, with resources and suggestions to help parents, caregivers, educators, and self-advocates rebuild skills that may have been lost during the pandemic. We thought that this would be a purely educational book. We were wrong.

As the chapters from a wide range of contributors rolled in, it became apparent that something else was happening. There were, of course, wonderful pieces by experts, reviewing the strategies and supports that will help during the transition back to a more expected life. But then there were stories, so many stories. People had profound experiences during the lockdown, and they wanted to share them. These stories always carried a message—of support, of advice, of sadness, of gratitude.

This book turned into something special . . . and unexpected. Everyone's lives have been touched by the pandemic, which is why we have chosen to present every contributor as a person first, and as a title or occupation second. The contributors to this book are all human beings who have shared an indelible experience. They are also people whose lives have been shaped by autism, whether professionally or personally. It gives us great joy to share their expertise, experiences, and advice with you. We hope that these chapters will educate and inspire you as much as they have us.

We have chosen to include all forms of descriptors—person-first language (a person with autism) to neurodiversity terms (autistic adults). We have honored the voices and choices of all contributors, without making any type of judgement. We have also included all points of view, whether they agree with our own or not. The book proceeds in five sections, with the last section offering questions that will hopefully drive discussion going forward.

Only forty years ago, people with disabilities living in state institutions were buried in graves marked only with a number. We knew some of those people, and we continue to grieve for the indignities that so many individuals with disabilities have experienced. Society has come so far, but we have so much farther to go. This pandemic has highlighted not only the differences between neurotypical and neurodiverse people, but also their similarities. Let us hope that this devastatingly impactful year serves as a wake-up call for us to improve the acceptance and inclusion of people with autism, and for us to embrace a more compassionate, inclusive way of life for us all.

The Life After Lockdown Editorial Team

SECTION 1
BECOMING SOCIAL AGAIN

One of the biggest changes in returning to life after lockdown will be the return to a more social world. During the pandemic, interactions were sharply curtailed and many people, both neurodiverse and neurotypical, interacted only with family members. Some adults live alone, and interacted with almost no one, due to the availability of grocery delivery, telemedicine appointments, and working from home. This actually provided a more enjoyable lifestyle for some individuals who do not enjoy social interactions and a more barren existence for others who have built a community of friends.

Whatever the benefits or limitations of the social isolation of the lockdown, returning to a more typical lifestyle presents its own special challenges. In this section, Temple Grandin shares her personal strategies and provides recommendations for helping children and adults adjust to the changes. Elizabeth Sautter and Jeffrey Jessum address the special needs of children and give suggestions to parents and caregivers to help their children thrive, while Carol Burmeister provides ways for parents to engage in self-care while simultaneously modeling sound strategies for children. Kiti

Freier-Randall, Maureen Bennie, and Kerry Magro explore the nature of anxiety and stress and talk about ways to combat the effects, while Vanessa Gill and Gail Shoffey provide personal insights into their return to a more social life and how they are coping with life after lockdown.

> **66** It was the hardest thing I had to adjust to in my entire life. Quarantine made me thankful for how much my friends and people mean to me. **99**
>
> Andrew Kruger, Wright State University Student

> **66** In March 2020 was the last day of school because of COVID. We had to stay home and stay safe. No traffic, no construction, but people dead of COVID. We stayed home to save people. **99**
>
> Jaden T, age 9

ADJUSTING TO LIFE AFTER LOCKDOWN

TEMPLE GRANDIN

Photo by Rosalie Winard

During the several months that we were locked down in the U.S., the thing that helped me adjust and not become totally stressed was a schedule. Every day I got up, had breakfast, took a shower, and got dressed for work by 7:00 in the morning. If I lounged around in my sleepwear, I remained tired and depressed. The other thing I did was start new projects to occupy my time in a constructive manner. I spent an entire year working on a new book about visual thinking. Before COVID-19, I traveled 85% of the time, giving talks on both autism and livestock handling. During COVID-19, I was grounded and did not fly for an entire year. Now that I am vaccinated, I have really enjoyed getting out and going on trips.

During the COVID-19 lockdown, there was an increase in mental health issues for many children and young adults. Many kids retreated to their rooms and became isolated. Making the transition back to a more social life may be difficult for all kids. For the autistic child, the transition may be even harder. It is likely that an autistic child may have a difficult time understanding why they need to wear a mask today and the next day, they can take it off. A basic principle with autistic individuals is that gradual transitions are easier and less stressful than abrupt changes. A better approach may be to phase the mask out gradually. When an autistic child is either going to a new school or a school with major changes, it MUST NEVER be a surprise. Surprises scare kids with autism. To reduce the surprise factor, the child should either have a prior visit to the school or see lots of pictures and videos about it.

Autistic people often have great anxiety when conditions are unknown. Since I am a scientist, I found that learning all about COVID-19 actually reduced my fear. I read scientific journal articles on every drug and every vaccine. Before being vaccinated, I was very careful not to catch COVID-19 because it is more deadly in older people. I still went out and carefully did things such as weekly lunches outdoors with my students and visits to our meat lab and a local lamb feedlot. I also had knowledge about every possible COVID-19 treatment, both the ones that might work and the ones that may have been worthless.

> 66 **When I was in primary school, I had a notebook that had an emblem on it that said, "Knowledge is power."** 99

When I travel, I carry medications with me. Maybe they are a useless security blanket and maybe they might make COVID-19 less severe. Due to all the crazy politics, I am not naming the medications I carry. They are common, easy-to-get drugs, but taking a pro-active approach makes me less afraid. I have gone deep into the scientific literature and read all the same things other scientists read. My knowledge is as deep as some of the best researchers. Google Scholar is the most wonderful thing that was ever invented. When I was in primary school, I had a notebook that had an emblem on it that said, "Knowledge is power." I completely avoid reading all the nonsense that people write on social media. As a trained scientist, it blows my mind that people believe so many really stupid things.

Going Back to School

At the time of writing this, my university where I work as a professor, Colorado State University, is planning to have full in-person classes. Could variants change this? I do not know. For kids going back to school, they may either be in fully in-person classes, hybrid, or online. Little kids between the ages of five and eight are the ones who really need to get back to in-person classes. I have talked to many elementary school teachers and half of their students failed to log on. Below are some tips that may help autistic students adapt.

1. **Wearing Masks**–If they are required, some kids may refuse to wear them. To help a child adjust, give them choices of masks. I have found some nice soft ones that are comfortable. My mother always gave me choices of new activities. Another tip is to wash new cloth masks before wearing them. I have to wash all new underwear to prevent rashes and itching. There are lots of fun masks. Since I like cattle, I was given a mask with a cow's nose on it. The child should practice wearing the masks at home before they go back to school. It would be best to start two weeks before school starts or before a trip to the airport. The airports in the U.S. require everybody to wear a mask. To encourage people to wear them, a pilot announced on a plane's public address system that he hates masks, but everybody has to wear them.

2. **Possible Sudden Shifts in Routine**–Autistic individuals often become frightened when the rules suddenly change. One day the rules are relaxed and it is possible they may get locked down again. It is best to tell a child up front that COVID-19

requirements may change depending on outbreaks. It is sort of like airplane delays due to storms. I have learned that this is part of flying on airplanes. They often get delayed so I always need to have books to read.

3. **Avoid Poorly Ventilated Places**—Outdoor activities are much safer than indoor activities where many people are in a room with poor ventilation. Masks are most important when you are inside with a lot of other people. Airborne transmission is the major route for catching COVID-19.

4. **Possible Loss of a Friend, Parent, or Relative**—This is the most stressful part of the COVID-19 pandemic. It has killed a bunch of people. I know people who have lost best friends and relatives to COVID-19. Due to my age, I was one of the first people who got an early vaccination. After my second shot, it felt like I was free. For maximum protection, two shots are needed. As I write this, I just read about the new Delta COVID-19 variant that may be worse. The virus is mutating and some scientists are worried. The good news is that updating the vaccines is easy. Getting a booster with a different type of vaccine may really increase immunity. In the U.S., we are so blessed to have vaccines. Other countries still have huge death losses and lockdowns due to a lack of vaccines.

5. **Get Kids Involved in Outdoor Activities**—Outdoor activities are much safer. Many people are hiking, going for bike rides, swimming in the river, and having other outdoor fun. One mom got her kid off the electronics and she discovered that looking at bugs in the grass was really fascinating. In my neighborhood during lockdown, several families got together and formed a quarantine group. This is really important so kids can have a social life with other kids. Parents need to get kids off the video games. This is why I have written two children's books full of activities that can be done outdoors. They are *Calling All Minds* and *The Outdoor Scientists*. The research is very clear: Video games are more addictive for autistics. I do not believe in banning them, but their use should be limited to one hour a day.

At the time I wrote this chapter, everything was opening up in the U.S. and I have been on five airplane trips. The airplanes are jam-packed with happy families getting out for a vacation. The research is clearly showing that the vaccines work. As an autistic person, I am appalled at the lack of logic in dealing with COVID-19. I am so happy that I have been vaccinated.

More about Temple . . .

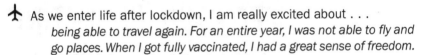 As we enter life after lockdown, I am really excited about . . .
being able to travel again. For an entire year, I was not able to fly and go places. When I got fully vaccinated, I had a great sense of freedom.

As we enter life after lockdown, I am concerned about . . .
some individuals on the autism spectrum who may have difficulty understanding sudden switching of the rules. One day you have to wear a mask and the next day, you no longer have to wear it.

Temple Grandin is a professor of animal science at Colorado State University. When she was two and a half years old, she had no speech and all the symptoms of severe autism. Early intensive speech therapy enabled her to speak by age four. Her mother always encouraged her interest in art and urged her to draw many different things. Good teachers and mentors were essential for Temple's success. Her high school science teacher challenged her with interesting projects where she had to figure out how to make things work. When studying in school became a pathway to becoming a scientist, she was motivated to study.

An HBO movie titled *Temple Grandin* was made about her life and Temple was inducted into The National Women's Hall of Fame and The Academy of Arts and Sciences. Facilities she has designed handle over half the cattle in the U.S. Some of her most important books are New York Times Bestseller *Animals in Translation, Thinking in Pictures, The Autistic Brain*, and *The Way I See It*. Riding horses and caring for them helped her get through difficult teenage years when she was bullied and teased.

Website for Autism

www.templegrandin.com

Website for Livestock

www.grandin.com

POSITIVE PARENTING AFTER THE PANDEMIC

ELIZABETH SAUTTER

As children head back into the post-pandemic world, things are bound to be challenging because so much has changed. There is still so much uncertainty, especially for those who struggle to manage emotions and navigate social situations. The silver lining is that social and emotional learning is now a part of almost every conversation when it comes to what can help. The social and emotional skills that kids need are more important than they have ever been. And the good news is that although there are some new and challenging situations, we can apply the same strategies to support children and adults through those situations. No matter what your role in a child's life—parent, family member, caregiver, educator, speech pathologist—you can be a valuable social coach by embedding social and emotional learning into everyday life, and by being intentional about what you are trying to teach them. You don't need to make life more complicated than it already is!

When we look at practicing social-emotional skills, let's think of how we can provide "add-ins" rather than "add-ons." In other words, by using strategies to support things we are already doing with children, we can provide maximum opportunities for practice while still maintaining our daily routines. Being intentional means that we pay close attention to the skills our child needs and that we use "teachable moments" to focus on those skills in the activities that we do every day. I have provided some effective strategies below that we can use, as well as some activities and ideas to try at the end of the chapter.

Priming

Children do better and have less anxiety when they have an idea about what might happen in a social situation. Priming is a way to set them up for success. Most adults use priming for new or unfamiliar situations on a regular basis. For example, if you are going to a party, you may ask for information in advance: Will there be parking? What should I wear? Will there be food? Similarly, if you haven't been to a restaurant in a year, your child may need priming to help them prepare for what will happen.

- **Find pictures or descriptions online** to study by looking up the restaurant on Yelp to see what it looks like or to check out the menu.
- **Observe in advance** either by driving by the day before, or sitting and watching from your parked car before you go in.
- **Review the rules** for going into a restaurant now, e.g., wear a mask until you get to a table, use hand sanitizer before eating, etc.
- **Write a social narrative** that describes where you are going and what it will be like. This can be in paragraph form or use drawings or other visuals, such as photos.

- **Role-play** what it might be like when the waiter comes to your table with or without a mask.
- **Map it out** by writing or drawing what is going to happen when you get to your destination, whether it is a restaurant or someone's home for a game night.
- **Use video or movie clips** to prepare for a situation. You can often find videos online that show stores, museums, doctors' offices—almost anywhere you might go with your child. Find a good video clip about where you are going, or even make a video of the place yourself, and have your child watch it in the days or hours before you go somewhere. You can also use video or movie clips to prepare for things like birthday celebrations at home, and can make your own videos of the people they might see there.

Debriefing

Just as it's important to prepare for what might happen, it is also important to talk about what happened after the activity is finished. Make sure to do this when your child is calm and focused. If the event was stressful, wait for a better time to debrief with a compassionate and curious state of mind.

- Talk about **what happened** and **what went well**.
- Ask **what could have gone differently.**
- **Validate any emotions** that come up.
- **Acknowledge the effort** that was put forth.
- Talk about **other choices** that could have been made.
- **Make a plan for next time**.

For example, perhaps you had family over for dinner for the first time in over a year. Despite priming your child for what might happen, there were still stressful moments, such as the house being noisier than it has been for a while or running out of your child's favorite dish when someone else took seconds. Later that night, after your child has taken a bath and is relaxing in bed, debrief with your child by helping them come up with ideas.

- ◆ **What went well**—You noticed that your child and their cousin played nicely together in the backyard so don't forget to mention that: "Wow, you looked like you had fun playing with your cousin!" Provide positive feedback but also let them come up with the things that they think went well, too. For example, you can ask them what they remembered about the night that went well, such as, "What were your highlights of tonight?" and maybe add appreciation and acknowledgement such as, "Thanks for helping set the table, that was really helpful!"
- ◆ **What could have gone better**—Your relatives spent a long time talking about their golfing vacation. Your child seemed bored and left the conversation and dinner table. You can validate them by saying something like, "It can be hard to sit at the dinner table while people are talking for a long time, like when Uncle Frankie and Aunt Liz were telling stories about their vacation. I noticed that you got up and left the table in the middle of them talking and they seemed surprised by that."
- ◆ **What could go differently next time**—Brainstorm with your child to come up with some ideas for other choices. For example, ask them "What could you do differently to help you stay focused when someone is talking for a long time and you are bored?" If they need help coming up with ideas, give them choices of some tools and strategies, such as doing some chair push-ups or using a hand fidget at the table to help them focus.
- ◆ **Make a plan for next time**—Write or sketch out what it might look like next time and what the better choices might lead to. Role-play what might happen.

Debriefing can be used for any type of social situation, familiar or unfamiliar, big or small. The important thing is to teach your child to reflect on a situation after it is over to figure out what worked and what didn't, so that the next time will go more smoothly.

Observing

This seems like such a simple strategy but it is highly effective. Too often, we jump right in to help our child with a difficult situation, or, worse, we push our child to tackle a new situation before they are ready. It is important for children to have social experiences, but it is equally important for them to be set up to succeed. Mindfully observing others and the contexts that we are in can provide helpful information and build skills such as reading facial expressions and nonverbal social cues, building situational awareness, and the ability to pause before jumping in to interact. This can be done as a standalone practice at home or in public but is definitely recommended when your child is confronted with a perplexing or unfamiliar situation. Don't jump in right away. Instead, teach your child to pause and watch.

Sitting and watching can help children with many different skills. By observing a situation before acting, your child can:

- **Watch** how others are acting.
- **Listen** to how others are speaking.
- **Develop perspective-taking** skills.
- Learn to **make inferences**.
- **Use self-talk** that helps them mentally prepare and builds confidence.

Much of this is accomplished with your intentional guidance and coaching. Let's pretend your child is going back to their special soccer team for the first time in a year and a half. What might you see, do, and say to help them be successful and enjoy the experience? Start off by sitting and observing as the practice begins before having your child join in.

- **Watch**—Point out children that your child may know or remember from before. Help your child look at the surroundings. Maybe the practice is in a new place. Where are the nets? Are there water fountains nearby if your child gets thirsty? Are other people wearing masks or not?
- **Listen**—Point out the coaches and help your child hear the differences when an adult gives a direction versus when a parent is yelling encouragement from the sidelines or when a teammate is talking to their friends. Help them listen to the types of words and the tones of voice. Do the adults sound pleasant? Do the children sound happy? Listen to how the children greet each other, and have your child practice the words, or use a wave to greet others.
- **Help them use perspective-taking skills**—This can build understanding, as well as empathy. Ask your child to look for children who are standing alone versus with a group. How might the child who is alone be feeling? Point out the child who is holding on to his mother and crying. Encourage your child to think of how that child is feeling.
- **Learn to make inferences**—Point out those same children (the one who is alone, and the one who is crying). Help your child figure out why the children might be feeling lonely or sad, and think of ways to help. You can also teach inferencing as a way of figuring out what to do. Most of the children are sitting on the ground in a circle around the coach. What does that mean, and should your child go over there and do the same thing?
- **Use positive self-talk**—Your child may still be nervous, so help them use self-talk, which is what most of us do inside our heads when we are anxious or unsure. Help your child develop a mantra that they can repeat to themselves over and over, such as: "I can do it!" Or "I am nervous but I know that I will be going home with dad in an hour." Or "Other kids are nervous, too. I'm not the only one."

Use these steps outside of the moment, so that your child can be successful in the moment.

Validation

The final strategy is possibly the most important. Children have feelings about the pandemic, and about the world around them. Just because they are children and may not be able to verbalize their feelings doesn't mean that their feelings are not as powerful or nuanced as our own. Children may feel confused, frightened, and anxious when they sense that the adults around them are feeling those things, too. It is incredibly important to validate our children's feelings by acknowledging them, and by letting them know how we are feeling, too.

- **Model talking** about feelings so that your child knows that we all have feelings and can learn new emotional vocabulary words.
- **Model behaviors** to reduce stress for yourself in front of your child so that they see what self-care and self-regulation look like.
- **Validate your child's feelings** so that they feel seen and heard. This in itself is calming for the brain.

Let's pretend that your child has just resumed in-person school and is having a very hard time with their anxiety about both COVID and about the classroom expectations. It is challenging to sit still for so long, unlike being at home for virtual learning.

- **Model talking**—Talk about your own fears about COVID. Be honest, and say you worry about being in a crowd.
- **Model behaviors**—You might model using self-talk: "I know I am safe because I am vaccinated." You might model taking a break when you are working on papers at home. "I think I will get up and stretch to wake myself up." Coach your child on how to request this at school.
- **Validate their feelings**—Let your child know that their feelings are natural, and that you understand by saying things like "I understand that you might feel nervous." Help your child realize that many other people are feeling the same way.

Children learn by watching their parents and other adults, and will try to imitate the behaviors they see as useful. Whether you are a parent, a caregiver, a family member, an educator, or a therapist, you have the power to reassure a child just by letting them know you understand. You do not always need to fix the problems they are having, or even to suggest solutions. Sometimes just letting them know you understand and are there for them is enough and can be extremely powerful.

Here are some activities you might try with your child to work on social and emotional learning during everyday activities and routines. (From *Make Social and Emotional Learning Stick!* Sautter 2020 and *Make Social Learning Stick Emotional Regulation Card Deck,* Sautter 2020)

☀ *Boxing Up Your Worries*

If your child has worries, fears, or even just a lot of thoughts that keep them up at night, suggest writing them down on a piece of paper and putting them under the pillow or in a "worry box" to symbolize letting them go.

☀ *Family Meetings*

Take time to gather the family together on a weekly basis to share news, go over the calendar for the upcoming week, and talk about any challenges that might need family members to problem-solve as a team. Remember to acknowledge any accomplishments and show appreciation or gratitude for each other. Family meetings can be a good way to stay connected, share information, and solve problems, just like any other groups that work together on a regular basis.

☀ *Calming Corner*

Designate a place in the house for quiet time, calming down, or just plain chilling out. Have your child help pick where that place will be, and make sure it's big enough for multiple people. Have them help with the design and props (e.g., bean bag, lava lamp, photos of things that bring them joy and good feelings, scents, and music that make them feel calm, etc.). Note: This is not a place for "time out" or punishment. It's a place to gather and relax, and calm down if needed.

Easing Fears

If you suspect your child is nervous about going to the doctor, explain that this is a common feeling for people before going to the doctor. Validate their feelings and provide some calming tools that you know work (bring a favorite toy or book, do some deep breathing, etc.). Tell your child how you keep yourself calm when you go to the doctor or go out someplace you haven't been for a while. Validating feelings can reduce anxiety in stressful situations.

Final Thoughts

Wherever you are or whatever you are doing, just remember that you can turn almost any routine activity into an opportunity for social and emotional learning. Look for the teachable moments in everyday life and use them to help you support your child in building the social and emotional skills that can help them survive a lockdown and return to a world full of social possibilities!

More about Elizabeth . . .

 As we enter life after lockdown, I am most concerned about . . .
people who are isolated, anxious, and disconnected socially. Loneliness can lead to such pain and even health issues and the pandemic has made this worse for so many. All of this uncertainty has made some people feel paralyzed and uncomfortable being around others or in public places. I'm concerned about the short- and long-term effects.

As we enter life after lockdown, I am most excited about . . .
Hugging! I didn't realize how much I miss hugging my friends, family, and those whom I love. I also am really enjoying seeing my clients in person again.

Elizabeth is a speech-language pathologist who specializes in social-emotional learning. She is an award-winning author, blogger, and trainer, including being a collaborative trainer for the Zones of Regulation. She is the owner and director of Communication Works which provides services to schools, individuals, and their families and provides online support to parents through her website MakeSocialLearningStick.com. Elizabeth lives in the Bay Area with her husband, two teenage sons, a cat, and a dog.

Books

o *Make Social and Emotional Learning Stick: Practical Activities to Help Your Child Manage Emotions, Navigate Social Situations and Reduce Anxiety*
o *Make Social Learning Stick* Card Deck
o *Make Emotional Learning Stick* Card Deck

Website

MakeSocialLearningStick.com

CONQUERING YOUR ANXIETY

MAUREEN BENNIE

As we emerge back into the world after months of lockdown, not only has the world around us irrevocably changed, but we have as well. No family remains untouched by the recent pandemic, protocols, policies, and new way of living. Although we were lucky to have the technology to keep us connected and communicating, it also introduced new problems. Connecting with others online brought new complexities and challenges to communication. With online interaction, social cues such as full body language, which add to meaning and understanding, were missing. *Zoom fatigue*—the tiredness, worry, or burnout associated with overusing virtual platforms of communication—is now a new term and a real thing.

Over 80% of children have had their education impacted by COVID-19 (Brandenburg et al. 2020). The lack of specialized instruction, individualized supports, and little to no assistance for parents at home made them feel anxious and frazzled. Hybrid learning, online classes, quarantines, and rotating lockdowns left children isolated, tired, and stressed.

Individuals on the autism spectrum have had to make enormous adjustments dealing with unpredictability, loss of routines, the shift to online learning, communicating through tech platforms, coping with the cancellation of programs and activities, and changes in family dynamics with everyone together for long periods of time. It will take time to recover from these huge daily life changes.

While we have gained much knowledge about COVID-19 since the pandemic began, there still remain many mysteries about the virus and how it will evolve as time goes on. The virus makes people anxious, as do the effects and influence it has on how we live our lives. It has power and leaves us feeling not in control. Its presence in the world has caused unpredictability and uncertainty; it has forced us to change even when we were not willing or wanting to do so.

What Are the Signs of Anxiety?

When addressing anxiety in autistic individuals about COVID-19, it is difficult to separate the idea of the virus itself from the changes it has caused. In order to best help individuals on the autism spectrum address and alleviate anxiety, we have to recognize the signs and causes of anxiety, then figure out what strategies can be utilized to help a person feel better.

It is important to recognize the signs of anxiety and not mistake these as problematic behaviors. Understanding and addressing anxiety is part of building a trusting, respectful relationship. A person will need support to get their anxiety in control. Punitive measures or thinking the person can control this on their own will only make the situation worse.

Some of the signs of anxiety to look for in someone on the autism spectrum are:

- Sleep disturbances
- Negative thoughts
- Perseverative thoughts (rumination)
- Feeling fearful or constantly worrying
- Upset stomach/digestive issues
- An increase in stimming behaviors such as fast, intense rocking, pacing, self-talk, hair twirling, hand flapping
- Increased echolalia
- Aggressive behavior
- Self-harm like picking or scratching skin
- Meltdowns
- Withdrawal or shutdowns

There can also be more subtle signs of anxiety that may be overlooked such as:

- Difficulty concentrating or paying attention to tasks
- Restlessness
- Agitation
- Difficulty settling
- Not wanting to engage in activities
- Sudden development of vocal or physical tics

What Are the Causes of Anxiety in the Current COVID-19 Climate?

Separation Anxiety

Entering back into the outside world after lockdown can cause a whole new set of worries or exacerbate old ones. After spending over a year at home, some individuals will experience separation anxiety. They may have become used to spending every waking hour with their parents and other family members, and feel fearful that something will happen to them once they leave for work or go out. Separation anxiety is driven by fear and is initially triggered by a negative event, such as COVID-19. In most cases, separation anxiety will be short-lived but for some individuals, this will linger. It can even start for the first time in adulthood.

Separation anxiety can be addressed by using these small steps:

- Practice going out. Start by just going out in the backyard or walking down the street and back. Gradually increase the time gone.
- Say goodbye before you go out. Do not sneak away unnoticed.
- Do what you say you will do. For example, "I am going to the grocery store. I'll be back in one hour."
- Create a Social Story ™ to let the person know what will happen to them while you are out and what they are expected to do. Social Stories ™ create predictability, which will ease anxiety (For more information on Social Stories ™ see https://carolgraysocialstories.com/social-stories/).
- Use visuals to say where you are and when you will be back.
- Have children engage in calming activities before a separation happens.
- Give children a special job or preferred activity to do to distract them from anxious feelings.

Changes to Routines and Protocols Outside of Home

Routines and protocols will be different depending on the organization. Create predictability for these new routines and protocols by preparing for them ahead of time. Preparation lessens surprises and anxiety around new protocols.

Some ways to create predictability are:

- Visit an organization's website or call them to see what their protocols are before going there.
- Review what physical or social distancing looks like. Make this abstract concept as concrete as possible through visuals. There are some great examples available on YouTube.
- Practice mask-wearing, as this may be required in tight, crowded spaces such as public transit. Find out when and where masks will be required for all activities.
- Contact the school before school starts and speak with the classroom teacher. Ask how lunchtime will work, recess, classroom spaces, etc.
- Use visuals to show what protocols look like. If directional arrows on the floor are used, take pictures of that. If a store expects a person to use hand sanitizer before entering, put that on a task breakdown visual strip for a shopping trip.
- Understand that protocols can change. Rules and measures are constantly shifting as more information about the virus becomes known. Explain that any rules and restrictions in place today may change in order to keep everyone safe and healthy.

Changes at Home

Life at home is changing as things open up. Parents are going back to work. Children have to get up in the morning for school. After a year of increased unscheduled time and a more relaxed pace, easing back into old routines will require support to get into the transition without increasing anxiety.

For any changes to the schedule:

- Start slowly and ahead of time. If a person has to start getting up earlier in the morning, establish the new rising time one to two weeks before the new schedule starts. Maybe use small increments of time.
- Use visual supports to show schedule changes.
- Do not change the schedule all at once as this is too big of an adjustment to make.
- Add one change to the schedule every few days and get that established before adding in another change. Small steps will lessen anxiety.

Ongoing Worries about COVID-19

Even with vaccines, there will still be issues to contend with around COVID-19. Not all of the world will be able to be vaccinated at the same time, but traveling will start again. New variants will emerge. As more information is learned about the virus, new concerns about it may surface. There is still so much we do not know about COVID-19, such as the long-term impact on physical and mental health. How long do vaccines last? How well does each type of vaccine combat each new variant? How easily can a person still get COVID-19 even if they are vaccinated?

All of these ongoing issues around COVID-19 can cause stress and anxiety. The best way to address this is by understanding what is in a person's control and what is not.

Helping a person on the autism spectrum focus on the things they can do to keep themselves safe and healthy will support them to feel in control. Share positive new information with them. For example, share the number of people that have been vaccinated or the success rates of the vaccine. This will lessen anxiety, show progress against the virus, and make a person feel empowered.

Some things we are *not in control* of include:

- How long this virus will last.
- If others are following the rules of social distancing.
- If people are wearing a mask or using hand sanitizer.
- How others react.
- The actions of others.
- Predicting what will happen next.
- Other people's motives.

The things that are *within our own power and control* include:

- Turning off the news.
- Limiting social media.
- Continuing to social distance.
- Following public health recommendations like using hand sanitizer and mask-wearing.
- Eating healthy.
- Exercising.
- Avoiding activities that may still pose a health risk, such as large indoor gatherings.
- Engaging in interests and passions that support happiness, especially during tough times.
- Our attitude and response.
- Kindness towards others.

How Can We Help a Person on the Autism Spectrum with Anxiety?

Figure Out What the Triggers Are for Anxiety

Be a detective by keeping a journal to pinpoint what is triggering anxiety. Is it too much screen time? Watching the news? Sensory overload from wearing a mask? The drying effects of using hand sanitizer? Waiting in a line to enter a favorite place?

☀ Reduce Unpredictability

Establish clear routines and schedules. Predictability and familiarity provide a sense of calm. Visual schedules show how the day will unfold. Task sequencing outlines the steps for task completion and fosters independence and a sense of control.

☀ Develop Some Simple Exercises or Routines That Are Calming

Since COVID-19 started, physical activity soared to the top of the priority list to support health and well-being. Regular exercise lessens anxiety, improves sleep, increases endurance, builds muscles, develops motor skills, and offers opportunities for socializing. Yoga and meditation are also great for calming and relaxing.

☀ Teach Interoceptive Awareness (IA)

The interoceptive system, the eighth sensory system, has little receptors located throughout the inside of the body, organs, muscles, skin, bones, and so forth. These receptors gather information from the inside of the body and send it to the brain. The brain helps to make sense of these messages and enables us to feel things such as hunger, fullness, itchiness, pain, body temperature, nausea, the need to go to the bathroom, and physical exertion. Interoception also allows us to feel our emotions.

People on the autism spectrum may not feel when their internal system is off. They are not aware of their interoceptive signals telling them they are hot, thirsty, or anxious. IA is needed in order to self-regulate. IA is also connected to executive function skills like flexible thinking, intuition, and problem-solving.

Teaching IA is a way to help a person on the spectrum understand what their internal body signals are telling them and how to react. The best source of information on how to teach IA is Kelly Mahler's book, *Interoception: The Eighth Sensory System*.

Teach Relaxation

Kari Dunn Buron wrote a great children's book called *When My Worries Get Too Big!* which teaches concrete relaxation techniques like deep breathing and counting. She also created a 6-minute video available on YouTube based on the book.

Offer Ways to Self-Soothe

Create a sensory basket or box that has calming things in it like a fidget spinner, squeeze ball, Tangle Toy, or Fidget for Your Digit. Some people like to chew, while others need deep pressure. Figure out what works best for calming down for the person you are supporting.

Try Distractions

While this may not work every time, providing a distraction can take a person's mind off what is bothering them. Talking about favorite topics and interests can brighten their mood right away.

Make Adaptations to the Environment

Have quiet, calming spaces available. This can be as simple as a one-person tent or draping a sheet over a chair to create an enclosed space that provides less visual stimulation. Figure out what the sensory triggers are and reduce those to prevent sensory overload.

Use an App to Track Anxiety

Using an app can help make anxiety more concrete and understandable. A good app to try is Molehill Mountain, which tracks mood, identifies triggers, and gives evidence-based tips on how to self-manage anxiety levels. Brain in Hand is another one to try that is not condition-specific but is often used by people who are autistic, who have learning difficulties, or who are managing mental health challenges. Brain in Hand is a digital self-management support system for people who need help remembering things, making decisions, planning, or managing anxiety. (Note: Some apps may not be available in all areas or countries.)

Consult a Professional

If anxiety issues are overwhelming and insurmountable, consider consulting a mental health professional who can do an assessment and provide some anxiety management strategies. You do not have to figure this out on your own.

Conclusion

As the world opens up again after months of lockdown, feeling anxious about COVID-19 and the changes and uncertainties it brings will be a part of this transition. It will be important to find ways to alleviate anxiety and reassure the person we are supporting that while things may be different, we will adapt to the new climate and find ways to feel good again.

Keeping informed about new developments and knowledge about the virus and sharing that information will help take the mystery out of COVID-19 and give predictability to the situation. Things will continue to evolve and change; this will be the new "normal" for quite some time. While we can still hold on to things we love and enjoy, some aspects of the world will never go back to the way they were. We will adjust and in time feel comfortable with the changes.

Going forward in the COVID-19 journey, there will be good and bad moments. Some days, these anxiety-alleviating ideas will work; other days, not. If a meltdown, outburst, or behavior of concern does occur, do not teach a calming technique in that moment. Try not to reason, argue, or talk until the person has recovered. Allow time for processing. Offer reassurance when the person is back in control and let them know that things are alright between you and them. Keeping a trusting and open relationship is the foundation for providing excellent support for positive mental health and well-being.

More about Maureen . . .

As we enter life after lockdown, I am most concerned about . . . *the emergence of new COVID variants that could put us back into lockdowns. I don't want to be fearful, but some days it is a challenge to be brave.*

As we enter life after lockdown, I am most excited about . . . *returning to figure skating and traveling again. I began figure skating in my 40s and the people I have met through training and competitions have changed my life. My international skating friends and I met online during the pandemic for weekly workouts to keep ourselves fit, connected, and motivated.*

Maureen Bennie is the co-founder and director of Autism Awareness Centre Inc. She manages all operations of the Centre—website, webinars, bookstore, Facebook page, bi-monthly blog, and the planning and management of conferences the Centre organizes. She is the author of over 400 articles and book reviews that have appeared in magazines, newsletters, and on websites throughout North America and the UK. She lives with her husband, Ron, and two autistic children—age 24 and age 22—in Calgary, Alberta, Canada.

Website

www.autismawarenesscentre.com

Reference

Brandenburg, Joline E., Lainie K. Holman, Susan D. Apkon, Amy J. Houtrow, Robert Rinaldi, and Maurice G. Sholas. 2020. "School Reopening During COVID-19 Pandemic: Considering Students with Disabilities." *Journal of Pediatric Rehabilitation Medicine* 13 (3): 425-431. https://doi.org/10.3233/PRM-200789.

CRACKING THE SOCIAL CIPHER

VANESSA GILL

Social interaction is hard. It's even harder when we've only been seeing small parts of each other through screens for the past year. As a neurodivergent person, before the pandemic I built up some tolerance to cope with the social, sensory, and emotional events going on around me in daily life. After the pandemic, however, that tolerance I built up is definitely not like it used to be. Interacting with others—even just being around others—is much more anxiety-inducing and exhausting than before. With some creativity and extra attention, though, I've been able to feel more comfortable and energized in social situations. Along with being an autistic person with ADHD, I'm also the CEO of Social Cipher, a company that makes social-emotional learning games for neurodivergent youth. Given that background, you'd be right to assume that I think about being autistic and social situations a whole lot. Below are the tips and tricks that have helped me most in integrating back into the world as we recover from this pandemic. I hope that they help you and your loved ones as well.

Go gradually to level up.

Think about the social "levels" of places in your area. The idea of higher-level places (more stimulating places with more people) like a party or a loud restaurant might sound terrible to you (they definitely do for me). A public park or hiking trail, however? That's much more manageable. If you or your loved ones are anything like me, it may take some time to work up to feeling comfortable, safe, and not completely depleted of energy in higher-level places. The best way that I've found to work up is by gradually "leveling up" the types of places I go to over time (see Social Levels chart below).

Social Levels

Level 0:   Home, of course!

Level 1:   A public park or hiking trail, a library, a parent or grandparent's home.

Level 2:   A quiet coffee shop patio, a beach, a playground, a close friend or family member's house.

Level 3:   This is where things might start to sound a little more difficult—but you'll get there! A small friends and family gathering, a restaurant patio at lunchtime, book stores, museums.

Level 4:   Indoors at a restaurant, shopping centers, department stores, larger family and friend gatherings.

The time you spend jumping between levels is completely up to you and your own comfort levels. The jump from a Level 0 to a Level 1 place may be easy, but a Level 2 to a Level 3 place may take a lot more time and feel a lot more difficult. This is completely natural and ok. I try to up my exposure to each level a bit. For me, I started by going to parks weekly, and then attending gatherings or going to busier places every two weeks. Then I challenged myself a bit more by doing some work in a busy coffee shop and then working up to having a small get together with trusted friends and family with an activity besides just conversation (board games, movies, etc.).

Make sure to pace yourself, and don't get frustrated if you or your child feel overwhelmed with the next step—instead, try heading into the space next time equipped with the tips I'll lay out in the next paragraphs.

Set time for self-care.

As you probably know, social interaction—even if you're not directly speaking to others—can be incredibly draining. That's why it's especially important to schedule "recharge time" both before and after events that tend to be anxiety-inducing or socially tiring. That recharge time can look completely different depending on you or your child's interests. If you're a neurodivergent person, think about when you feel the most calm or comfortable. Is it when you're engaging in a special interest, reading, listening to music? If you have a neurodivergent loved one, where do they seem to enjoy themselves most, or feel at peace? Schedule time for that care and compassion for yourself or your loved one in order to give yourself a good foundation of grace before and after potentially stressful activities.

Have some backups.

We're humans. Sometimes we have no idea what might make us more anxious than usual—especially in times like these, where we're facing unprecedented scenarios. Triggering situations can include anything from a flustered conversation to too many people in close proximity without masks. That's why I've always got a tool kit (with both physical and mental tools) on me at all times. One thing that I use consistently is a stim ring—a spinning piece of jewelry that allows me to fidget inconspicuously and ground myself to reduce my anxiety in crowds (bonus: it's pretty!). Stimming is the act of carrying out repetitive movements (blinking, flapping hands, rocking, etc.) to gain control of an environment when you're feeling overwhelmed, and it's common with many neurodivergent folks.

> 66 Stimming is the act of carrying out repetitive movements to gain control of an environment when you're feeling overwhelmed. 99

With subtle objects like these, I can keep my anxiety to a minimum without being nervous or self-conscious that my stimming is disruptive or noticeable by others (though stimming should be more widely accepted in society and is sadly still stigmatized, but that's another conversation.) My stim jewelry also serves as an indicator for family and friends, especially when I'm feeling too overwhelmed to notice that I need a break. They know that when I'm spinning my ring like crazy, it's time to check in with me and ask how I'm feeling. Other options for these physical tools can be chew jewelry, earplugs, headphones, and finding quiet spaces, like your car, bathroom, or a walk outside. If you're a neurodivergent adult and anxious about certain social events and gatherings, try to arrange your own form of transportation rather than going with friends or a group. By taking your own form of transport, designating a friend or family member not attending to pick you up, or a ridesharing service, you're able to put yourself in control of leaving an overwhelming event without depending on others who may want to stay. It is completely fine to leave early if you need to—your true friends and family will understand.

Advocate for your needs.

In these times, everyone is feeling the difficulties of interacting to some degree, which means that you're not alone in your anxiety.

Before diving into tips for advocacy, it's important to remember that even the most extroverted, socially skilled people have also been out of practice with social interaction for the past year, and they won't be perfect at it. Nearly everyone you know has been at least a little nervous to get back into pre-COVID social interactions at one point or another. It's important to know this because though everyone may be feeling this, not everyone is going to talk about it. Whether you're a neurodivergent person yourself, a parent, or a loved one, these conversations need to be had. When my friends started getting vaccinated, they couldn't wait to hang out. I was excited too, but incredibly overwhelmed by the idea of booking my calendar up with social engagements. I had just had my first social event a week before, and it took me about two days to recover from the social exhaustion of a simple get-together. To save my own mental health, I set a rule for myself: I'd start with only one social event each week. I had to turn down a lot of gatherings and, initially, felt bad about "letting my friends down."

> 66 I set a rule for myself: I'd start with only one social event each week. 99

Time after time, though, I realized that my friends and family were perfectly understanding of my situation, and gladly rescheduled to another time in the next few weeks. Some even adopted the rule for themselves!

In another situation, I learned that being at social gatherings (especially those that include new people) made me incredibly anxious. What if I forgot how to engage in small talk? How do I even start and keep up a conversation with someone I've just met? What if I say something inappropriate, or I overshare, or I don't recognize that the other person wants to leave the conversation? The spiral would continue like that for a good while. The best way to solve this? I brought my own activities, like board games, to parties. That way, I knew that I could turn to an activity to engage in with others, but my presence at the party wouldn't have to depend on my ability to have a conversation. If I was anxious about the gathering, I would also talk to the host to learn about who would be there, what activities would be involved, and if I could bring or help with an activity to take the core focus of the engagement off of just conversation.

In situations where you don't have much control, it's good to have a buddy. Bring a friend, parent, or family member who can check in with you a couple of times throughout the gathering to help you reflect on how you're feeling. Let them know what your anxieties are about the upcoming gathering, and brainstorm solutions to make you feel more comfortable. It's also helpful to have this buddy as an advocate when you're feeling overwhelmed since they can cover for you and let other people know your whereabouts so you can take your break in peace.

Forgive, learn, and try again.

Reintegration after COVID won't be an easy path for anyone. When you get right down to it, most folks (the folks who truly care about you, anyway) will not judge you or your loved one for having difficulties and needing time to readjust to post-COVID social life. You shouldn't either.

If you think about it, none of us have actually ever experienced something like COVID, and we especially have never experienced social interaction after a global pandemic like this. In the future, there will be lots and lots of awkwardness, apologies, and learning as we all try to figure out this new world. You are not alone in this. When you feel like you've made a mistake, when you feel exhausted or overwhelmed by a social situation that "shouldn't have affected you so much," when you feel that you or your loved one has "regressed" socially, just remember:

You've survived a global pandemic. We're all learning how to live life again. You became stronger. You've learned. You've grown.

Give yourself the grace that a friend or family member you trust would give you. Listen to your body and thoughts. Rest, think about how you can help yourself do better next time, or ask for help. Try again, and keep moving forward.

You're going to be great.

More about Vanessa . . .

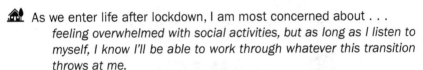 As we enter life after lockdown, I am most concerned about . . .
feeling overwhelmed with social activities, but as long as I listen to myself, I know I'll be able to work through whatever this transition throws at me.

As we enter life after lockdown, I am most excited about . . .
seeing my friends and family again! Seeing live music again is also going to be fantastic.

Vanessa Castañeda Gill is an autistic advocate and the CEO + Co-Founder of Social Cipher, a game-based social-emotional learning platform for neurodivergent youth and the professionals who work with them. Through her work with her incredible team, she's earned recognition as a Forbes 30 Under 30, a Facebook Global Gaming Citizen, and an AT&T Aspire Fellow.

STRESS AND ANXIETY: AN ECHO OF COVID

KITI FREIER-RANDALL

We find ourselves in times we could not have imagined even a short while ago. We are experiencing feelings of vulnerability due to limited resources and the primal need for survival. In this global battle, particularly with an unseen enemy, we are all experiencing an enormous amount of stress and anxiety. And yet while it is global, it is so very personal! There is heightened stress and pressures in families and relationships, and we each have a story to be told about this uncertain time: A journey of changes, loss, hopes, fears, and anxiety; a time when social support is critical. Yet, with our social networks also stressed, our experiences and stories go largely untold and anxieties fester.

While it was initially critical to "flatten the curve" and our community entered a stay-at-home phase, we are now transitioning to the important phases of reintegration. However, as our environment opens up, and COVID shows no signs of just disappearing, many of us are asking ourselves: "What is safe?" We are anxious about the ambiguous realities of *what is* versus *what is desired* for ourselves and most pointedly for our children. While it was difficult and anxiety-provoking to go into lockdown and other restrictions, there will be even more challenging issues that arise from a return to "normal" life. The ongoing adjustments and ever-changing regulations of what is recommended or required create more anxiety as we are constantly moving back and forth from less restricted to more restricted environments. The impact of these constant changes will be even more pronounced for people with ASD and those who have significant trouble with changes in routine. For these individuals and families, the stressors are magnified.

We lost services and supports during lockdown that we relied on to meet our needs and the needs of our children. The more that was lost because of the stay-at-home status, the more stress we faced and the more anxiety we experienced. But now, as these services are opening back up to in-person availability, our anxiety seems to be in direct correlation to how many services or supports we need to re-start. The process of reintegration can be daunting.

It is important to understand and accept that in any change or transition there are multiple factors that can create anxiety. Certainly, the current situation brings multiple levels of stress and uncertainty—a formula for heightened anxiety. Some say we are in an *echo pandemic,* meaning that its impact echoes through every level of society. This *echo pandemic* has made reentry into society critical for everyone, particularly for children (Bezane 2021). Our children lost stability in every facet of life: Peers, education, daily routine, sports, interventions, and more. And, sadly for many children, they lost the safety of being in the public eye. For these and many other reasons, reintegration is necessary. The consequences should not be greater than the cause. We are at the tipping point, and many believe we are well beyond that.

Risk

> **"** As we move forward, it helps to acknowledge that we have all experienced trauma. **"**

As we move forward, it helps to acknowledge that we have all experienced trauma. We must also realize that we will all handle this situation differently. Anxiety and stress from this type of trauma are similar to how we experience grief—we all do it differently. For some, reintegration is going too fast and for others, it is going too slow. As diverse as we are as individuals or persons with ASD, so is the diversity of our responses. Anxiety and risk work in tandem. How we face life after lockdown and how we feel about others' behavior during reintegration highlights this.

One thing that this pandemic has shown is that we live in a state of risk. We constantly make decisions about how much risk we are willing to take—even if we are not consciously thinking about it. *Risk can be defined as the possibility of something bad happening.* Risk is in everything we do, but how it affects us is personal. Every time you get into a car, you are taking a risk. For some, skydiving is too risky while for others it's an acceptable risk. Every time you wash your hands after using the restroom, you are reducing risk.

Risk is in everything we do, but its calculation is personal. Anxiety is heightened when the calculation of risk is *necessary* but is also *unwanted.* It isn't surprising that both we and our children may currently be anxious. We are in a novel situation and the impact may not be known for some time. The good news is that we are also resilient. We can draft our own future by moving forward with hope, faith, support; by educating ourselves; and by making decisions to the best of our ability. Having a plan for life after lockdown is crucial. Flexibility is imperative.

Anxiety

The more predictable our environment, the less anxiety we experience. COVID provides an environment of unseen consequences. In order to mitigate our anxiety, we need to make choices about what types of situations or environments we feel are safer. We also need to learn behaviors that will help us to venture more effectively into a more normal life experience. Families need to be clear about their comfort with risk. Agencies need to be clear about their strategies to mitigate risk. Our choices should match our risk comfort levels. Choosing comfortable activities in safe environments will decrease anxiety and offer a smoother transition into desired experiences.

> 66 The more predictable our environment, the less anxiety we experience. 99

For those who are particularly anxious, we will need to do more to encourage their participation in life after lockdown. For those where anxiety is high, purposeful planning and reassurance are paramount. Sometimes identifying faulty thought patterns (e.g., "I cannot go outside or I will make grandma sick") and logically addressing them with facts can be a starting point. If someone is experiencing heightened anxiety that is not lessened by implementing planned and deliberate steps to reintegration, they may need mental health counseling or professional services.

Some of us are anxious about our child's difficulties with required safety protocols. There are strategies you can engage to alleviate anxiety for both you and your child. Prepare your child for what an activity will be like. Provide experiences that simulate what it will be like. Practice new routines and behaviors until everyone understands how to do them correctly. Making repeated attempts with increasingly realistic approximations, providing reassurance, and making a full disclosure of your anxiety (to yourself or others that will be in the environment—doctor's office staff, etc.) can help to make the situation more successful and less anxious. Remember that the more predictable we make things, the less anxiety is experienced. Hint: This is one of the primary reasons why routine is critical for children.

Strategies to Reduce Anxiety

Remember, this is an adjustment for everyone! Acknowledge that this is an ambiguous situation and that stress will need to be addressed and managed. Since we are in uncharted territory, we may need to experiment with what works best for ourselves and/or our children. Below are some strategies that may help lessen the anxiety of our children.

1. **Be prepared for some specific conversations with your children.** *Information to be given depends on what the child knows and what they ask.*

   I am afraid of getting sick.

   - Washing our hands keeps us from spreading germs.
   - We have enough tests now to test you if you feel sick.
   - We have treatments now that can help you if you get sick.
   - If you get sick, we can take you to the doctor to get you better.
   - Not all sick people die.
     ⇨ Some children need to know details of the symptoms, so help them to understand that you will be there to monitor symptoms with them. They should let you know if they don't feel well.

   I am worried and afraid.

   - It is normal to worry.
   - We are here to keep you safe.

- Yes, I do sometimes feel anxious, but I do things that help me to not feel anxious. This is expected.
  - ⇨ Sometimes if children feel that nobody seems to be listening to them or don't know how to tell you how scared they are, it can come out in other ways (e.g., temper tantrums).
  - ⇨ Negative behaviors may escalate to get attention – they still might not know how to say what they need, but at least they will have your attention.
  - ⇨ Be patient with them.
  - ⇨ Let them know that they are loved.

2. **We are most likely to forget the safety rules when we are anxious.**

    - Making sure the activity is *developmentally appropriate* AND providing preparation and predictability are critical.
    - Routine and boundaries provide an environment that can lessen anxiety.

3. **Children need you to comment on emotions.**

    - Recognize and acknowledge both their feelings and your own.

4. **Identify if children may need professional mental health support for anxiety.**

    - For example, they do not enjoy things they used to enjoy. They are having trouble sleeping. They are not eating well or eating too much. They cannot function in activities of daily living.

5. **Help your child by adjusting time demands.**

    - Children may not have had practice with on-task focus during the lockdown, and anxiety decreases your ability to sustain attention. As such, children will need less time on task to build to pre-lockdown attention capacity.

- The environment may need more structure than before. The environment should be firm but flexible to help them adjust. *When the parent/caregiver exudes confidence, firm boundaries, and caring to the children, it makes a huge impact to decrease anxiety and tension AND can make the environment feel safe and peaceful.*

6. **Most of all, keep it simple.**

   - Don't overwhelm yourself or your children in the beginning.
   - Identify what really matters and focus on that.

It is important to match your expectation and life after lockdown demands with your child's ability and tolerance for that activity. Remember, when children are overwhelmed or anxious, they tend to have an increase in negative behavior.

Resiliency and Relationships

The good news is that we can be resilient! We have the ability to handle stress and anxiety and maintain competent functioning. However, it is important to know that the PRIMARY FACTOR IN RESILIENCY IS **RELATIONSHIP.** There have been tens of thousands of articles written on resiliency and the one common factor among them is that relationships promote both mental and physical resiliency. As we face the stressors that create anxiety, our positive social connections can be the most important supports for our resiliency and mental health. Meaningful doses of social contact, even with physical distance, can be brief and make a huge difference.

In the book *From Neurons to Neighborhoods*, the authors share their understanding of child resiliency and relationships. They offer, "Relationships are among the most significant influences on healthy growth and psychological well-being" (National Research Council and Institute of Medicine 2000, 264). Of course, the corollary for this requires us to realize that children, any child, typically only do as well as their caregiving environment is doing. Children absorb and react to how they sense their environment, so it is important that we self-check and see what environment we are creating. When children are anxious it is our responsibility to share our calm and not join in their turmoil. We need to shore up supports and provide the environment that will promote calm and peace.

There are three primary resiliency factors (adapted from Perry 2007) that we can offer our children during times of stress and anxiety that will help to stabilize their functioning:

- **ROUTINE**–keep schedules
- **BOUNDARIES**–have requirements/keep them safe
- **NURTURANCE**–It's all about relationships–love

This may have been one of the most difficult times you and/or your family has experienced. If everything seems insurmountable right now, that is how it feels to your children too. If it is difficult to balance the multitude of needs and waves of feelings that you and your family are facing at this time you should look for support. While for some, family and other social supports can assist, others may also need to find professional services (particularly if you or your child is having difficulty functioning in everyday circumstances). You should find a mental health counselor. A neutral and safe environment can be helpful to address your concerns. **We are stewards, not just of those whom we care for, but also of our own capacities.** It is important to find ways to do self-care that will allow you to create an environment that your children need.

Remember the transition to life after lockdown is uncharted territory and we will need to give each other grace as we navigate it. Like grieving, we all experience stress and anxiety differently and we will all do this transition differently. We should not tell others how they must grieve, so let us be careful not to dictate to others how they should transition—but we can ask for respect and we can give each other GRACE!

More about Kiti . . .

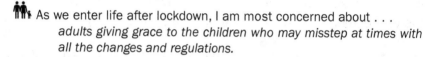 As we enter life after lockdown, I am most concerned about . . .
adults giving grace to the children who may misstep at times with all the changes and regulations.

As we enter life after lockdown, I am most excited about . . .
traveling to see friends and making new friends.

Dr. Kiti is a pediatric neurodevelopmental psychologist with extensive experience in infant high-risk populations, neurodevelopmental disability, trauma, and pre- and postnatal substance/toxin exposure. She is the medical director of the Inland Empire Autism Assessment Center. Dr. Kiti has dedicated her career to children, families, professionals, organizations, and communities to enhance the physical, cognitive, emotional, and spiritual lives of children and their families to promote optimal and healthy living.

References

Bezane, Conor. 2021. "The 'Echo Pandemic' is Real and Your Mental Health is at Stake." *The Mighty*, March 10, 2021. https://themighty.com/2021/03/covid-19-echo-pandemic-mental-health/.

Children's Hospital Colorado. 2021. "Children's Hospital Colorado Declares a 'State of Emergency' for Youth Mental Health." May 25, 2021. https://www.childrenscolorado.org/about/news/2021/may-2021/youth-mental-health-state-of-emergency/.

National Research Council and Institute of Medicine. 2000. *From Neurons to Neighborhoods: The Science of Early Childhood Development*. Committee on integrating the Science of Early Childhood Development. Jack P. Shonkoff and Deborah A. Phillips, eds. Board on Children, Youth, and Families, Commission on Behavioral and Social Sciences and Education. Washington, D.C.: National Academy Press. https://doi.org/10.17226/9824.

Perry, Bruce D. 2007. "Stress, Trauma and Post-traumatic Stress Disorders in Children." The Child Trauma Academy. https://www.mnadopt.org/wp-content/uploads/2017/12/B-Perry-Stress-Trauma-and-PTSD-in-Children.pdf.

TALKING HEAD SYNDROME

JEFFREY JESSUM

After what has seemed like an eternity, the world is beginning to come back to life. Vaccines are readily available, cases are down significantly, restaurants and businesses are opening. And of course, high up on this list, schools are transitioning back to in-person learning. A whole generation of blossoming humans who have been placed in a developmental deep freeze for the last year is coming out of hibernation and preparing to rejoin the world after sheltering in place. It's a cause for celebration, without a doubt. But for many, the road back to normal might not be as smooth as we would hope. This is especially true for children and young adults with special needs.

Technology has made social distancing more bearable in many ways. Because of video conferencing, we've been able to see the faces and hear the voices of our loved ones in real-time, even when they are miles and miles away from us. Many of us have been able to continue our work and be productive contributors to society because of video conferencing and other virtual technologies. And even though the circumstances are far from ideal and many kids have fallen behind both socially and academically, we've been able to continue providing an education to students. Video games and social media have offered a medium for kids to connect. Netflix, Hulu, YouTube, and other platforms have helped us all, young and old, fill the void that social distancing and stay-at-home has created.

The virtual world that technology has brought forth has helped us stay connected in many important ways. However, virtual connecting is not the same as in-person, full-spectrum connecting. Virtual connecting offers us some interpersonal popcorn instead of much-needed, nutrient-rich relating. And like popcorn, virtual connecting gives us the illusion of satiation without providing the real relational nourishment we need to grow and thrive as humans.

> 66 Talking Head Syndrome: A pervasive disconnection from one's own body. 99

In the virtual world, we are all reduced to disembodied talking heads. Our coworkers now appear solely as two-dimensional boxes on our screen. Their hair might be combed and their shirts pressed and cleaned, but there is a good chance that outside the limited range of the camera lens, they are wearing the same sweatpants they've worn all week. We don't wear sweatpants to rebel or because we are not able to conform to social norms. We wear them because it does not matter. Because in the world of talking heads, everything outside the realm of the camera's eye is irrelevant.

This is true for our kids as well. With the exception of the few other humans within their immediate pod, kids' social interactions have been limited to two-dimensional, animated thumbnails of their peers on Zoom or Microsoft Classroom. And as is true for most of us, those thumbnails primarily show only the head.

During the pandemic kids also lost the important opportunities for embodied social nourishment that happen at school outside of structured learning. With distance learning, there is no opportunity for casual chit-chat before class, or when the teacher is not looking. There is no opportunity to interact in the hallways or at lunch and recess, or when waiting for pick-up after school.

What happens to kids in circumstances like these when most of their daily interactions are with disembodied talking heads? And when all they present to others is a talking head? What happens to kids when they spend the majority of the day sitting inside, staring at their screens?

They develop what I call *"Talking Head Syndrome"*—a pervasive disconnection from one's own body. In the virtual world, the incentive to focus on the body fades away. There is no need to be authentic. Other talking heads don't notice a body, so there is no need for us to focus on it. Sitting all day also makes it easy to ignore our bodies. In the world of virtual relating, the body only gets in the way and takes our attention away from the screen. Altogether this creates a pandemic-induced, disembodied *Groundhog Day*, in which the world of the body and of authenticity is replaced by a digitized, fabricated echo of the social world we once lived and thrived in.

Talking Head Syndrome is a challenge for all of us. The truth is, it has been a challenge long before the pandemic. The virtual world has pulled our attention away from the embodied world. We all have been trained to respond to the dopamine hits of screen engagement, which has resulted in us channeling more and more of our attention away from embodied relating and *towards* disembodied talking-head relating. But the measures we have needed to take to keep ourselves, our loved ones, and our fellow human beings safe during the pandemic have brought this habit of talking-head relating to another level.

The not-so-surprising reality is that for many kids already struggling with interpersonal difficulties, living in the pandemic-induced world of talking heads has offered some respite. Many of our kids struggled with Talking Head Syndrome long before the pandemic. Only having to relate from the neck up has provided many of them with a sense of relief. The world of embodied relating has always been chaotic and mysterious to them and only having to relate from the neck up has made their lives simpler and more manageable. But not having to relate in more embodied ways atrophies the skills kids may have been struggling to acquire prior to the pandemic. For many kids, the social gains they made pre-pandemic have been lost. And unlike neurotypical kids, it will be more of a challenge to limber up and reacquaint themselves with their bodies and the nonverbal body communications of others as we now resume connecting in person.

The Importance of Body Awareness

Connection to our body is incredibly important socially. When we're connected to our bodies, we tend to feel more comfortable in our own skin. When we suffer from Talking Head Syndrome, we're much less likely to feel comfortable in our own skin, which inevitably translates into feeling more awkward when relating to others in embodied ways. Body awkwardness can be more easily pushed to the sidelines in virtual screen relating, but we can't ignore the body when we are relating in person.

> 66 When we suffer from Talking Head Syndrome, we're much less likely to feel comfortable in our own skin. 99

Our bodies also give us important information about what others are feeling and about appropriate ways of responding socially. When someone falls and hurts themselves, we often feel a twinge of pain in our own body. If someone is sad, we often feel a heaviness in our chest. But when we are not connected with our bodies, we will not sense these things. In addition, the majority of social relating is nonverbal. When we're disconnected from our own body, we will inevitably be at a disadvantage reading others' nonverbal communication, as well as communicating nonverbally ourselves.

Nonverbal, body-centered information helps us form a comprehensive social map. Awareness of our own body helps us to not only sense interpersonal communications, but also to organize and make sense of all the social information coming our way. One of the reasons people on the spectrum have so much trouble interpersonally is because they already have some degree of Talking Head Syndrome, and lack awareness of the important information their body contributes to a comprehensive map of the social world.

When we can't rely on the body for important clues about our social world, relating becomes much more difficult to understand and navigate. This leaves kids in a situation where they don't have the tools to organize the large amounts of social information that comes their way. For many kids, this results in higher anxiety around transitioning back into the complex social dynamics that occur when relating with peers. And often this kind of anxiety is followed by other problematic behaviors, such as resistance, withdrawal, agitation, and defiance.

Being disconnected from our body also interferes with our ability to regulate our nervous system. Awareness is the first step in regulation. It helps us to identify what's going on inside us so we can engage in effective regulation strategies.

Feeling uncomfortable in our own skin, lacking important information necessary to understanding and navigating the social terrain, anxiety, and trouble regulating our nervous systems create a perfect storm for a difficult transition back to in-person learning and face-to-face relating. But the good news is that even for kids who are more susceptible to Talking Head Syndrome, there are things that can be done to reacquaint oneself with the body. Even if skills were not great to begin with, there is muscle memory. Skills that have atrophied because of lack of use can come back with practice, and with intention and targeted remediation, new skills can be built.

Antidotes to Talking Head Syndrome

One of the most powerful and simple ways to get more in touch with the body is to move it. When we spend our days staring at the screen, our attention is on the screen, and we are therefore only aware of the screen. However, when we take our attention off the screen and move our bodies, our attention will naturally be drawn to what the body is doing – how it moves, balances, and feels inside. How you move the body is not as important as the act of moving it.

Most importantly, we need to get kids off the couch, out in the world, and back in their bodies. You can go on hikes with them or have them help you garden in the backyard. Sign them up for a summer sport or an activity-based camp. Shoot some hoops with them. You can do yoga or go to the gym with them. Maybe sign them up for martial arts or gymnastics. Biking, skating, swimming, bowling, golfing, laser tag, trampolining . . . there are countless ways to move the body that can be fun. And as much as possible, do these things *with* them.

> 66 Most importantly, we need to get kids off the couch, out in the world and back in their bodies. 99

You can have a dance party at home or in class where you all move your bodies to music. Some might feel self-conscious dancing, especially after a year of talking-head living. If this is the case, you can put on some music during your less-structured family or class time and just start moving to the music while you are doing your individual or collective projects. Let them see you moving your body to the beat and invite them to join the fun. Feel the rhythm of the music and ask them if they can feel it. Music with a pronounced bass rhythm can be particularly effective because deep bass is more easily sensed in the body. Ask them if they sense the low-frequency rhythm of the bass in their bodies and share your experience of that as well.

You can also intentionally infuse these kinds of embodied activities with mindful awareness. In my book, *Social Detective Academy,* and in our classes at Social Detective Academy, we have a series of practices aimed to increase mindfulness of one's body as well as awareness of our other senses.

The body scan is a simple practice kids can do on their own or incorporate into other body-oriented activities. You can use it with kids before bed, or during the day at home or school. With practice, it has a cumulative effect on one's ability to sense their own somatic world. I have included an excerpt from my book at the end of this chapter that offers a written script for a basic body scan. I've also provided a link to an audio body scan meditation we use in our Social Detective Academy programs: https://www.socialdetectiveacademy.com/body-awareness-practice/

The goal of the body scan is to increase awareness of one's own body—to shine a "spotlight of attention" on the body, rather than shining it onto the attention-grabbing screens that exist in the realm of the talking heads. Awareness of the body includes awareness of physical sensations, as well as feelings. Helping kids become more aware of states of tension and relaxation, comfort and discomfort, energy and fatigue, as well as the full spectrum of feelings they might experience, has broad-reaching positive effects.

The body scan is a practice we can all benefit from. It is a wonderful way of sharing embodied experiences together. I encourage you to practice this with the people in your life, both young and old, and share your experiences with one another. Move away from the realm of the talking head and incorporate this embodied realm into your exchanges with one another.

I believe that the importance of skills in all these areas extends beyond helping kids transition back into in-person learning and face-to-face relating. These skills are also important for helping them be more socially competent and satisfied in their lives, and to become contributing members of society. The kids of today will be the authors of tomorrow's world. Social and emotional competence in all its forms will bolster our children in ways that increase the likelihood that they become the protagonists of the next generation so that their intentions and actions can help to make the world a better place—a hope so many of us have for the kids we parent, care for, and work with.

More about Jeffrey . . .

As we enter life after lockdown, I am most concerned about . . .
our ability to learn from our mistakes.

As we enter life after lockdown, I am most excited about . . .
our ability to learn from our mistakes.

Jeffrey Ethan Jessum is a clinical psychologist and long-time practitioner of Mindfulness Meditation. Dr. Jessum has worked at UCLA Neuropsychiatric institute, Children's Hospital Los Angeles, the Veterans Hospital, Los Angeles and a variety of community outpatient settings. He is currently in private practice, serving a diverse clientele with a wide variety of issues. One of his areas of specialization is social emotional intelligence training.

Books

- *Diary of a Social Detective: Real-life Tales of Mystery, Intrigue and Interpersonal Adventure*
- *Social Detective Academy: How to Become Your Own Social Detective* (Fall 2021)

Website

https://www.socialdetectiveacademy.com/

The Body Scan

(from the book Social Detective Academy)

Start by getting in a comfortable position. Close your eyes and imagine your spotlight of attention. Shine that spotlight on your feet so that all your attention focuses on your feet. Let everything else go dark except the place where your spotlight is going. And as you do this, allow yourself to notice what it feels like in your feet.

Are your feet hot or cold? Do they feel heavy or light? Is there a comfortable feeling in them, or do they feel uncomfortable? Or maybe there is just a neutral feeling. Be poetic in how you describe the feelings in your feet. Maybe they feel bubbly or tingly, or like there is a little river of energy running through them. Maybe they feel as if they are tightening or releasing. It might feel like static in there, like when the radio is not tuned in properly. Or like water flowing, or feathers tickling, or little rubber balls bouncing up and down in there. Let your words and your imagination find ways to describe what it might feel like in your feet.

You may also find that as you shine your spotlight of attention, the feeling seems to have a shape or color to it. It may seem like the feeling is moving in a certain direction or as if it is very still. It may seem like your feet are as hard as steel or as soft as tapioca pudding. It may even feel as if the sensation is stronger in one spot and weaker in other spots of your foot, or as if there is one specific spot the feeling is starting at and then radiating out to other places.

Once you have spent a little time shining your attention on your feet, let your spotlight move up to your lower legs. Do the same thing here that you did with your feet. Notice if there are comfortable, uncomfortable, or neutral feelings. Notice temperature and tension. Be poetic in your description of what you are feeling in the same way you did with your feet. After spending some time with your lower legs, move your spotlight to your upper legs, then to your waist, and then your stomach and chest.

Often people feel a lot of the more subtle sensations, like emotions and tensions, in their chest, so make sure to give some special attention to this area. Keep moving the spotlight slowly to cover all the places in your body. From your stomach and chest, you can move up to your throat, then to your shoulders and arms, then to your back and up the back of your neck, all the way to the top of your head. Come to the front again, and let your spotlight shine on your face and eyes and mouth. Notice all the different flavors of sensation you might be feeling in your body in different places. (Jessum 2021)

THE NEW NORMAL: HOW I MANAGE ANXIETY

KERRY MAGRO

After being nonspeaking till two and a half and diagnosed autistic at four, I thrived in early intervention, receiving physical, occupational, speech, theater, and music therapies. The words started coming at age three and complete sentences at seven. I went from nonspeaking to having a career in professional speaking as one of the few openly autistic certified public speaking professionals in the country. During my travels I have had the opportunity to write several books on my life growing up autistic, consult on several films to bring a realistic portrayal of disability to our entertainment industry, and be a mentor/consultant for businesses, schools, and self-advocates alike.

Through all these journeys, and with speaking later becoming a strength, the majority of my parents' challenges after helping me discover my voice were sensory, emotional, and anxiety-related. During the COVID-19 pandemic, my anxiety came to the forefront as a public speaker. Most of my speaking events were either canceled or postponed as physical distancing became part of the "new normal." Some people were able to deal better with COVID-19 than others, but because of my autism, my challenges grew.

As part of my speaking efforts up until COVID, I also had the opportunity to bring a camera and sit down with self-advocates to hear them share their stories, while also nurturing their self-advocacy. Unfortunately, many of these opportunities got pushed to Zoom meetings during COVID, which was awkward. Thankfully, now that we are moving forward and things are changing again, I can finally go back to meeting more members of our community in person. So let us talk a bit about managing potential anxiety that you or someone you know may face when reentering society.

Seeking Professional Support

Autism is a vast spectrum, and as my dear friend Dr. Stephen Shore says, "If you have met one person with autism, you have met one." One of the first universal steps I always recommend is ruling out as many associated mental health conditions as humanly possible. Suppose you have anxiety and talk to your physician about it. They may evaluate you and diagnose you with one or several different anxiety-related diagnoses, including general anxiety. They may also be looking at obsessive-compulsive disorder or other anxiety-related disorders. Many in our autism community have a dual diagnosis that can fall under the radar. For example, even though I was diagnosed with pervasive developmental disorder – not otherwise specified (PDD-NOS, another form of autism) at four, I was in my teens before I received the diagnosis of dysgraphia, a handwriting disorder.

Speaking of diagnoses, social anxiety disorder and some of its characteristics may be more prevalent in life after lockdown because of the fear of going back out into social situations. Today in the United States, anxiety disorders are the most common mental illness. That is why understanding preexisting anxiety and post-COVID-19-related anxiety can help with identifying triggers that may require treatment. Negative thoughts may linger for those who have lost someone during the pandemic, for those who are still recovering from testing positive, or for those who lost their job. Those who have autism, which is fundamentally a social and communication disorder, were already struggling with social skills before COVID-19 and will still need guidance in this area. It is crucial, though, to push yourself. Temple Grandin says it is important to "stretch yourself and remember not to stretch yourself too thin." Self-reflection exercises such as meditation or journaling can help you in this area to avoid burnout and added anxiety.

> 66 Those who have autism . . . were already struggling with social skills before COVID-19 99

As a young child, when I was dealing with challenging behaviors, my parents sought out medical and mental health help for me for a short time. It was helpful to talk to someone about what I was feeling with someone who understood what I was going through. I would also recommend educating yourself about the facts of COVID-19, so you are not getting any false information from other sources. The Centers for Disease Control and Prevention have data trackers that not only break down the prevalence of COVID cases in your area but also have information about what, if any, restrictions are still happening in your area. There is also information on health and safety guidance that may be beneficial for yourself and your loved ones to review.

Establishing a Schedule and Preparing for Social Outings

One way you may manage anxiety is by establishing a routine schedule. Many like myself use structure to avoid uncertainty, and this leads to a decrease in anxiety. One issue I have seen in my consultant work with autistic youth is the challenge of transition and changes, ranging from something small, like moving from one activity to another, to something big, like moving to a new school. With things opening up, we will see these transitions and routine changes again as many return to in-person therapy and school, and interacting with others socially face-to-face.

In building this routine, you should consider creating a daily schedule. In this daily schedule, you should have times for meals and breaks. The following is an example of what a daily schedule would look like for me.

8:00-9:00	Wake up	Shower, get dressed, morning TV, have breakfast
9:00-11:00	Emails/Phone calls/ Complete assignments	Look at Google Calendar to see what is on the schedule for the week, follow up with speaker inquiries sent to me from the weekend, review action items on the to-do list
11:00-11:45	Cardio	Walk/run on a treadmill, read a book if using a standing desk
11:45-12:15	Personal time	Catch up with friends – texts
12:15-1:00	Lunch	
1:00-1:30	Creative time	Write a blog for one of my social media accounts
1:30-3:30	Emails/Phone calls/ Complete assignments	Assignments done in the morning, then work on creative projects (next book, new presentations, video projects)
3:30-4:00	Break	Go outside for a walk, get fresh air

4:00-5:30	Emails/Phone calls/ Complete assignments	If assignments from morning work are completed, work on creative projects (next book, new presentations, video projects)
5:30-7:00	Dinner/Relaxing time	
7:00-11:00	Socializing/Relaxing time	
11:00-12:00	Slow down time/Go to bed	

You can use this template to set up a daily schedule for you or someone else. When creating daily schedules, some people forget to add meals, which are essential because some in our autism community need reminders to eat. Some individuals may find it easier to follow a daily schedule with more structure. In that case, you can implement a visual schedule or social narrative to break down tasks into smaller steps. Google Calendar is a free application that I use on all my devices. I receive a push notification an hour and 30 minutes before each of the transitions, which helps whenever I have to alter my schedule.

When you think about scheduling social outings, you can consider priming or roleplaying to help ease concerns. For example, if you are going to a restaurant with a few friends, you can jot down on a piece of paper some questions you might have like, Is it ok to hug them? Or, Will we shake hands or just greet each other with a wave? Thinking about the possibilities beforehand may ease some of the anxiety of the outing. Role-playing was helpful for me as a kid in understanding things such as friendships and speaking up about bullying situations to help decrease my anxiety and depression due to loneliness.

It may also be helpful to plan social gatherings ahead of time versus spontaneously. Thinking about certain times in the day when there may be fewer people around can hopefully relieve some anxiety. Be mindful of dating as well and what will help you feel the most comfortable. Many are still pursuing virtual dating via platforms, such as video chatting, versus in-person dating for the time being. If you are dating in person, openly communicate with each other as much as possible about your needs and what you feel comfortable with when it comes to levels of intimacy.

Other Ways to Relieve Anxiety

Exercise is something I have found to be helpful in relieving stress. I would recommend at least 30 minutes of physical activity each day (nothing strenuous, could just be walking). Regular exercise releases endorphins, decreasing muscle tension which can help with anxiety. When the pandemic began, I bought a treadmill and a standing desk, so I focused on my physical health when we were on lockdown. Now that we are coming out of lockdown, I am still doing my 30 minutes a day, but I switch it up to doing it outside, as many people believe the fresh air can have psychological benefits. Spending time outdoors has led over time to my passion for photography. I now bring a camera everywhere I go to take photos and turn them into fine art photography.

Eating a healthy diet could be beneficial. Also, do not forgo sleep. Keeping a routine also means self-care and getting the right number of hours based on your sleep needs. At the end of the day, your physical health can have benefits for your mental health.

Now, if new anxiety forms in this new normal and leads to either high- or low-sensory stimulation, you may want to consider different sensory and deep pressure products to help with self-soothing. Music can also provide some soothing effects for those managing anxiety. I have noticed myself listening to more music recently since things have opened up to ease my anxiety. R&B music, which has soft, slow tones, has been of benefit. For me, it has always been helpful to focus on specific sounds within the music. As a child who hated loud noises, there was always something soothing about music that helped me tremendously as a part of my therapy during my early development and intervention.

In addition to using music to ease anxiety, you may consider meditation, deep breathing, and diaphragm exercises. Writing in a journal can also be a helpful avenue to consider in life after lockdown for additional anxiety. I find it very therapeutic. As we are opening up again, I plan on doing more journaling. If you are suffering from any panic attacks or meltdowns from anxiety, a journal is a good place to keep track. Take note of how long they occur, of what you remember feeling (sensory challenges, stimming), and if applicable, what may have led to the incident.

Those who are autistic, like myself, may have a key interest they can focus on for long periods. Focusing on these interests after the lockdown has helped me "get lost" and get out of my head. For example, when outdoor seating first opened during COVID-19 pandemic, I found bars where I could watch football and basketball games to lose myself and not be so worried about being out in public. Focusing on interests may help ease the transition into life after lockdown.

Final Thoughts

> **"** If your child is in school, please consider prioritizing mental health over grades . . . . **"**

If you have a nonspeaking loved one, make sure to try to meet them as much as you can at their level. Read their body language. Are they making any odd body movements you have never seen before? Are they stimming and flapping their hands? Are they sweating or refusing to eat? Also, are they having more occurrences of self-injurious-related behaviors? All these things can be an indicator of a potential increase in anxiety.

If your child is in school, please consider prioritizing mental health over grades, with most schools going back to in-person learning. That first semester may be a time of intense routine change and uncertainty due to social distancing and the possible elimination of masks. As bullying is often more common for those with an autism spectrum disorder, this may cause extra anxiety.

As I stated earlier in this chapter, autism is a vast spectrum. No two people are affected in the same way. What is effective in reducing anxiety for one individual may not be effective for another. I've shared what has helped me manage my anxiety in the past and what I am currently doing as we enter this post-pandemic phase of our lives. I hope you can take from this chapter what might be helpful for you or your child to make this transition more successful.

Finally, as we move down the road into life after lockdown, I continue to tell my mentees: It is ok to fail. It is ok not to be where you want to be yet. These feelings are valid. You are on your path. As someone who still deals with anxiety to this day, know that you are not alone while you manage your anxiety. As for me, I am managing my anxiety by knowing the facts. I still feel more comfortable wearing my mask in some crowded areas, bringing hand sanitizer with me whenever I go out in public, and speaking and doing meetings virtually when possible. I know it will take some time for me to get used to this transition. Include others, like friends and allies, in your plans, and help them create their own comfort zones. In a world that looks very different, it could make a world of difference.

More about Kerry . . .

- As we enter life after lockdown, I am most concerned about . . .
  how our autism community deals with the change in routine going back to a "new normal life."

- As we enter life after lockdown, I am most excited about . . .
  getting back on the road. As a full-time speaker, I was used to being on the road and out of state 3-4 times a month. Can't wait to meet more members of our community!

5

Dr. Kerry Magro is an award-winning public speaker, best-selling author, autism entertainment consultant, nonprofit founder, anti-bullying activist, and autistic self-advocate. For his efforts, Kerry has been featured in major media and worked with amazing brands including NBC's Today Show, CBS News, Inside Edition, Upworthy, and HuffPost, among others. He is based in New Jersey and can be contacted about speaker inquiries at Kerrymagro@gmail.com.

Books

o   *Defining Autism from The Heart*
o   *Autism and Falling in Love*
o   *I Will Light It Up Blue!*

Website

http://kerrymagro.com/

HELPING YOUR CHILD WHILE HELPING YOURSELF

CAROL BURMEISTER

The COVID-19 pandemic has affected our lives in a variety of ways. Many of us have had to establish new routines, find new ways to communicate and interact with others, and learn and use new technology that, however useful it may be, frustrates us at times. For some, fear and fluctuations in how everyday tasks are conducted have made the world an overwhelming place to navigate, causing anxiety and stress levels to escalate. When stress overwhelms, skills that allow us to function successfully can disappear. As adults, we may not be able to hold information in our minds. We may not be able to organize daily tasks. We may not be able to see the big picture. We may not be able to make decisions. We lose our cool when something seemingly minor happens. We may not be able to successfully juggle a multitude of commitments. How can we best support our children if we can't support ourselves?

How You Can Help Yourself

You can help yourself with **being flexible** by realizing that what you may experience when reentering society may be vastly different than what you experienced before, and adapting to varied situations and expectations by being able to change your mind and make changes to plans or routines as needed.

You can help yourself with **leveling or managing your emotions** by understanding the causes of frustration and anxiety and learning coping strategies that support self-regulation.

You can help yourself with **controlling your impulses** by thinking before blurting out comments or taking actions such as waiting your turn to speak in a conversation, and by staying focused on a task until it is completed.

You can help yourself with **planning and organizing** by making plans, keeping track of time and materials, and staying organized so that tasks are finished on time. This may include prioritizing, breaking tasks down into manageable chunks, and understanding and using visual organizational tools to effectively manage time.

You can help yourself with **problem-solving** by recognizing when there is a problem to be solved, determining possible solutions, choosing one, and evaluating the outcome.

How You Can Help Your Child

You can help your child by modeling appropriate behaviors and talking through your thoughts and actions as you do so:

Flexibility: *You have a lot on your agenda for the day, which starts with making an important phone call. You are put on hold, with the auditory message that the wait time will be 47 minutes. "That's okay, I can be* **flexible.** *I can put the phone on speaker mode, then finish folding the clean laundry and chop the vegetables for dinner while I wait."*

 Leveled Emotions: *You have to go in to work for a few hours and you've left your preteen son and daughter a list of chores to be completed during your absence. Upon returning home, you find that they did not complete their chores and are instead playing video games. You are pretty upset, and your first thought is to shout at your children that you are taking away all their electronics for a year. Attempting to* **level your emotions,** *you tell your children to start their chores while you cuddle with your dogs for ten minutes, letting them know that after you calm down you will discuss the consequences of their behavior.*

 Impulse Control: *Just before sitting down to help your daughter on a school project, you receive a group text about a party invitation. As you work with your daughter, you get text notifications continuously as multiple responses to the original text come in. "I'd like to check on the activity, but I'm helping you right now and my focus should be on that. I am going to* **control the impulse** *to look at my phone. I can wait to check the messages later."*

 Planning and Organizing: *You and your child have multiple errands to run tomorrow and a limited time to accomplish this. "Let's make a* **plan and organize** *our day. We will make a list of what we have to do as well as the places we have to stop. After that, let's estimate the time we think we might need at each stop. We have to be back home by 4:00 so we need to make sure we can get all of our errands done in time."*

 Problem Solving: *You receive a phone call informing you that a relative is bringing four additional people to a long-planned*

*family dinner. You express to your children, "I have a problem. I planned our meal for ten people and now we have fourteen coming for dinner. How can I **solve this problem**? What are some options for solving this problem? I can serve smaller portions, I can take leftovers out of the freezer, I can ask the relative who just called to stop at the supermarket and pick up a quart of potato salad and a deli chicken, or I can tell the relative that we can't accommodate four additional people. I think asking that relative to make a stop to pick up a chicken and some potato salad would be the best solution."*

You can also help your child by supporting and coaching your child when you see them struggling with a situation:

 Flexibility: *Your children's grandma has suffered a fall and needs to be cared for by you. That means that the family's trip to an amusement park must be postponed. Your young son doesn't really understand Grandma's situation, but he is devastated by what this turn of events means for him. You explain that plans sometimes change and, even though you know he is sad that the family has to postpone the amusement park trip, being flexible helps us all get through situations we might not like.*

 Leveled Emotions: *You are grocery shopping when your pre-teen daughter calls you in a panic to tell you that something very scary has happened and she doesn't know what to do. Once you determine that there doesn't appear to be a real emergency, you ask her to calm down and tell you exactly what's going on. She clarifies that the problem is that she has seen a huge spider in the living room. You ask her, on a scale of 1 to 10, how big the problem is. When she responds that, in her mind, it's an 8, you remind her to use one of her calming strategies, such as putting on her headphones and listening to music or drawing on her sketchpad in another room until you return home.*

Impulse Control: *Your children are playing a game based on a game show theme. They are supposed to take turns answering questions, but your younger son struggles with waiting for his turn and blurts out answers, even when it's not his turn. His siblings are tiring of this behavior. You remind your son that even though he may have all of the answers, everyone gets to have a turn. When he controls his impulse to shout out the answers, the players have more fun.*

 Planning and Organizing: *Your child has been invited to accompany their friend and family on a week-long camping trip. Your child has never been camping before and will need to pack and organize their items so that they fit into one large duffel bag. You suggest they ask their friend about the activities they will be participating in. You encourage your child to try to get the "big picture"—to visualize in their mind what they will be doing on that trip so that they can figure out what they might need to pack.*

 Problem Solving: *Your teenage son has just been asked by his employer to work an extra shift over the weekend. Before he responds to his employer, he tells you that he has a problem and he's not sure what to do. He defines the problem as the fact that his employer wants him to work, but he has already made plans with his friends. You ask, "How can you solve that problem?" You coach him through determining some possible solutions. Your son decides the best solution is to work the extra shift and reschedule his outing with his friends.*

These scenarios demonstrate the appropriate use of executive function skills. The term executive function (EF) refers to a group of mental processes that help us to be more mentally flexible, less impulsive, able to control our emotions, and capable of planning and problem solving—aiding us essentially in carrying out any task successfully. When executive function is working well, life goes smoothly.

There is no universally agreed-upon definition of executive function components, but one way to recall the types of skills that fall under the category of executive functions is to remember the acronym FLIPP: **F**lexibility, **L**eveled Emotionality, **I**mpulse Control, **P**lanning, and **P**roblem Solving (Wilkins and Burmeister 2015; Burmeister, Wilkins, and Silva 2021). These five components of executive function, which have been defined earlier in this chapter, are ones that are consistently evident in people who have well-developed EF skills. Another component of EF is working memory, which works in concert with the other skills by supporting individuals in holding information in the mind long enough to process it, make a decision, and then act on that decision.

> " As we reenter society and we all adjust to new expectations, this is the perfect time to be strategic in paying attention to our own thoughts, behaviors, and actions. "

We are not born with executive function skills, and they are not fully developed until young adulthood. Executive function deficits are closely linked with individuals with autism, but many individuals of all ages, with or without a diagnosed disability, struggle with executive function. The good news is that EF skills can be taught and strengthened.

Conclusion

As we reenter society and we all adjust to new expectations, this is the perfect time to be strategic in paying attention to our own thoughts, behaviors, and actions. Find teachable moments during which you can model those behaviors that demonstrate the traits of flexibility, leveled emotions, impulse control, planning and organizing, and problem-solving—all components of competent executive function. Ask others who interact with your child to do the same. When we use appropriate EF behaviors, we can reduce our stress and anxiety. When we model the appropriate behaviors while articulating this to our children, we can support all of us in building the EF skills critical to success in all environments.

More about Carol . . .

🏠 As we enter life after lockdown, I am most concerned that . . .
individuals who are struggling with stress and anxiety have the resources available that will help them learn to cope in a healthy way.

😊 As we enter life after lockdown, I am most excited about . . .
seeing smiles on unmasked faces.

Serving as an educational assistant, general education teacher, special educator, program specialist, university instructor, and consultant across a variety of settings has provided me with so many opportunities to work alongside remarkable students, their families, and the professionals who support them. For the past several years, my work has focused on the crucial topic of executive function (EF), helping students and parents as well as educators understand the complexity of social, academic, and behavioral challenges that accompany EF deficits and how teaching specific skills in childhood and adolescence can have a positive impact on adulthood. I hope I have made a difference and I am truly grateful for all of these experiences!

Books

o *FLIPP the Switch: Strengthen Executive Function Skills*, with co-author Sheri Wilkins
o *FLIPP the Switch 2.0: Mastering Executive Function Skills from School to Adult Life for Students with Autism*, with co-authors Rebecca Silva and Sheri Wilkins

References

Burmeister, Carol, Sheri Wilkins, and Rebecca Silva. 2021. *FLIPP the Switch: Mastering Executive Function Skills from School to Adult Life for Students with Autism*. Shawnee, KS: AAPC.

Wilkins, Sheri, and Carol Burmeister. 2015. *FLIPP the Switch: Strengthen Executive Function Skills*. Shawnee Mission, KS: AAPC.

MOVING FORWARD: FINDING THE SUNSHINE

GAIL SHOFFEY

Daylight hurts my eyes, so I wake up before dawn and enjoy the gradience of sunlight. Most mornings, I wake up with a fair amount of energy. I like to hike every morning with my chocolate Labrador, Reign, my service dog. I started walking during lockdown because walking a dog was considered essential. My walks were for miles. My thoughts were intense.

Once I got over a media-induced feeling of panic about catching the virus, I began to enjoy lockdown. Everyone had to stay home during lockdown; I loved staying home. Services that were previously unavailable to me were now accessible online. I did not have to go into public places. The pandemic has permanently changed how I feel about going to public places. I enjoyed how the world opened up to me during the pandemic, and now I face reintegration.

Biopsychosocial Stress

The following are the stressors that I feel in life after lockdown and how I deal with them. I am not a medical doctor; therefore, I am presenting my ideas as entirely my own program of living with autism and coping with stress. The stress markers are bio-psychosocial—physical, psychological, and social. Biologically, the various body systems, organs, and tissues are all affected by stress. Psychological distress, anxiety, or even fear must not guide my thoughts, feelings, and actions; therefore, I need external and internal coping methods. Social efficacy is a struggle without all the social rules quickly changing in our current environment. The intersection of these three elements is the core of solid mental health.

Physical

The physical issues with reintegration involve my body, my mind, and my senses. It was hard getting used to wearing a mask because I was not used to covering my face. After some time, I began to feel comfortable behind the façades because I did not have to worry about my facial expressions being *appropriate*. Reintegration is allowing for masks to be optional in some places. When I am in a crowd of people without a mask, I do not know if I am being seen or not. I do not know what face I should be wearing. Am I supposed to smile at everyone? If I look down, will people not see me? I feel very uncomfortable in crowds. I will struggle with showing my face again.

I followed my doctor's recommendation that I get vaccinated against the COVID-19 virus. Considerations before going into public places include not knowing who has been vaccinated, recently exposed to COVID-19, or has not seen a doctor for other infectious diseases. People may be in poor general health and be susceptible to increased health issues because they or their doctor postponed routine care and elective procedures.

Physically, I feel the stress on my body in many ways, such as headaches, teeth grinding, neck aches, and increased nervous habits (stimming). To combat these stressors, I first follow my doctor's orders, take my prescribed medications, exercise, and watch my diet. I walk every day with Reign. I try to eat primarily plant-based foods.

Psychological

Psychological stress is a normal reaction to changes in environments, new routines, new expectations, and responsibilities. There is a new normal where isolation and social distancing are practiced. As people reintegrate after lockdown, there is fear of infection, personal issues like interpersonal conflict, a sense of loss from missed activities like graduation ceremonies, financial stress, the widening political polarization, and anxiety of social unrest.

> 66 Psychological stress is a normal reaction to changes in environments, new routines, new expectations, and responsibilities. 99

Growing up, I was expected to know the proper behaviors and responses to social situations. I learned what was "right" after I was "wrong" a few times . . . the equivalent of social narratives, but going through them in practice instead of in theory. I recognize that the psychological stress symptoms have affected me in the following ways: My executive functions have slowed down, I have more problems communicating, more nightmares, increased irritability, and frequent mood swings.

People with disabilities often have co-occurring mental issues. Doubts, distractions, and worries can lead to depression or exacerbate other mental health problems. I feel the psychological stress challenging because I find it difficult to know who, what, where, and when new rules apply. What others often refer to as *common sense* has been a source of frustration because these are ordinarily unspoken rules of engagement. I need explicit instructions. My best resource is the autism community. When I ask particular questions, the autism community explicitly shares these *secret* rules that everyone else seems to know.

As an aside, I can give you an example of a common-sense rule. You have a five-foot-wide board that you want to put into the truck, and I am standing in your way. If you come towards me, I will try to figure out what to do. I would think: Is this a test to see if I will not move, or am I sup-posed to take the board from you? I may not think about moving out of the way. Plainly asking me to move out of the path is explicit instruction.

To combat my anxiety about becom-ing social again, I practice keeping my mind active by learning declarative knowledge through reputable sources. I tutor advanced education, currently with one student earning his Bachelor of Science in Sociology. He is in his third year with a 3.67 GPA. What I do is learn what he has to know, template all the tools he needs to submit successful work, and gear his brain in the learner mode. Arizona State University is a reputable source.

I work on the skills I am good at to increase my potential. During the pandemic, I joined the Autism Society's free online art lessons and discovered that I could draw and paint. I never thought that I could draw and paint; but I can. I create goals and commitments for self-motivation by developing detailed lists and calendar items.

Social ease

The social stressors include having to deal with *all* the sensory inputs and people. All my senses work well; most times, too well. I can see the sun all over my body and all the colors that are reflecting around me. I hear the wind, a heated conversation, a baby crying, and so much more. I feel the different floor coverings, even through my shoes. The best analogy that I can share with neurotypicals is, "Someone scraping their nails down a chalkboard." For many, this sound produces a physical effect. Physical responses to environmental stimuli are the norm for many with autism.

I freeze in a crowd. It just feels overwhelming to move. Reign helps me to keep moving unless I am talking to someone. I grew up learning to deal with crowds at a young age as my parents hosted parties of over 40 people. I remember everything in the form of pictures. I have to make an extra effort to memorize words and contexts consciously.

Fortunately, I drive and have my transportation. I have learned how to have a small circle of friends that I see. The only strangers that I see are in my daily routines. COVID has not changed my limited social access much, though I do even more things alone. I usually wear a mask, and when I meet someone new, I typically choose not to stare them in the eyes. I prefer to process the interaction—the nuances, tone, subject matter, and possible role—before deciding how to respond. One of the biggest favors I can ask is to give me time to process what is said.

Coping Strategies

I learn implicit new social expectations and manage changes to my social *rules-of-behavior* by looking for help from the autism community. There are leaders in the autism community that offer support and explicit instructions. I try to stay cheerful when experiencing any changes. I live with the knowledge that change is certain, and having a positive frame of mind is another skill in which to invest my time.

Individuals with whom I have relationships also provide some comfort. Cultivating relationships are worth the extra effort it takes to be social because everyone needs a friend.

When returning to work or school, it is essential to have a flexible arrangement; gradual reintegration is the key. Accept your feelings because it is possible to be both scared and excited as you ease into new activities or take short trips. You must keep informed of the pandemic status and turn off the information when it no longer becomes productive.

> 66 When returning to work or school, it is essential to have a flexible arrangement; gradual reintegration is the key. 99

Keeping remote activities is vital to me. I have had more help since COVID-19, and I do not want to lose the services that I now have. It is crucial to keep live events low-key and in familiar environments. I usually keep a sensory bag with me. A sensory bag has something for all the senses like sunglasses, different fabrics, noise-canceling headphones, oil scents, music, and some treats.

Keeping my hands busy with crafts or something to fidget with helps my insides stay calm. I like to work with paracord and make bracelets and belts, etc. Other hobbies help keep me calm because I use them as positive reinforcement, such as drawing, painting, and photography. Once I go out and do my necessary errands, I reward myself when I get home by doing something I like, such as my crafts.

The ingredients for happiness include the mind, body, and soul. I regularly exercise my mind. I love patterns of anything from writing programming code to knitting. I learn something new most days by reading or applying new knowledge. I work on my body by hiking with my pets and keeping a balanced diet. Spiritually, I try to be the best person I can. My soul likes the sunshine.

More about Gail . . .

🏠 As we enter life after lockdown, I am most concerned about . . .
    losing, or not being offered, remote services.

🎬 As we enter life after lockdown, I am most excited about . . .
    travel.

Dr. Gail Shoffey, DCSc has a Doctorate in Computer Science and is on the autism spectrum. Dr. Shoffey is passionate about bringing Autism Acceptance to the public through example and education.

SECTION 2

BACK TO SCHOOL

A year of virtual or hybrid-model school left many children and families feeling lost and frustrated, while others felt successful and comfortable with the quiet and greater control over sensory input and social interactions. Whatever the reactions, in-person school is returning. Chapters from Tracey DeMaria, Jennifer Cork, Cathy Pratt, and Amy Gaffney address the challenges of in-person learning and provide strategies for successfully navigating the school environment and addressing a possible loss of skills from the last year. Christa Smith, Gaby Toledo, and Lisa Kistler add insights to the school-home relationship and the IEP process. And Cort Rogers and Jennifer Schmidt share the joy of returning to campus and some positive steps for an enjoyable experience.

This section not only provides great advice, but also invites some interesting questions. As we learn about the ways that virtual school both met the educational needs of some children while being less than ideal for others, how can we plan for a future in which a variety of options may be available? How can we assist parents in supporting their children in all types of learning? And how can we make changes to current in-person learning situations to decrease the sensory overload while maximizing the social benefits?

> 66 I didn't like the lockdown. We are not back to real life yet. I want to be at school with my friends. 99
>
> Lucas G, age 10

> 66 The best part of doing school at home was not having to wake up early. Also, you don't have to worry about turning papers in and you can do all your work online, making you feel less overwhelmed. My favorite part about going back to school is seeing your friends, going to recess, and seeing people in person rather than online. Also, the school has some good lunches. 99
>
> Ava A, age 10

> 66 I am most looking forward to my teacher to stop telling me to pull my mask up. 99
>
> Ocean L, age 10

LEAVING THE COVID ZONE

CORT ROGERS

Have you ever felt like you just entered an episode of *The Twilight Zone*? Well, my first day back to my school after the COVID lockdown felt like I did, and, let me tell you, it was very strange and peculiar. Not seeing anybody for, like, five months was weird so when we had to go back to school it kind of felt like I was at school with a bunch of strangers. When you are on the autism spectrum like me, things like a global pandemic can pretty much change everything about how you see the world.

Let me take you back to March of 2020 when it all started. I remember my mother coming home from a meeting she had at school telling her that they were closing down the schools due to the COVID pandemic. We were on Spring Break at the time and when she sat us down and told us, I immediately got happy because who wouldn't want to be told they didn't have to go back to school? It was like a vacation. Actually, it was an early start to our summer, right? It wasn't.

We had to do distance learning where you have classes on Google Classroom and join Zoom with your teacher and learn like you're in school. We had to finish the school year out that way, which was hard because I work better when my day is planned, or when my schedule is the same every day. I mean don't get me wrong, I feel like I could do distance learning until I graduate because being behind a computer screen is a lot easier than having to talk to someone one-on-one, not to mention making eye contact, which is just painful for me. But if I didn't go back to school and did online learning, I couldn't get better at being social, right?!

Anyway, during the online learning, we were muted most of the time so we didn't talk to our friends that much nor see them in Zoom. However, I did have this one teacher who insisted we all turn our cameras on so she could see our faces while she taught the lesson. I thought to myself, "I don't look at anyone's face that much in normal life, what makes her think I can stare at a screen looking at all 23 kids that are in my class for 40 minutes?" Well, all I knew was that I had to find a solution to this quickly because I wasn't about to do this every day, so I found a picture of myself my mom had on her dresser and propped it in front of my camera, and BAM! Problem solved.

One of the things I have learned to do because of my Asperger's is to problem solve when things are too difficult to handle. My parents want me to go through uncomfortable things and to practice learning how to cope with these things to make it easier for me. I feel like it is very important to make a child who has autism go through situations they may not want to go through because they need to learn how to overcome them on their own. One strategy I use when things get too out of control in my brain is to find a private place to go and escape from everyone around me, every person, every sound, every noise, and I count. Yes, count! At school, it's in the bathroom. If I were at my house, it would be my bedroom. I find that when my brain is too "overloaded" all I need to do is focus on one thing or one subject, and for me, it's math or numbers. It always makes me feel calm and feel like I can face my problems a lot better than when my brain was going "nuts." Being able to learn how to live in this world with Asperger's has been a challenge so when COVID hit it just made it more challenging.

All I have to say about distance learning was it was a pain to get in the meetings because either you have bad internet at your house or lag problems while communicating with others or you didn't understand the teacher's instructions. Online learning wasn't the only thing that made the COVID lockdowns hard—all restaurants in my town were closed and I couldn't go to church which was very weird to me. Either way, it was hard to adjust.

Now let's flashback five months later to the beginning of August when we started school (on school grounds) and communicated with one another in real life again. I know that communication is something I always have to work on but the COVID restrictions made things a little bit harder. For example, how was I supposed to practice reading people's facial expressions when they all had masks on? Having masks on allows you to see only someone's eyes and everyone

1st Day of School 2020

knows that someone with Asperger's (like me) can hardly stand to look someone in the eyes, so what was I supposed to look at, their feet? Luckily, I went to a small school where masks were just recommended and not mandated so it was something that only happened if I was around someone with a mask. There is another boy on campus who has autism and he wore a ski mask that covered his entire head except for his eyes. It was kinda scary, in fact even after the COVID restrictions were gone, he still wore his mask. He said he liked being able to hide from the world. I guess even those of us on the spectrum are all different.

My parents didn't make me wear masks because of my sensory issues. I don't know about y'all, but wearing a mask was like suffocating in cloth and it made my nose itch so much it drove me nuts. It made it hard to talk to others and you smelt your own breath all day which isn't the easiest thing to do. When my body goes through a "sensory overload" like wearing a mask put me in, I couldn't even concentrate on what my teacher was teaching or hear what was asked of me. It was so awful!! I couldn't imagine having to wear my mask every day, I wouldn't survive. I hope teachers around the world understood that when a child with autism was required to wear a mask and was having a hard time, it was because it's just plain uncomfortable.

Wearing masks wasn't the only thing different about going back to school. At my school, not only did the bell schedule for lunch change, meaning not all classes were in the cafeteria at the same time, but there were posters everywhere saying things like "Wear a mask" or "Always stay 6 feet apart." They were mainly in the halls and the library, but it was a constant reminder of how much COVID has changed our lives. Because of COVID, our schools took down all water fountains and bought plastic water bottles for every student, having us carry our water from class to class. Some of the teachers had adjusted their lessons to teach about COVID. I mean, that to me was going too far! My brother had to write a poem about what he felt like during the lockdown and I think it's so good I want to share it with you so I added it here.

I think that the more negative things you hear about anything will only make you fearful of it. For this reason, my parents didn't want me to watch the news because it just made everybody fearful of the world and now I had to sit through a whole reading lesson and slide show of how COVID spreads and how to prevent it from spreading.

My teacher even made a PowerPoint presentation with slide after slide of stats on how many people have died from it. I mean if you ask me, they should teach lessons on how it feels to be in the world with autism and make it mandatory for all teachers to learn how to help kids that may be different. Also, the teachers had to spray and wipe down the desks with this strong disinfectant in between every class to help from spreading any germs.

Ever since the whole COVID thing even started, I feel like some people acted differently than they usually act which made me feel like they were strangers. I figured out that according to their behavior and attitude they probably allowed fear of COVID to somehow take over their thoughts, but some people, like me, stayed the same the whole time. I encourage everyone out there in the world, whether they have autism or not, to always try your hardest to adapt and adjust to the world around you, even during a pandemic.

Trapped

Written by Cayden Rogers

Locked, Caged, and Suffocated

All is lost in a fallen world

Where a virus spreads through the lives of the living

My heart sinking into the deep

I reach out but no one is there

Till I realize that hope was lost

Then I finally felt that hand, it pulled me out

Now that I am back on my feet, I can finally see that there's still hope after all.

More about Cort . . .

My name is Cort Daniel Rogers. I am 12 years old and I live in Graham, TX. I have always had a passion for writing, in fact my mother said I always carried a notebook and pencil everywhere I went and was always writing stories. I want to become a children's book author or a scientist when I grow up. I enjoy playing the piano and spending time with my family. I hope this book will help someone who has just been diagnosed with Asperger's and make them feel like they are not alone.

SURVIVING THE TSUNAMI

TRACEY DEMARIA

March 2020 . . . what a time for the world and humanity. What created change and challenge universally for people across the planet certainly did not miss impacting individuals with an autism spectrum disorder. Over this past year, I have seen a full range of responses from the perspectives of being a therapist working with individuals with ASD, a family member of those with ASD, and more intimately, the parent of a teenager with ASD. Responses have ranged from the complete loss of ability to function that involved a high level of psychiatric care to thriving and a marked improvement in quality of life. It is said by so many and bears saying again: Autism is as diverse as the people who have it. While there are some common groupings of observable traits and characteristics, it is impossible to generalize across the board.

The lockdown periods faced by the world during the COVID-19 pandemic undeniably prompted a huge change in the daily lives of most people. Changes can create distress for so many, even neurotypical individuals. However, those with ASD often struggle more with adapting to change. As a result, children and adults with autism faced additional challenges when they had to adjust to these swift and severe life changes. Some welcomed the changes with relief at the chance to isolate themselves from demands, social pressures, sensory stimuli, and to simply slow down, while others lost the structure and supports that helped them to be functional. Regardless of where a person stood in their response to these changes, the light is flipping back on, and change will be happening again. While the world did not have the luxury of preparing for the first round of change, we know this next one is coming and are better suited to prepare for the impact.

For those people who breathed a sigh of relief due to the decreased demands of life in lockdown, returning to society, school, and work will present challenges because they have gotten used to a life that is less taxing on the nervous system. Too often there are situations in the world that trigger emotional distress or dysregulation of the nervous system, situations that are out of a person's control. But during lockdown, the frequency and intensity of such situations decreased, or was eliminated altogether. It cannot be overstated how difficult it will be for some to go back to a life where the amount of uncontrollable, stressful, and exhausting situations is dramatically increased. We can prepare ourselves and we can prepare children for this process from a cognitive perspective, but the nervous system will likely still experience some degree of shock. It will take time, and it is ideal to begin this gradually whenever possible. It is not a skill like riding a bike. It is more akin to a muscle that can lose strength and mass without use; it may take time to build up a tolerance as the nervous system reacclimates to social, environmental, and sensory triggers.

Before lockdown, most people with ASD spent a great deal of their energy "holding it together" or "masking" when out in the world. The concept of autistic masking is becoming better understood recently due to the increase in self-advocacy among autistic adults. Masking is a way of social camouflaging that allows a person to appear non-autistic so as to conform to neurotypical social expectations (Mandy 2019). Masking is a process that requires a person to hide or suppress their internal state, motor and sensory stims, feelings, emotions, and thoughts to fit in social situations or to meet the expectations of others. People with ASD inevitably learn to do some type of masking from a very early age.

> 66 Masking is a way of camouflaging that allows a person to appear non–autistic so as to conform to neurotypical social expectations. 99

Masking is incredibly exhausting. It can be a large factor for someone who "holds it together" when out in public, at school, parties, play dates, work, etc., then comes home and completely falls apart and needs a lot of recovery time. It is common for parents of children with ASD to hear that their child is not experiencing any problems in school, while this same child comes home completely drained, with meltdowns and severe difficulties while performing everyday tasks at home.

The nervous system, specifically the autonomic nervous system, directly impacts emotions and behaviors and vice versa. So, the increase in nervous system stress because of re-exposure to the stimuli of society and people after lockdown will have an inevitable impact on emotions, which in turn affects behavior. Emotions are not permanent, but they are continually present and vary in type and intensity. Consider the wave analogy when thinking of emotions. Just like waves on the ocean, emotions are always present. It is even possible to physiologically feel emotions, especially intense ones such as fear or terror, wash over you like a wave crashing on the shore.

Emotions, like waves on the ocean, can sometimes be massive, while at other times they are slight; sometimes the waters are calm and other times they are very choppy. Similarly, our emotions can be mild or intense and positive or negative, but they all are a vital part of our human experience. Learning to navigate or surf the waves of emotion in our daily life can be synonymous with learning to regulate emotions. The use of an analogy such as waves and surfing can provide a visual representation of an abstract concept. This more concrete representation can be very beneficial when trying to explain and understand more complex or conceptual ideas.

Returning to life after lockdown will completely change the pattern of the water we are in. For some, the waves will go from smooth calm waters to intense waves or even tsunamis. The key to surviving the tsunami and navigating this change and influx of stressors from so many angles is emotional regulation. No person is perfect with emotional regulation 100% of the time, though some are innately better at it than others. Some people have nervous systems where emotional regulation comes more easily to them. Perhaps their synapses are firing slowly or perhaps their personality type is more chill. No matter what lens is used to look at it, emotional regulation is clearly harder for some than others. For example, an individual with ASD is not guaranteed to have poor emotional regulation skills, but there is a lot of research to suggest there will likely be some impact on an individual's ability to regulate emotions. However, no matter how a person is neuropsychologically set up, being human means that some situations and combinations of triggers or stimuli can prompt a person to lose their capacity to regulate emotions effectively. However, with practice, everyone can learn to improve their emotional regulation skills.

Strategies for Surfing the Waves of Daily Life After Lockdown

 ### *Predict the Waves*

The waves are the emotions people experience. Just like waves on the ocean, it is normal for them to change in intensity throughout the day and from one day to the next. They can be positive or negative emotions. Predicting the waves, or times of higher emotional intensity, can be critical for effective emotional regulation. What are the high-risk situations throughout the day—those times of day, situations, or environments where they are most likely to become distressed or dysregulated? Are there days of the week that are harder and bring bigger waves? Sunday or Monday are often tougher days for many because they will soon have to go back to the demands of work or school. For others, activities like shopping or going to crowded events like ball games, concerts, or parties can be triggers for big waves.

 ### Get a Good Surfboard

Surfboards are the tools that help us surf the waves of daily life. They are the many tools we use to regulate, cope, tolerate, and feel at ease in our minds and bodies. Know what works for you or your child.

- *Sensory, environmental, and body tools*: What sensory, environmental, and body strategies help, and what input increases discomfort or distress? Do you need to run every morning? Do compression or weighted materials increase body awareness and help maintain calm and ease? Consider everything that is a physical sensation and how it can help or hurt regulation. This includes oral sensory/taste, tactile/touch, pressure/compression, sound/silence, limbs/trunk/head movement, visual input, smells, hunger, constipation, temperature, and anything in between. What about being around a lot of people? Are you able to take a break from being around people if you become dysregulated?

- *Cognitive or brain tools:* Some people can regulate better by distracting their mind or by actively thinking about the situation. Looking at situations logistically and cognitively can be beneficial for some. Examining fears and thoughts for facts versus fiction or verbally reviewing details of a schedule multiple times can provide a sense of control and help ease distress with change. For some, reading helps or even talking about a favorite subject. Then there are ever-popular video games, the internet, YouTube, and TV. Often these activities get a bad rap, but they are a vital coping skill for many individuals with ASD and can be very helpful with emotional regulation. However, it is important to remember that removal or transition away from these activities can instantly dysregulate some, especially children.

 ### Get a Lifeguard

For most children and those who struggle greatly with emotional regulation, it is important to know your skill level and understand when to have help available. It is important to prepare for challenges and big waves and to work toward self-sufficiency. It is also just as vital to know that learning to regulate when overwhelmed, either from a sensory or emotional perspective, takes a great deal of practice and is also reliant on developmental readiness. Realistically, caregivers, teachers, and other helping adults may need to act as a co-regulator for a child for many years. Partners, family, and close friends often fill these needs for adults with ASD. And depending on the level of physiological impact in the brain, such as with more severe autism, this need for co-regulation or assistance can continue indefinitely. However, with practice and time, trust is built between the individual with ASD and the co-regulator, and the process becomes more habitual and more effective.

 ### Watch Out for Sharks!

Sharks are dangers lurking in the water that can make it difficult to surf the waves of your life. Sharks can be a situation (change in routine, doing homework, going new places), a person (a specific boss, teacher, or peer you have a history of conflict with, a sibling), an experience (parties, shopping, homework), something in the environment (loud noise, flashing lights, a lot of people, strong smells), a time of day (bedtime, after school, transitions from preferred to non-preferred tasks), or internal body feelings (sick, hungry, tired, hot).

As with real sharks, it is always best to be prepared and aware of their presence. Knowing what your sharks are and the potential dangers they pose are keys to successfully navigating the waters. While surfboards and lifeguards are important and helpful, there might be times when an emergency plan, or life vest, is needed. Unfortunately, sharks can cause crises, even if prepared for. When a person is in crisis, the life vest may be removal from the environment to regulate the individual to stay safe or out of trouble. It may be limiting demands on a particular day because the shark was just too big and fast and the crisis or meltdown could not be averted. Or the person may need to stop what they are doing and engage in intense sensory input such as taking a bath or shower, swinging, running, etc.—anything that can help re-regulate after a meltdown or crisis.

While the goal is to surf the waves of our daily life smoothly, we all face large waves and sharks in the water. Ultimately, life after lockdown for those with ASD is likely to come with some challenges and growing pains. But if people manage expectations of themselves and are prepared, it will make the transition less stressful and more successful. Parents, caregivers, spouses, teachers, therapists, etc. should understand that showing empathy and patience will be key. Trust will need to be rebuilt. Not because it was broken, but because the individual may feel the changes and increased demands as distressing or as a threat to their sense of comfort and what they have grown used to. Demands should be small, breaks should be built-in, plans should be made for each individual person. Whether a person with ASD or a support person, continue to focus on improving emotional regulation skills. It's a lifelong process that involves learning, feedback, experience, and practice. Sure, you will still wipe out and sometimes take spills, but with enough practice, you can be catching waves and surfing like the pros!

More about Tracey . . .

🏠 As we enter life after lockdown, I am most concerned about . . .
all those struggling with fear and anxiety about returning to demands of school, work, and social environments and personally about balancing typical life stressors while maintaining time for self-care.

👫 As we enter life after lockdown, I am most excited about . . .
people and connection—being back with all the amazing children and adults that I have missed so much. And live music!!

Dr. Tracey DeMaria, OTD, OTR/L has been an occupational therapist for 24 years, is passionate about helping people of all ages learn about emotional regulation, and currently works in the Phillipsburg School District in NJ. She is the mother to one amazing teenage son with ASD, is married to her best friend Christopher, and is dog-mom to two loving and crazy dogs.

Website

TraceyDemaria.com

Book

o   *How to Surf the Waves: A Program for Children With Emotional and Behavioral Regulation Difficulties* (Fall 2021)

Reference

Mandy, Will. 2019. "Social Camouflaging in Autism: Is It Time to Lose the Mask? *Autism* 23 (8): 1879–1881. https://doi.org/10.1177/1362361319878559.

COMMUNICATION IS EVERYTHING! SCHOOL AND HOME CONNECTION

CHRISTA SMITH

Why won't anyone return my calls?
Is anyone actually doing anything in the schools?
Who can help me?
Will my child/my students regress?

These were some of the questions during the time we were under stay-at-home orders. Every one of us was thrown into the unknown. Being forced to stay home by the federal, state, and county government, how were we to keep the education system functioning successfully?

This year we learned a lot about how we function as a society when the unknown occurs. We also learned how our schools function in a crisis. In the past, it was easy to stop by a school to speak to a teacher, set up an IEP meeting, or call to make an appointment. Once the pandemic hit, all of that stopped. Our world suddenly became virtual. Schools went into overdrive trying to develop a distance learning model, provide students with technology, and ensure internet access. All of these were crucial in order to support students and to get better access to communication though online video calls, email, and internet calling.

Parents became frustrated by their lack of teaching or internet skills, inability to access materials, and children's possible regression. Parents were also struggling to work from home while supervising their child with special needs' online schooling. Meanwhile, educators were juggling the same things—trying to work as online teachers for their students while supervising their own children's online schooling. Teachers became frustrated by the sudden change in teaching requirements and strategies and even the prohibition in some places about providing physical materials because of potential health risks. Both groups wondered: How will we be able to help students regain the skills they may have lost?

This situation placed new pressures on the school-home relationship. However, out of these challenges came awareness of the basics of that relationship, especially the fragile and crucial role of communication. We learned some valuable lessons about communication that continue to support the relationship between school and home as we move forward.

---

1   *Be calm* – Trying to get answers was and is frustrating for both parents and educators. In many instances, answers aren't available for anyone. If there are answers, it often takes time to get things organized for the solution. The more time went on during the pandemic, the more frustrated, scared, and upset each of us became.

Positive Communication Strategy

In a situation where you can feel yourself getting upset, you can do a few things to help re-center:

- **Take a few slow deep breaths.** When people are upset, it is hard to keep communication going. It's hard to even stay on a call or video call. When you are upset, your breathing becomes more rapid and shallow. By simply slowing down and taking a few deep breaths, you can help regulate your breathing, which can have a calming effect. Slower, deeper breathing helps to reduce your stress.
- **Use a calm voice.** If someone is speaking to you with a raised voice, respond with a calm voice. If one person is upset and the other person responds by getting upset, the conversation may go nowhere and things will continue to escalate. Using a calm voice can help reduce the tension for everyone.

---

2 *Always be polite* – Having to communicate with everyone via phone or computer made for an interesting jump to life online. Whether we return to in-person meetings or continue to meet online, we still need to be professional and polite to each other.

Positive Communication Strategy

In a situation where a meeting is being held virtually or via phone, some ways to keep things on track are:

- *Introduce everyone* at the start of the meeting.
- *Identify yourself* when speaking so everyone knows who you are.
- *Follow an agenda* so everyone knows what is being discussed and in what order.

- When you are meeting online, *stay silent after speaking*, as there is often a delay when others are processing what is being said.
- *Stay muted* when it is not your time to speak. There is sometimes an echo or feedback if more than one microphone is turned on at the same time.
- When you are meeting online, *raise your hand* if you have something to share.
- Keep the conversation *child-centered*.

---

3 **Go into each conversation believing that everyone has good intentions** – Both families and school personnel all have the student's best interests at heart. Sometimes beliefs are different, but people typically do not go into meetings or conversations with bad intentions.

Positive Communication Strategy

If you are starting a conversation with a predetermined belief that the other person has bad intentions, try to allow that person to share before forming an opinion.

- *Ask questions* to figure out if what you have previously decided will happen is really what is occurring.
- Allow the person to *speak uninterrupted* to share their message.
- Be sure to *clearly understand* what that person is sharing before forming an opinion without all the facts.
- Use open and *welcoming facial expressions*. (Non-furrowed brow and no frowns.)

---

4 **Be aware of other people's perceptions** – If tensions are high in a conversation, others may hear an inflection in your voice, see a facial expression or body language that may lead them to misinterpret what you are saying. This misperception can throw a conversation off track and lead to distrust.

Positive Communication Strategy

When you are sharing information with a group:

- Start conversations with a smile and be aware of your facial expressions.
- Maintain open body language.
- Be mindful of how you are saying your words. Putting emphasis on one word instead of another can change the whole meaning of what you are saying. An example would be saying, "*That's* great" with a furrowed brow and emphasizing "That's" and not "great," which makes it seem negative. However, by saying "That's *great*," emphasizing "great" with a smile, the two words take on a whole new meaning.

---

5 **Follow the chain of command** – If there is an issue that needs to be resolved, start with the person involved first, then work your way up the chain of command, if necessary. The person with whom you have an issue should be the first person you speak with in determining what occurred. For example, if you decide not to speak with a teacher and jump right to the superintendent, the situation may take longer to resolve, as the superintendent does not directly work with your student, won't be familiar with the situation, and will probably need to refer back to the person who does know about the situation, which is the teacher.

Positive Communication Strategy

If something occurs in a classroom:

- Be sure to start with the teacher for clarification. Teachers are the ones working directly with your student. If you are not able to resolve your concerns at that level, you may then need to speak with the assistant principal. This may lead to the principal, who may refer you on to the district office to speak with someone within the special education department for resolution. At this level, you may start with a program specialist, then coordinator, assistant director, or director, then even further up, if necessary, to an assistant superintendent or the superintendent.
- Get your information from the source. Each person will be gathering information along the way and can direct you to the person that you would need to speak with regarding your issue. In these instances, they may jump you to a different level but are able to provide that new person with prior information to help in resolving issues.

———◆———

6 *We are all human* – When communicating with others, always remember that what you are seeing is only a part of that person. You are seeing the professional or parent in a virtual meeting or hearing their voice on a phone call without knowing what has been happening in their life. Everyone has things happening in their lives. Stressful events tend to make each of us react differently than we normally would.

Positive Communication Strategy

With any communication you have with others, you are not seeing or knowing that whole person at that particular time. During the pandemic, many teachers were home trying to teach both their own children and their school classes. Many people were ill or were caring for others who were ill. Some people dealt with the death of a loved one. Many people experienced financial insecurity. Almost everyone dealt with fear, uncertainty, and stress.

- *Think about others as people* who are coping with many circumstances in their lives.
- *Be kind* when communicating with others.
- We all need to approach each other with a *friendly, open outlook* and with grace.

Some Final Thoughts

In looking at the tips above, remember that we all want to be appreciated for what we have accomplished. We want to be validated for the things we do to empower children and students. Remember that we are all in this together—whether it is the pandemic or students' education. Over the past year, some things have changed. We have seen some changes that were for the better and some that were not. If we are mindful about our communications and interactions with one another, we can rebuild the school-home relationship to be stronger and better, because we truly have been—and are—all in this together. As always, communication is EVERYTHING!

More about Christa . . .

🏠 As we enter life after lockdown, I am most concerned about . . .
   the mental health and well-being of ourselves, families, students and staff. I am hopeful that supports will be readily available for everyone to help us heal.

💻 As we enter life after lockdown, I am most excited about . . .
   all the wonderful online platforms and resources we have been utilizing. I am confident we will continue to use them to improve our systems and services to our students and families.

I am blessed to have been in the special education field for over 29 years, as a teacher, program specialist, and coordinator. I have been fortunate to have had the opportunity to work with amazing people over the years and have learned many life lessons from them which I use daily in my work.

A SUCCESSFUL TRANSITION TO AND FROM SCHOOL

JENNIFER CORK

In an average year, the back-to-school transition is full of emotions. Excitement as new clothes and supplies are purchased, stress on how to pay for them, dismay for kids as their summer comes to an end, and relief for parents. It is also potentially a time for increased anxiety, especially for kids and teens on the autism spectrum. Each year around August, my office is full of kids struggling with the stress of going back to school and parents with questions on how to best support them. This transition is often difficult, especially for people on the spectrum, who thrive on routine. Questions about who their teacher will be, whether their friends will be in their classes, what the rules will be, and a whole host of other unknowns come to the surface. This happens each year as we go into a typical or average school year.

This next school year will not be typical or average. Going back to school after a year of lockdown will be a new challenge. Not only will there be all of the regular unknowns to contend with, but there will also be a whole new list of unknowns as school administrators and teachers make plans to adapt to life after lockdown. On top of that, many kids have spent the last year doing school at home where they are comfortable. They may not be in a hurry to leave that safe place to go back to school, which can be its own source of stress.

Parents, your child might be feeling excitement, fear, and anxiety. You might have all of these feelings as well, along with a sense that you should know all the answers about how to help your child cope. Teachers, you may also be feeling unprepared and like you don't have answers. Take a breath and remind yourself that no one knows all of the answers. Then take a few minutes to review a few strategies that you can use to help children make the successful transitions to and from school each day.

Parents: Start Talking about the Transition

Don't wait to start talking about the transition back to school. You don't have to have big official discussions, just start casually mentioning it in conversations. Begin the usual back-to-school process of shopping for supplies, buying new school clothes, and implementing other back-to-school routines. You might watch TV shows or movies about going back to school or look for books on the subject to help your child get used to the idea of the upcoming transition. Answer any questions that your child has and make sure that when you are talking about going back to school, you remain calm so your child will be more likely to remain calm. Make sure to involve your child in the back-to-school process as much as possible.

Taking a trip to the library is a great way to find books about going back to school. Librarians are experts in helping you find just the right book and will usually have displays set up on this topic as it gets closer to the first day of school. Here are a few recommendations for younger kids who might be anxious about the first day of school:

- *How Do Dinosaurs Go to School?* by Jane Yolen
- *The Kissing Hand* by Audrey Penn
- *Miss Bindergarten Gets Ready for Kindergarten* by Joseph Slate
- *Wemberly Worried* by Kevin Henkes

There are also lots of TV shows and movies on the topic of going to school. You can do a quick search either on a streaming platform or on a search engine to find titles that will be appropriate for your child. Look for shows that your family can enjoy together and can potentially start back-to-school conversations.

Normalize Your Child's Feelings

When someone is feeling anxious and that anxiety feels out of control, it's common for them to also feel like no one else is struggling as much as they are. Make sure to help normalize an anxious child's feelings by talking to them about how common it is to be nervous on the first day of school. Point out characters who feel anxious in the books, movies, or TV shows that you have been reading and watching. Talk to them about how other members of the family or the classroom are feeling about the start of school if you have that person's permission. This can be especially helpful if they have siblings or friends who are anxious too. Share that the adults in their life, especially teachers, are probably feeling anxiety as the first day of school approaches. There will be changes and new ways of doing things for them too. Change and transitions are difficult for everyone and everyone will be going through it together.

Start Talking About What Will be Different

School after lockdown may be different than it was the last time children were in the classroom. While change is difficult for everyone, it is even more difficult for children on the spectrum who have had to deal with many changes over the last year. Parents, contact your child's school and find out what is going to be different in their school routine this year. Meet with teachers and administration to get a full list of changes, which may include cleaning routines, how children will be seated in classrooms, new materials, what the lunch routine will look like, how they will play outside, etc. Teachers, write a letter to be sent out to families before the school year to help them process things that might be different. Think about creating a Social Story™ or Social Article about these changes (for more information about Social Stories™ and Social Articles, look for books or articles by Carol Gray or you can visit: https://carolgraysocialstories.com/). Arrange times when children can come in before the first day to take a tour, even if they have gone to the school in the past. Let them tour their classrooms, the library, lunchroom, art rooms, playground, and any other places that they will use during the year. If possible, try to arrange a time for the tour when teachers and staff will be present so that kids can meet or get reacquainted with them before the year begins.

Make a Schedule

Parents, making a schedule of things your child needs to do each morning to get ready for school is a common and effective strategy. Routines not only outline expectations, they are also a source of calming for many people on the autism spectrum. A few weeks before school starts, sit down with your child and make a list of everything they will need to do each morning to be ready for school.

After you have your schedule completed, hang it up where you and your child will see it and then start practicing. You may want to add deadlines for each item to help

> 66 Routines not only outline expectations, they are also a source of calming for many people on the autism spectrum. 99

stay on track. You may want to add a reward at the end that your child can earn. As your child practices their schedule, you may notice that some things need adjusting. Practicing a few weeks before school starts will help you find things that need changing ahead of time so when the big day comes, you will be ready to go.

Remember that this is your child's schedule, so let them help you personalize it. It can be handwritten on paper, written on a white-board that can be erased, or printed out on a piece of paper from a document on your computer. The schedule can include pictures that are copied from search engines online, your or your child's own drawings, or just writing alone. The schedule can be as simple or as complex as it needs to be. Examples of visual schedules are available online, so if you need ideas, just type "visual schedule" in a search engine. If your child works with an occupational or behavioral therapist, check in with them to get suggestions or help in completing the schedule.

When working with kids in my office, I like to fold a piece of paper in half three times so that it makes eight rectangles on the page, then I draw a stick figure comic strip to illustrate their morning schedules. This type of schedule is pretty simple, but it can help anxious children rehearse what the morning will bring. You don't have to be a gifted artist to make this type of schedule, so don't worry if you can only draw stick figures.

Comic Strip Schedule

Whatever type of schedule you make, put it somewhere that your child will easily see it: For example, on the refrigerator, on a bulletin board they walk by and look at often, or even on the bathroom mirror. The bathroom is a place kids will go to frequently during the day. This means that they will see their schedule the night before while they are getting ready for bed and doing their night routine and again in the morning when they wake up so that they have a lot of time to process the morning's events.

For the transition from school to home, parents and teachers can use the same techniques, starting with making of list of all the things that will happen to help them get ready to come home. This may require coordination between parents and teachers to see what their afternoon routine looks like at the school, home, or childcare setting. You will also need to find a place to put the afternoon schedule where the child will see it, such as their school notebook. It is a good idea to have someone at school help the child review their schedule in the afternoon, especially during the first few weeks of school.

Positive Self-Talk

When there is a big transition coming that brings along anxiety, it is very common for people to struggle with negative thoughts like, "I can't do this" or "This is impossible." If people struggle with these types of thoughts, then it makes anxiety bigger and the task more difficult. Listen for negative thinking and help model and prompt changing these thoughts to more balanced and positive ways of thinking. For example, unless this is a child's very first day of school, they have had other first days of school in the past. Help them replace "I can't do this" with "I have gone through other first days of school, and I can do it again." If this is a child's very first day of school, remind them of other times they did something very big or very difficult. Another way to think of this is by teaching kids to be their own cheerleaders. A great book to read with younger children to review this concept is *The Little Engine That Could* by Watty Piper.

Parents: Don't Forget to Take a Break

When your child gets home from school, they will likely have homework. You or your child may want to sit down as soon as they get home to finish their homework so that it will be done and out of the way. This can lead to increased frustration and anxiety, and may even end up in a meltdown. Your child has been in school all day and deserves a break. Let them come home, put their school things away, have a snack, and take some time doing a preferred activity before they have to go back to any kind of academic work. Break time should be part of their daily afternoon schedule.

> 66 Your child has been in school all day and deserves a break. 99

Having specific time limits that your child maintains each day will help them transition from their preferred activity back to their homework, but don't be surprised or discouraged if it takes a while to get this routine into place. It is normal for kids to be upset when they have to stop doing something they want to do and transition to doing something they have to do and may not want to do. To help with this, you can give them something they can earn when they are completely done with their homework. The use of a visual timer that helps them see exactly how much time they have can be helpful as well.

Since your child has likely had to sit a good part of the school day, their after-school break should involve physical activity. Have them help you make a list of physical activities they enjoy. They will be more likely to engage in the activity if they helped choose it and it is something that they like to do.

Many children will want to play video games after school. If your child has a difficult time stopping video games in general, they will likely have a much harder time stopping a game to do their homework. These kids may benefit from doing a less preferred activity as their after-school break, saving video game time as the activity they earn when all of their homework is done.

Make Sure That There Are Coping Skills and Tools Available

If a child did all their schooling at home this last year, they may have used coping skills and tools that won't be available in the school setting. If this is the case, take a look at the child's preferred calming tools and look for replacements that can be available at school. Remember, kids are a full year older and have been through a lot this past year, so strategies they used at school in the past may not work as well as they did before. Coordination between parents and school will help ensure that the right tools are available.

> 66 Coordination between parents and school will help ensure that the right tools are available. 99

It is recommended to consult with a child's outside therapies to help find the right supports to stay regulated in the school setting.

The After-School Meltdown

It is very common for individuals on the autism spectrum to go through their whole school day without any incidents or problem behaviors, only to get home and let out a full day's worth of anxiety, anger, and frustration when they walk in the door. Children spend the whole day masking or trying to blend in with neurotypical peers, which can take tremendous effort. Once they get home to their safe place, they can no longer hold in their anxiety anymore and may go into full meltdown mode. This is difficult for the person, as well as parents, and is often not fully understood by school staff who do not see these behaviors.

While you may not be able to fully prevent an after-school meltdown, you can help support a child as they transition from school to home. First, parents can make a note of any behaviors that occur and consult with any professionals working with the child if there is a healthier and effective replacement behavior that they can engage in. For a replacement behavior to be effective, it needs to be just as easy to do as the current behavior and give the child the same result. For example, if a child typically engages in physical aggression like hitting and kicking during an after-school meltdown, see if a punching bag would help. Give them time when they get home to use the punching bag until they calm down. If a child tends to shut down or run away when they get home, make sure that they have a safe, quiet place to go to with limited sensory input. Leave them alone and give them space until they are ready to engage with you.

As with any skill, it will take time for them to learn how to use their replacement behaviors effectively. Make these activities part of the afternoon routine each day. The more they do this, the more of a habit it will become. There may be days when the stress is too high to prevent a meltdown, but on days that stress is more manageable, they will know that when they get home, they will have an outlet and relief and be able to transition more smoothly.

Scheduling additional breaks to be given during the school day as an accommodation on an Individualized Educational Plan (IEP) or 504 Plan is also a good idea. These breaks should be no longer than 15 minutes and scheduled at least once in the morning and once in the afternoon at times when the child has additional downtime to engage in a calming activity. This will help them process the day's events and hopefully help prevent the buildup of stress that leads to an after-school meltdown.

Conclusion

Since the beginning of the pandemic, almost all our routines have changed—how we interact with each other, how we go to school, how we shop, how we celebrate holidays, and so many other aspects of our lives that it would be impossible to name them all. These changes have been hard for everyone, but for many individuals on the spectrum, this may have felt like going from one crisis to the next. One of the primary symptoms of autism spectrum disorder, is an insistence on routine and distress if the routine is changed. The distress that I have observed in the individuals I work with over this last year has been very real. Just as everyone is getting used to the new normal, we will now be asking everyone to go back out into the world where things will be the same, but also different. This may feel like an insurmountable task, but remember that you have been through big transitions before and you and your child or students can do it again. Look for supports from friends, family members, colleagues, or other individuals on the spectrum. Find out if there is a local support group that can offer encouragement and assistance during this year's big transition back to school. Finally, don't forget to take time for your own self-care and don't compare yourself to others. This is you and your child or student's story, and you can do this.

More about Jennifer . . .

🏠 As we enter life after lockdown, I am most concerned about . . .
>   *the toll the pandemic has taken on our society as a whole and on our working professionals. Not just medical professionals, who bore the brunt of caring for individuals with COVID-19, but also other professionals whose work was directly affected by the pandemic. In my region, there has been high turnover rates in our health district, public school administrators, mental health professionals, and other needed professions. I worry about the impact that the pandemic will have for years to come.*

 As we enter life after lockdown, I am most excited about . . .
>   *going back to coffee shops. I like quiet and everyone in my family is loud. One of my coping skills was a weekly trip to a quiet coffee shop with a good book and I miss it!*

My husband, three children, and I live in beautiful North Idaho. I work as a licensed clinical social worker (LCSW), specializing in treating neurodiverse individuals with co-occurring mental health diagnoses. My favorite question to ask new clients is, "What is the difference between Legos and Minecraft and which one is better?"

BACK TO SCHOOL: WE'RE IN THIS TOGETHER

LISA KISTLER & GABY TOLEDO

It's finally happening—we are going back to school. With all of the chaos and changes of the last year, watching your child transition back to full-time, in-person instruction may bring mixed feelings. From the excitement of seeing your child in a classroom setting to the anxiety of worrying about your child's adjustment, it is bound to be an emotional time. But with planning and collaboration, a successful transition can be a reality.

Before School Starts

Most of us and our families have been impacted by the pandemic to varying degrees. Many children may have thrived in the virtual classroom while others may have experienced a halt or a loss of previously learned skills. As we all, parents, students, and teachers, navigate through this transition, it is imperative that collaborative partnerships are formed to support the success of all students— and especially those with autism. Individuals with autism thrive with well-established routines and structures so it will be important for all of us to work together to re-establish rapport or build new relationships. This process, which includes input from educators, parents, as well as students, should start before the beginning of the school year and will be the foundation for a positive transition.

 Educators, you should reach out to parents before the first day of class and spend some time talking about the student's progress over the last year. Be sure to chat with families and, if possible, with the student directly to identify interests, preferences, and favorite things.

 Parents, this would be the time to share with school staff how your child has been doing at home, especially around the areas of communication, social interactions, and overall behavior.

 Students, you also can use this opportunity to talk to your teachers and share with them how you feel about returning to school and what would help you be successful.

Planning ahead will be key for everyone; set up school visits, meet the staff, use social narratives, videos, or simply review the schedule for the first day or first week of school.

During the School Year

Educators, once the school year gets underway and you have built rapport with students and parents, you will need to start assessing the child across all areas of functioning. Do this by taking note of daily interactions and setting up activities embedded within the classroom routines that will provide you the opportunity to see a variety of skills. Do not forget to use any district-adopted assessment, curriculum measures, and informal assessments you have created. In addition to academics, also prioritize functional communication, social and emotional skills, adaptive skills, and behavior. Next, plan to have informal conversations about how the student is doing and start prioritizing areas where the student may need more support.

Parents, before you call or go in for your appointment, make a list of your concerns, and also the things about your child you are proud of or are satisfied with regarding their performance. During the meeting use phrases like, "I would like to see (child's name) be able to . . ." or "I want (child's name) to be able to (insert skill) because . . . ." These types of statements allow you to define your priorities and help the teacher or administrator collaborate with you on goals, lessons, and activities. Whenever possible look toward the future—returning to past problems or what didn't happen during COVID will slow down the process.

Students, as you get comfortable with the school routines, reflect on what is happening during your school day that is helping you to learn. Also reflect on whether there are ways that your learning can be improved. Be sure to talk to your teacher about what your learning goals are and share any ideas on how school staff can support your learning.

Collaboration Through the IEP Process

A positive way to plan and collaborate is through the IEP. Parents or educators can request to set up an individualized education program (IEP) meeting at any time. IEP meetings are a process, not just an hour of time to review paperwork. In fact, IEP meetings are one of the strongest tools in everyone's tool box. The IEP process is designed to bring parents and educators together to develop a plan to support the student's learning and growth. This starts with the IEP agenda which provides context for everyone at the table and structures the time to allow the IEP team to understand how the child's disability impacts their learning and participation in school.

Parents, everyone knowing your child's strengths and preferences, as well as your concerns, places your child in the middle of the conversation. This child-centered focus then guides the team as they move through the rest of the meeting. Regardless of previous experiences with this process, you are a key participant in building this plan for your child. Therefore, it is extremely important that you are an active participant. So, what does that mean? Well, it simply means that within each area (i.e., academics, social, communication, adaptive, etc.) you provide your input by describing your experiences, preferences, and priorities for your child. You can work with your child's teacher before the meeting to provide feedback on their progress, share your ideas about areas you feel your child needs support to grow, and share your thoughts on what worked best for your child this past year.

Educators, you can support parents' participation in the IEP process by reaching out early, not only to set a date and time but also to start gathering their input and sharing your view of how the student is performing in the school setting. Remember to support parents in identifying the student's areas of strength both in the school and the home settings. These areas should be used as anchors to build skills and support areas of need. The chart below offers you an example of areas to consider to guide the conversation, or as something you can send home for feedback. Asking questions about these skills will help parents identify areas of strength or areas to add support.

Home Skills	What It Looks Like	School Skills	Supports
Meal Routines		Snack Break & Lunch	
Play/Leisure		Recess	
Self-Care		Self-Care	

Educators, the pandemic impacted learning in different ways for every child and family, increasing the need to focus on where the student is at this time. Review progress on previous goals and identify areas of success. If any of the goals were not met, they can serve as a starting point for the present levels of performance section of the IEP. Pay close attention to areas and skills previously mastered that may have been lost during the pandemic. This will form the basis for identifying areas of regression to note within the present levels of performance and then be addressed systematically through IEP goals and services.

Parents, the present levels of performance are the foundation for the IEP and should be written with input from every IEP team member. This is the place where you can share what your child can do. Over the past year, you have supported your child's learning alongside the school staff. Now more than ever it is crucial that you share areas in which your child has exceled as well as those areas that still need support. Once this section is complete, identify the areas of need across academics, communication, social/emotional/behavioral, vocational, and adaptive skills.

Parents and Educators, work together to narrow down specific skills in the areas of need that will be targeted for the remainder of the year as IEP goals. Make sure that you are identifying areas that are meaningful to the child and will have a high impact. In other words, identify skills that can be worked on across multiple settings and that will allow the child to increase their participation in other parts of their lives. A great example is functional communication skills. Functional communication allows your child to make requests, ask questions, and share vital information. Some examples are asking for basic items like food, water, clothing, or letting you know that they are not feeling well or have to use the restroom.

Parents, when you meet as an IEP team to address concerns regarding learning loss it is important to talk through a typical day or week for your child. The classroom is one of the strongest places for learning, both academically and socially. When considering additional services, it is important to create a balance that will maximize your child's learning. Although it may sound like a good idea to add additional ABA services, speech services, and OT services to your child's school day, consider the impact and how much time your child be separated from their peers. The more time they are working outside of their classroom, the more likely it is that they will miss important instructional activities. Consider other service options and activities that are available before or after school or on weekends as a positive alternative.

Students, talk to your parents and teachers prior to the IEP meeting to discuss your role and participation during the meeting. Share your strengths and preferences and the learning areas you would like to focus on. Think of school work or anything else that you have done this past year that you feel you excelled in and share it with the IEP team.

Learning Opportunities Outside of the Regular School Day

Many districts have received money to address potential learning loss or to help accelerate learning. This should create many programs and opportunities for activities and services to increase academic and social skills.

Parents, a week or two before school starts, call your child's school and ask about the different learning opportunities available, such as before or after school tutoring, Saturday School, online programs, enrichment programs, or social skills groups. These programs are open to all kids and do not need an IEP to access. Clubs or intramural sports are also a great way to help your child's motivation to return to school as well as provide an opportunity for social engagement. Being with other children and having fun may help lower any anxiety your child may have, and also give them an opportunity to see kids they know from school. The routine of having to be somewhere on time or follow a schedule will also provide activities with structure outside of your home. Clubs and other outside hobbies provide another setting to practice the functional skill we have discussed. You can also explore the district website for extra-curricular activities and parent engagement classes or programs. Attend back-to-school activities and check with the local PTA, Boys and Girls Club, city parks and recreation department, and Community Advisory Committee through your special education department for additional resources and activities your child can participate in after school or on weekends. Once you are aware of what is available, work collaboratively with your child's school staff to identify supports available for your child that can be accessed early on and that will meet the specific needs of your child while still being manageable with your family life.

We Can Do It!

When coming back together in the fall, we are going to experience a variety of emotions; some may feel eager to be back at school, while others may feel apprehensive and unsure. Hopefully, starting the school year with options designed to provide students with the support needed for a successful transition will assuage any anxieties. We have discussed some of the emotions and concerns both educators and parents might be feeling about a child's education and progress. Positive and effective communication, rapport, and structure will be the tools you can implement to ensure student success.

 Parents, trust that the IEP team is on your child's side;

 Educators, parents are key participants of the IEP team and need to be a part of the process from the beginning to the end; and

 Students, do not be afraid to share what you need and what you would like from your school experience.

We have all been apart for more than a year. Now that we are coming back together, it is an opportunity to regroup, rebuild, and strengthen our relationships. Educators and families are the cornerstone of a rich and satisfying school experience for children. By using practical strategies, focusing on relationships, and good communication, this can be a great year. And by treating one another—families, students, educators—with respect, this can be one of the best years ever. We have an opportunity here to use our collective experiences to continue to improve for a brighter future. Let's do it!

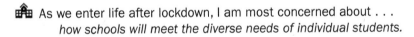

More about Lisa . . .

🏫 As we enter life after lockdown, I am most concerned about . . .
how schools will meet the diverse needs of individual students.

👪 As we enter life after lockdown, I am most excited about . . .
the opportunity to improve how we provide a quality education for students with disabilities.

Lisa Kistler, M.A. has over 30 years of experience working with students with special needs. She has held teaching and administrative positions in both the private and public sector. Helping individuals and organizations build capacity and working collaboratively with educators and families to provide quality education programs are Lisa's passions. Lisa and her husband, David, love spending time with their family, especially their two grandsons. Lisa enjoys playing with her dog, Mooshu, reading, gardening, and watching science fiction and superhero movies.

More about Gaby . . .

As we enter life after lockdown, I am most concerned about . . . *ensuring individuals with autism and other abilities receive the support to continue to grow and thrive.*

As we enter life after lockdown, I am most excited about . . . *continuing to nourish the skills we developed throughout the pandemic both in education and as a society and hope that we have renewed energy to look into the future and remember the importance of supporting one another.*

I always try to live my life with purpose, love, and in service of others. My husband and two amazing children are the force that keeps me grounded and balanced. As a teacher, principal, director, and university professor, I have dedicated my career to serving children with disabilities and their families to ensure they receive high-quality educational opportunities through equity, high expectations, and positive relationships.

ADDRESSING CHALLENGING BEHAVIOR: TRANSITION BACK TO SCHOOL

ROBERT PENNINGTON & MONIQUE PINCZYNSKI

One of the greatest challenges facing individuals with ASD, their families, and educators is the emergence of contextually inappropriate or harmful behaviors. These "challenging" behaviors can limit an individual's full access  to inclusive school and community environments, negatively impact the development of relationships, and in some cases, result in harm and hospitalization. Challenging behavior is not unique to ASD and occurs because it "works" for an individual in changing their current circumstances. For example, a child might protest when asked to transition from playing video games to dinner because, in the past, a protest has produced extended time in a preferred activity.

Individuals with and without ASD continuously behave, appropriately and inappropriately, to create more preferred conditions (i.e., accessing preferred or escaping unpleasant items, activities, tasks, sensory experiences). Understanding this relationship between challenging behavior and the environment is essential. We must find ways to change the environment to reduce the motivation to engage in challenging behavior or teach a more effective way to change one's situation.

For example, a high school student with ASD might engage in disruptive vocal outbursts when asked to perform difficult math tasks because in the past it has produced an escape from similar tasks. The teacher might then reduce the student's motivation to escape the task by decreasing the difficulty of the task and providing more instructional support, or she might teach the student to ask for assistance or a break in lieu of the vocal disruption. These functional approaches to challenging behavior have been demonstrated to be highly effective in school and home environments (Jeong and Copeland 2020; Walker, Chung, and Bonnet 2018).

Since all behavior is directly related to the environment, it is likely that the interruption in school services as a result of the COVID-19 pandemic produced changes in students' behavior. For many students with ASD and other learning differences, especially those with extensive support needs, instructional demands changed significantly as teachers struggled to implement full days of high-quality instructional programming in virtual formats.

Many parents had difficulty maintaining daily instructional routines for their children as they labored to adjust to their own new employment routines while balancing childcare and adhering to national and local pandemic restrictions. Within these new evolving routines, many students found increased access to preferred noninstructional activities, less time spent in instruction, and in some cases, lots of 1:1 parent-delivered instructional support. As many students were exposed to these conditions for an extended period, it is reasonable to expect that some will have difficulty transitioning back to typical classroom routines.

Be Prepared

Most people do not enjoy major disruptions to their daily routines and as a result, may engage in a range of challenging behaviors from minor "vocal gripes" to full-blown "tantrums." It is important that educational teams acknowledge that a return to school presents a disruption to students' routines to which challenging behavior is a logical response. Educational team members should take the time to review existing behavior support plans, but also note that they may no longer be applicable as circumstances likely have changed since their development. They should be prepared to provide all supports and if necessary, implement emergency procedures for responding to severe challenging behavior (See https://iris.peabody. vanderbilt.edu/module/beh2/cresource/q2/p08/).

> 66 . . . a return to school presents a disruption to students' routines to which challenging behavior is a logical response. 99

Prepare the Learner

As previously mentioned, it will be important to prepare students for a return to school. This may be accomplished by direct exposure to school-related materials, activities, and personnel or by adjusting student's home schedules to more closely approximate those of the typical school routine.

Teachers and family members can develop social narratives, which are brief narratives describing an upcoming event and the behavioral expectations of that event (See https://afirm.fpg.unc.edu/social-narratives) or gradually introduce returning to school as a topic in daily discussion. Social narratives and discussion should focus on strategies for success during the return to school but also emphasize potentially rewarding aspects of the school experience (e.g., access to peers, seeing a favorite teacher, preferred content areas).

Families also can prepare learners for social distancing and mask-wearing protocols by embedding these skills in their daily routines before returning to school. These strategies might be enhanced by scheduling brief visits to the school prior to returning and planning visits so that students experience preferred activities or interactions with favorite staff members.

Finally, family members should gradually begin adjusting students' daily schedules to more closely reflect the school day. For example, caregivers might consider adjusting students' morning routine so that they must get up, get dressed, leave the house, and drive by the school in the weeks before returning. They also might begin reducing students' amount of time engaged in non-instructional or free time during typical school hours.

Reteach and Support Routines

Once students return to school, many will require refamiliarization with educational routines. It may be necessary for teachers and family members to reinstitute schedule supports (e.g., calendars, visual schedules, prompting strategies) that may have been faded in the past. In general, incoming students should have continuous access to an object, picture-supported, or written schedule. Students should then be provided an opportunity to preview the schedule at the beginning of the school day and then prior to transitions.

When possible, students should have an opportunity to make choices within scheduled routines. Though teachers may need instructional activities to occur in a particular sequence, they can embed opportunities for students to select materials, peers with whom to work, and the order of tasks within scheduled activities.

Finally, some students will require prompting from teachers to assist them in transition. For example, after presenting the next picture on a visual schedule, a teacher might wait ten seconds for the student to transition independently and after no response, provide a model of how to access materials for the next activity. As students are relearning these routines, it will be important that educators and family members provide positive feedback and other rewards following successful transitions.

> **When possible, students should have an opportunity to make choices within scheduled routines.**

Responding to New or Resurging Challenging Behavior

Some students returning to school will bring with them new behaviors acquired in the home setting, and some will revisit old ones. The first step in addressing these behaviors is to determine what purpose they might serve for the learner (Cooper, Heron, and Heward 2020). In some instances, the purpose might seem clear (e.g., a child dives under his desk to escape a demand), but in others, the educational team might need to reconvene to conduct a new functional behavior assessment (FBA; For more information see https://autisminternetmodules.org/ or https://practicalfunctionalassessment.com).

Once the purpose or function of the behavior (i.e., access, escape, or avoidance) is determined, the educational team might find minor changes to the educational environment (e.g., simplifying instructional tasks, providing more attention to students) are effective or they may determine the need to develop a behavior support plan (BSP).

The BSP outlines strategies for educational team members to use in teaching new skills to students and in responding to challenging behavior (See https://autisminternetmodules.org/). The BSP must be accompanied by continuous data collection so that the team can determine whether the selected strategies are effective and if modifications to the plan should be made.

> 66 Teachers also must remember that students will be adjusting to their new schedule. 99

Teachers also must remember that students will be adjusting to their new schedule during the first few weeks of their return and should be cautious in sounding the alarm before determining whether the challenging behavior persists. A single student meltdown may not warrant a meeting of the IEP team, but a persistent pattern of meltdowns over a few weeks should occasion a convening of IEP behavior support team members. In addition, educators should be careful to not reward new behaviors in the school environment. Teachers can provide a consequence with minimal value as a reward following challenging behavior. For example, a teacher might respond to a vocal outburst (i.e., previously rewarded with teacher attention) with a brief neutral statement of what the student can do instead to access attention (e.g., "Izzy, if you need help, raise your hand.").

Teachers should simultaneously focus on consistently rewarding contextually appropriate behavior and when possible, prompt students to make requests for preferred access to and escape from educational conditions. This might involve providing a vocal model (e.g., "Break") or a gestural prompt to select a "break" icon on a speech-generating device when the teacher detects a student might be frustrated.

Final Words

The COVID-19 pandemic introduced significant changes to the ways individuals with and without ASD navigated their daily lives. As schools reopen and students transition from home and virtual instructional settings, some students will struggle in relearning educational routines and adjusting to vastly different expectations and contingencies within the traditional classroom. Teachers and family members should expect challenging behavior to arise, be empathetic towards students engaging in challenging behavior during this difficult transition, and carefully guide students to more successful ways of coping with this new reality.

More about Robert . . .

As we enter life after lockdown, I am concerned about . . .
the stress some might face as they return to contingencies that were absent or significantly altered over the last year and half. I worry that some will think that "just like riding a bike" people should be able to get right back to their old lives and lack understanding towards those that struggle in the transition. We will need to take our extra "compassion" vitamins over the next year.

As we enter life after lockdown, I am excited to . . .
reflect upon what we have learned during the pandemic and alter our old tools for navigating the world in ways that are more efficient and potentially bring more joy in our lives.

Robert Pennington, PhD, BCBA-D is the Lake and Edward J Snyder, Jr. Distinguished professor in Special Education at the University of North Carolina at Charlotte and has over 30 years of experience working with individuals with disabilities, their families, and teachers. He publishes, teaches, and engages in service in the areas of applied behavior analysis, communication instruction, and educational programming for students with extensive support needs.

More about Monique . . .

 As we enter life after lockdown, I am concerned about . . .
students and teachers getting their emotional, social, and academic needs met after being away from the physical school environment for over a year's time for some.

As we enter life after lockdown, I am most excited about . . .
students being able to reconnect and build new relationships with peers, friends, and teachers.

Hello! My name is Monique Pinczynski and I am from Henderson, NV where I have been teaching students with disabilities for the last five years. This fall I will begin my doctoral studies at the University of North Carolina Charlotte in special education, with an emphasis on autism and academic/behavioral interventions in the school setting.

References

Cooper, John O., Timothy E. Heron, and William L. Heward. 2020. *Applied Behavior Analysis*. Third edition. Hoboken, New Jersey: Pearson.

Jeong, Yunji and Susan R. Copeland. 2020. "Comparing Functional Behavior Assessment-Based Interventions and Non-Functional Behavior Assessment-Based Interventions: A Systematic Review of Outcomes and Methodological Quality of Studies." *Journal of Behavioral Education* 29 (1): 1–41. https://doi.org/10.1007/s10864-019-09355-4.

Walker, Virginia L., Yun-Ching Chung, and Lauren K. Bonnet. 2018. "Function-Based Intervention in Inclusive School Settings: A Meta-Analysis." *Journal of Positive Behavior Interventions* 20 (4): 203–216. https://doi.org/10.1177/1098300717718350.

A RECIPE FOR STUDENT SUCCESS

AMY GAFFNEY & CATHY PRATT

We are now living in a time of many transitions. Teachers, students, and their families have lived through over a year of school during a pandemic. There was no instructional manual for how to do this; we have all been doing our best to find our way. Teachers have worked hard to find ways to educate children and children have worked hard to continue learning during these strange and uncertain circumstances. Some positives have come from this period of learning—new ways to use technology, more collaboration with colleagues, and stronger family relationships. The pandemic has also left some with challenges . . . anxiety, stress, grief, social isolation.

As teachers prepare for more and more students to return to school, now more than ever it's critical that we are thoughtful about how we will prepare a place where students will feel safe, be able to have fun, and be successful. After months of school during a pandemic, whether socially distancing with masks in a school building or at a kitchen table watching a lesson on the computer, students' attention skills, independence, and pace of learning have been affected.

One thing that we can all acknowledge as we enter the new school year is that nothing is static. Mandates and policies will continue to change. School rules and routines will have to change to meet student needs. For students entering school after virtually learning from home for an extended period, familiar expectations and experiences from school may be different now. Schools need to use the best evidence-based practices (EBPs) to support students from the moment they enter the school building to teach new routines and expectations, as well as support their' emotional well-being. Though there are a variety of EBPs that can be effectively implemented in school settings, there are three that may be especially helpful to focus on as we return to school—visual supports, social narratives, and video modeling.

Visual Supports

We know that most students on the autism spectrum learn best when information is presented visually. Visual supports provide concrete information about a concept or routine and help in clarifying expectations. Everyone can benefit from these visual supports. A variety of formats can be used, including objects, photographs, drawings, and written words. Since information presented via visual supports will not disappear, it becomes more tangible than the spoken word. The students can refer to them as often as needed and this can help reduce anxiety and assist with self-management. With visual supports, a student with ASD can build their confidence and become more independent. Three types of visual supports that we highly recommend being used at school are visual boundaries, visual cues, and visual schedules.

Visual Boundaries

Visual boundaries can be used to give meaning to the environment and clarify expectations in the learning environment. Students may need more defined boundaries due to COVID-19 protocols. Boundaries can be defined by the way furniture, carpets, and materials are arranged. Visual boundaries can be  useful in the classroom to define workspaces and to promote appropriate social distancing. These supports can be helpful for students to understand and respect personal space, or to clarify behavioral expectations, such as staying in a specific area during a break or group work.

Visual Cues

Visual cues present information to support comprehension by giving a visual representation of the meaning of the message. They also allow the student more time to process the information. Visual cues allow for multiple opportunities to reference and rehearse the information. Visual cues can be used to support a wide variety of needs, including choices, directions,

Keep your thoughts in your thought bubble.

behavior expectations, and the sequence of steps in a routine. A visual cue can be a poster outlining choices for greeting teachers and friends at school; a sign, such as ENTER or EXIT, to help with the flow of people entering or exiting the gym, cafeteria, or school building. A visual cue can be a sequence posted in the bathroom to remind students to do all needed steps, along with washing their hands for the proper amount of time. A visual cue can be a small picture taped to the hand sanitizer bottle to remind students to only use one pump.

Visual Schedules

Visual schedules tell the student what activities are going to occur and in what order the activities will occur. With this information, a student is better able to predict what will happen next during the day. Some students may be out of practice with moving through an entire school day so knowing what to expect can help reduce anxiety. Schedules are a good way to support a student through transitions, such as moving from one subject to the next, from class to class, or from summer break to the school year. By teaching a student to use a schedule, the schedule becomes a tool to teach flexibility. The student is learning to trust and follow the schedule, and by doing so, we can see rigidity decrease. Finally, by using a visual schedule, a student can function more independently. They will be able to move through the day and require fewer prompts from others to get to where they need to be. This tool will benefit them into adulthood. A schedule can be created using objects, pictures, or written words, depending on the comprehension abilities of the student. The length of the schedule should be individualized according to the needs of the student.

A.J.'s Schedule

___ Morning Job
___ Class Meeting
___ 1:1 Work
___ Independent Work
___ Break
___ Group Work
___ Lunch
___ Independent Work
___ 1:1 Work
___ Class Meeting
___ Bus

By using visual supports throughout school, students, especially those with ASD, will have the information they need to be able to move through the many changes and transitions that the upcoming school year will bring. The visual supports will deliver consistent messages to the students and examples of the visuals can be sent home, so families can also be familiar with any new routines.

Social Narratives

A social narrative is an evidence-based practice that shares relevant social information, clarifying the relevant social cues, perspectives, and appropriate responses in a reassuring, nonthreatening way. A social narrative can take one of many forms and uses words or illustrations to explain a variety of social situations. Options include a short narrative that has been typed or handwritten on paper or a slide show such as PowerPoint. The important thing about a social narrative is that it provides information regarding a situation about which a student may lack understanding and offers a sequence or process of how to respond appropriately. Social Stories™, developed by Carol Gray, is a type of social narrative strategy written in a precise format and style specified by Gray. Information about this explicit format can be on the Social Stories™ website, https://carolgraysocialstories.com.

Sometimes, it can be helpful for students to connect more with the information if the person's favorite interests are used as part of the story information and illustrations. Power Cards (Gagnon and Myles 2016) are a type of social narrative that capitalizes on a student's special interest, hero, or role model. It is an easy-to-implement strategy that addresses a behavior of concern in two parts: A hero or role model with a problem and a scenario for solving it, and a card that acts as a visual support, sharing what the hero does to solve the problem. Power Cards can be an effective strategy for individuals of all ages and developmental levels.

Scenario: Football Player

Due to COVID-19 restrictions, this year my favorite football team players live in a bubble environment to protect themselves and their teammates from the virus. They live in a specific hotel and stay with their team for practices and meals. They do not interact with the public. When they are not playing football, they wash their hands often, keep their hands away from their faces, and they wear a mask when it is required. I can be safe just like the football team by doing these things and staying in my bubble environment with my family and interacting with just a small number of people. This is how it will be until we have more information about COVID-19 and how we can stay safe.

Power Card

Staying Safe During COVID-19

1. Wash my hands frequently.
2. Keep my hands off my face.
3. Wear my mask when told.
4. Stay in my bubble.

Power Cards are effective because they capitalize on the characteristics of many individuals with autism: a keen visual sense, a highly-focused interest, and the fact that the hero has a non-threatening way to solve the problem. Power Cards can be used in any environment. For example, one family developed a Power Card for their child, who has a highly-focused interest in their local football team. Their child was motivated to use safe behaviors during COVID because these are behaviors their favorite football team members used.

Another family developed a unicorn Power Card for their child who loves unicorns and needs support following social distancing rules standing in line. This card is designed to support the learning needs of this student who responds best to structured information with fewer words.

Scenario: Unicorns

I love unicorns and unicorns always follow the social distancing rules.

They wait in line and stand six feet away from other unicorns.

When I stand in line, I will remember to wait and stand six feet away from other people, just like unicorns.

Power Card

The unicorn waits in line and stands six feet away.

Cartooning is another type of social narrative that uses simple drawings to portray dialogue or back-and-forth communication, which can help individuals who struggle with the rapid pace of conversations. Simple symbols or stick drawings can be used to turn abstract conversation into concrete representations of thoughts and speech. This allows an individual to reflect on an exchange and to understand the implicit messages being communicated. Thought bubbles, such as those used in cartoons or comic strips, can emphasize what others may be thinking, which is helpful for individuals who have trouble understanding other people's thoughts, beliefs, or motives.

The "hidden curriculum" of a situation is the information that most neurotypical people know, but is often not recognized by individuals on the spectrum without explicit instruction. Social narratives can include this information and clarify it. They are always written positively, describing the desired or targeted behavior. They can be an effective strategy to help individuals comprehend social information and respond appropriately.

Video Modeling

Another evidence-based practice we can use to teach a routine or activity to our students is video modeling. Once the targeted skill is defined, determine which point of view to use—first person or third person (e.g., "I walk quietly through the halls" versus "Jesse walks quietly through the halls"). Create a script or outline that indicates the steps that need to occur to complete the target skill. Plan for the video recording (e.g., Where? When? Who?) and make the video (using a video camera, smartphone, tablet, digital camera, or other recording device) by filming step-by-step exactly what is expected. The student for whom the video is being created may be the main character (video self-modeling) or others (such as a similar-age peer) may be filmed modeling the target behavior. Once the video has been created, introduce the video and allow the student to watch as many times as needed. The video should be watched prior to participating in the routine or activity, such as "See, then do."

Video modeling can be used to teach or reteach behaviors such as:

- Routines for entering the classroom, completing morning work tasks, going through the cafeteria line, participating in a fire/emergency drill, attending assemblies, packing up for the day
- Asking for help
- Listening to someone talk
- Waiting for a turn on playground equipment
- Getting homework after an absence
- Letting someone know you don't feel well

Many of us turn to videos for a visual example when learning a new skill. Appealing to those who are motivated to learn through technology, video modeling is an instructional tool that teaches to the strengths of students with autism and involves few materials. During this time of transition, as students learn and adjust to new routines and expectations, video modeling can be an effective strategy to support them.

There are also a number of pre-made video model examples on platforms such as YouTube. Simply search using the term "autism video modeling" plus the skill the individual is working on. There are numerous examples that address everything from daily living skills to abstract social skills, and are for a variety of ages. If you are creative, you can create your own YouTube channel with videos that you have made, or better yet, that your child has helped make.

Final Thoughts

Students will be reentering classrooms with unique traits and circumstances that affect their learning. The good news is we have a wide range of resources to inform and guide our efforts at supporting them. The three EBPs described in this chapter have sound research to support their efficacy. Though this chapter focused on supporting students at school, the practices described in this section can also be used by parents and others in the home and community settings. You can find additional information and step-by-step instructions on how to implement these EBPs and some terrific resources on the Autism Focused Intervention Resources & Modules website: https://afirm.fpg.unc.edu/afirm-modules.

Much of the success in addressing the challenges of a return from lockdown will rest on using already-existing resources and strategies, but in using them more often, more creatively, and more strategically. Tailoring any visual to an individual's special interests will not only make the strategy more powerful, but also more motivating. And when children and adults are enjoying school and work, it's a win-win situation.

More about Amy . . .

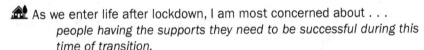 As we enter life after lockdown, I am most concerned about . . .
people having the supports they need to be successful during this time of transition.

As we enter life after lockdown, I am most excited about . . .
utilizing the teaching tools, skills, and opportunities that have come out of this experience.

Amy Gaffney is an educational consultant and Speech-Language Pathologist with the Indiana Resource Center for Autism, located at the Indiana Institute on Disability and Community at Indiana University. She has enjoyed working with and learning from people with autism and their families for over 20 years.

Website

https://www.iidc.indiana.edu/irca/

More about Cathy . . .

🏠 As we enter life after lockdown, I am most concerned about . . .
   the continued health and safety of others, including their mental health.

👪 As we enter life after lockdown, I am most excited about . . .
   spending time with family and friends again, and being able to hug those I love and have not seen.

Dr. Cathy Pratt, BCBA-D, is the Director of the Indiana Resource Center for Autism located at the Indiana Institute on Disability and Community, Indiana's University Center for Excellence in Disabilities. Because of the co-occurring mental health experienced by some on the autism spectrum, Dr. Pratt has become the director of the Indiana School Mental Health Initiative. This role is focused on addressing policy, working with individuals, supporting families, and creating sustainable change statewide.

Website

https://www.iidc.indiana.edu/irca/

Reference

Gagnon, Elisa and Brenda Smith Myles. 2016. *Power Card Strategy 2.0: Using Special Interests to Motivate Children and Youth With Autism Spectrum Disorder.* Lenexa, KS: AAPC Publishing.

IT'S TIME TO SHINE, YOUNG ADULTS!

JENNIFER M. SCHMIDT

"Emergency staff meeting in the auditorium, right after dismissal!" The conclusion of the announcement on the loudspeaker coincided with the arrival of an immediate flutter in my stomach. Emergency staff meetings are never good news, and I began thinking that maybe the rumors that had been spreading in the hallways among students and staff of an "extended spring break" because of coronavirus might hold some weight.

As the staff filed into the auditorium, tension filled the air. After taking our unofficially assigned seats near each other, our principal began the meeting by asking us to "socially distance." What in the world does that mean?! My once-voted "most friendly" self immediately decided this social distancing they spoke of did not sound like my cup of tea; a math colleague behind me, on the other hand, sat herself in an isolated corner of the auditorium and declared, "Social distancing? I've been training for this my whole life!" Although I was happy to hear that my colleague felt this was her time to shine, her declaration immediately made me think of the young adults with autism that I work with every day. How would these unforeseen changes affect them now and in the future?

Many of our students with autism find it challenging to interact socially, and may have breathed a collective sigh of relief at the thought of a mandated reprieve; as an educator with 25 years of experience, one of the biggest struggles for my high school students with autism is often social connection. Many, if not all, of my students describe the social world as a foreign land where everyone else seems to magically understand how to interact, make friends, and maintain strong social connections. Because of this, my former speech-language pathologist colleague and I developed the PEERspective Learning Approach, designed around evidence-based practices in the field of autism. The year-long course uses intentional social skills/communication lessons and peer-mediated instruction and intervention to teach students how to communicate, advocate, and make social connections. Many of the strategies we teach through PEERspective, thankfully, are also strategies that can be used to help young adults with autism overcome the challenges of reintegrating back into life after lockdown. Read on for some specific strategies that can help young adults with autism merge back into society and hopefully find that it is their time to shine!

1 Take baby steps back into society; don't try to get back to life as you left it.

In PEERspective, we often talk about breaking large or intimidating projects into small parts, and reintegrating into life after lockdown shouldn't be treated any differently. At the time of our mandated shutdown due to COVID-19, we were about to end our year with prom, graduation parties, and so many other social events, giving students many opportunities to utilize the social skills they worked so hard to improve over the course of the year. As lockdown ends, the thought of diving back into all these types of activities at once may be daunting. Consider choosing one social event each week or month and baby step your way back to your pre-COVID normal—or better yet, challenge yourself to grow beyond where you were! Remember that all of us are a little out of practice socially after being mandated to isolate ourselves, and it's okay to be a little nervous about putting yourself back into the social world. My students with autism often lack the perspective that other people are also nervous about social events. Those people are just faking it a little more confidently.

2   Journal and reflect on how you are feeling and what you can and cannot control.

Just as the pandemic proved to be especially challenging for many reasons, integrating back into "normalcy" can be challenging, too. For example, for people with social anxiety or cleanliness phobias that are sometimes comorbid with anxiety, the idea of being thrust back into the world around others and their germs is likely difficult, especially after a year where so much emphasis was placed on distancing and disinfecting. Journaling and reflecting on things that you can and cannot control is a way to acknowledge these feelings and work through fears that might come with stepping back into the world. Reflecting can help create concrete action items for things we can control and helps us let go of things we cannot control. Below is an example template from our book, *Yes, Please Tell Me* (Schmidt and Barrett 2021). Below each box, answer the journal prompt and "dump" all of your worries and associated thoughts and feelings in the space provided. Remember, feelings are not wrong or right, they just are feelings. This is a safe place to get worries out of your mind and create a plan to deal with them.

Write your worries here . . .	How does this worry make you feel?	Is this worry a **Can** or **Can't** control for you?	If you **Can** control it, what will you do about it, starting right now?	If you **Can't** control it, what calming strategy will you use to over-come this thought?
I am worried about . . .	I'm feeling . . .	❏ I Can Control ❏ I Can't Control	I can control this by . . .	I can't control this and need to . . .

3 **Create a daily schedule and several items you'd like to accomplish each day.**

Most people thrive on routine, especially those with autism. Unexpected changes can be difficult to handle; a worldwide pandemic clearly changed things in unexpected ways! Many of the students and families I've talked to about COVID and lockdown have said that one thing that helped them through the shutdown was keeping a somewhat similar schedule or structure. Most people with autism are schedule-driven and like to know what is coming next, so now that we are heading back into pre-COVID life, this is an easy strategy to focus on and can give some sense of control.

4 **Focus on what you are thankful for; list three each day.**

The pandemic took so much away from so many. Prior to the pandemic, a former student of mine, Peyton, lived on her college campus and was doing exceptionally well. Then, in an instant, her plans to study abroad in Japan were canceled, and she was told to move back home. While Peyton's family is supportive and living at home was not a negative thing for her, her future plans were definitely on hold. I remember sharing with Peyton's mom that this type of change would be devastating for any young adult, autism or no autism. Then she shared the final blow that Peyton's program of studies (the one she had two semesters left to complete) would not be offered any longer due to budget cuts associated with, you guessed it: COVID.

In these circumstances, it would be understandable to focus on the negatives and all that was lost as a result of the pandemic. However, a way to combat these feelings is to practice gratitude journaling as a form of perspective-taking. Identifying three things each day that you are grateful for can help to create a positive mindset and a framework that can help create positive feelings around reintegrating back into the world.

5 Create social opportunities through goal setting.

During the period of lockdown, I thought a lot about how I had challenged my students to try social outings, connect with friends, and practice socializing, yet now the whole world had shut down. As we come out of lockdown, the opportunity to connect socially has returned, but now my students who have graduated do not have me there challenging and encouraging them each day. It's my hope that maybe they remember our lessons on the importance of goal setting. Setting actionable goals allow us to find successes, and small successes build upon themselves. Consider setting small goals that will create social opportunities.

Social Goal Bank:

- Use a conversation starter with a friend or family member daily.
- Text, call, or interact online socially with one person each week.
- Set up a coffee date once a month with a new person.
- Invite a friend to do something social with you.

6 Be kind to yourself and focus on having positive self-talk.

We created PEERspective because we saw so many amazing individuals with autism struggling to feel connected to those around them, which sometimes appears to take a toll on their self-esteem and overall fulfillment in life. Because of this, we teach the importance of positive self-talk. Consider choosing a mantra that you can use to encourage yourself as you dive back into post-pandemic life. Something as simple as "I got this" can be enough to coach yourself back towards social success. Our brains believe what we tell them, and at the very least it can't hurt to be our own cheerleader and remind ourselves that although these past few months have been challenging, we are stronger now because we did make it through the lockdown.

Take a Breath . . . It's Time!

The bottom line is that we are all hesitant to bound back into the social world after such a tumultuous time. As social as I am, it's taken me a little time to start intentionally getting together with friends and planning social events and family gatherings again. Life is not going to be the same as it was before COVID, which is perhaps both good and bad. It is so important to be kind to ourselves as we navigate this so-called "new normal" post-COVID world, reminding ourselves that we are not the only ones adjusting back into social lives. Use positive self-talk as you reflect on how you are feeling each day and ease back into activities you enjoy. Push yourself outside of your comfort zone through goal setting and structured to-do lists, and use these strategies to grow each day. We have so much to be thankful for each day and having the ability to make connections with others is just one of the gifts we've been given. Taking small steps towards your goals and focusing on what you can control may help you find that as you transition into our post-COVID world, it can indeed be your time to shine!

More about Jennifer . . .

🏠 As we enter life after lockdown, I am most concerned about . . .
how my students and my daughters will adjust back to life and how the life we knew prior to COVID has changed. I get a little sad about all the experiences they've missed because of COVID, but then I remember that this is a part of their life's journey and that this experience, although not ideal, has taught each of them so many vital life lessons they will use now and in the future.

🏟 As we enter life after lockdown, I am most excited about enjoying . . .
the small things that we all missed; a bonfire with friends, dinner out at my favorite restaurant with my husband, sporting events and performances that my daughters are involved in, and a postponed family trip.

I am a high school special education teacher at Beavercreek High School in Beavercreek, Ohio. I co-designed the PEERspective Learning Approach in 2006 and published my first book entitled, *Why Didn't They Just Say That?* in 2017 with AAPC publishing. My second book with co-author Megan Barrett is due out in fall of 2021 and is called, *Yes, Please Tell Me.* I am also an adjunct professor at Wright State University and The University of Dayton, and most importantly I am a proud wife and mom of two amazing daughters.

Books
o   *Why Didn't They Just Say That?*
o   *Yes, Please Tell Me* (Fall 2021)

Website

PEERspectiveLearningApproach.com

Reference
Schmidt, Jennifer M., and Megan Barrett. 2021. *Yes, Please Tell Me.* Shawnee, KS: AAPC.

SECTION 3
ADULTS IN TRANSITION

Adults on the spectrum share a unique set of challenges as they deal with the return to employment, higher education, and social lives. The changes in these important parts of life also created additional stresses for many autistic adults who have sought to preserve their hard-won relationships and skills during the pandemic. This chapter contains first-person accounts of life both during and after lockdown and offers tips and suggestions for successfully mastering a return to a more "normal" way of life. It also questions whether virtual options may provide viable choices for some autistic adults.

Tony Attwood provides a provocative and eye-opening account of the dangers of addiction to online video games. Linda Murdock offers clearly-written guidelines for college students which could apply to both neurodivergent and neurotypical young adults in a wide range of settings. Amanda Backer offers practical strategies for employment and education, while Kelly Londenberg and Wilma Wake talk about friendships and how to navigate important relationships in the new world. Sandy and David Petrovic offer two perspectives on how the pandemic affected their family, and Lesley Clark contributes a poignant chapter about the challenges and choices involved in living through a pandemic with an autistic adult.

> 66 COVID made people more lazy. And you use your phone and other electronics a lot more. No going out. No fun. Bored easy. With COVID is more yuck than without COVID. 99
>
> Gabe LL, age 18

> 66 I would love to be able to shop or go to huge social events without using a mask again. 99
>
> Tiffany Baran, age 31

MY TRIP TO CANCUN

KELLY LONDENBERG

My childhood was spent with few friends. I did not comprehend how to play the games of my neurotypical peers and their gossiping nature always seemed cruel. Likewise, they could not relate to my fascination with chimpanzees; and they were baffled when I would scream and throw myself to the ground as each activity would end. Our differently-wired brains made it difficult for us to understand each other, often leaving me to play on my own. Luckily, as I grew into adulthood, I began making the social connections I desperately wanted. I now have a variety of autistic and neurotypical friends whom I cherish.

One of my long-time circles of friends is a group of neurotypical women. We all work in the school system supporting children in special education. Our scheduled times off are similar, so we always plan a girls' trip together each summer. Las Vegas was our annual destination for over a decade. There, we spent our days talking about life by the hotel pool. The evenings were spent applying make-up, putting on dresses, and curling our hair, skills they helped me with as I have no sense of fashion. We would then spend the evening dancing, singing, or watching shows without a care in the world. I always felt like I belonged when I was with them.

The Las Vegas girls' trip tradition was one of the highlights of each summer, but we longed to try something new. In 2019, we decided it was time to expand our horizons and planned to go international in 2020. We researched activities and resorts. Dates and flights were discussed and we booked our first trip abroad, to Cancun. We were elated! Unfortunately, Mother Nature had other plans for us.

Early in 2020, I started hearing stories on the news about a virus called COVID-19. At that time, I could not predict a pandemic was about to sweep the world. By mid-March, I realized the seriousness of COVID-19 when the schools closed and my state was locked down. I was afraid to go outside of my apartment. Even going to the store seemed too dangerous. I definitely did not want to be around people or friends. I was scared of catching the virus myself but was terrified of passing it on to a vulnerable person. I stayed inside of my four walls; first it was for weeks, then months. I was once again isolated from the relationships I had worked so hard to achieve.

As the summer approached and the virus was in full swing, I knew our annual girls' trip would be canceled. I would not get to swim with dolphins in Cancun with my beloved friends. We would not see the Mayan ruins. I was lonely and missed them dearly, but staying home was the best decision that summer. We rescheduled the trip for the summer of 2021. The pandemic would surely be over by then, right?

The second half of 2020 I continued to stay home as cases of COVID-19 were skyrocketing in the United States. Finally, in early 2021 a vaccine was available. I received both doses and felt a sense of relief. Slowly, with great anxiety, I began entering public places. First, I went into a store to get one item. I had to adjust to the social distancing rules, plexiglass, and masks that were all foreign to me. New rules are difficult because I have to learn them one by one. Was I still supposed to shake people's hands when we meet? Would shaking their hands be an exception to the six-foot social rule? It was all so confusing.

Schools opened back up part-time in April 2021 and being in the classroom with new restrictions was another change, another set of new rules. As spring began to turn into summer, I was unsure if I could join the girls' trip. Going to work was hard enough, so a vacation seemed impossible. My decision wavered day by day as questions plagued my mind. Could I get on a plane with so many people? Could I tolerate wearing a mask for so many hours? What if I got sick in Cancun and could not go home? Is it responsible to go on vacation now? I spoke with my friends and they answered some of my questions. They were all vaccinated and would not leave me alone in Cancun. They knew I had difficulty with changes in social rules and reassured me they would be there to help me navigate the novel situations. Eventually, I decided to go. I missed my friends and knew we would all follow the precautions.

I packed my suitcase, hand sanitizer and masks included. I made sure to have plenty of both. My friends picked me up the morning of the flight and we headed to the airport. Once I entered the airport, my heart began to race. There were so many people and anxiety was dominating my mind. Surely, one or more of the individuals there was carrying the virus. I made sure my mask was covering my nose and refocused on getting through security. People were not standing on the socially distancing dots that were placed on the ground to keep us six feet apart. Some people were pulling their masks down. It worried me. They were not following the rules, but at the same time, I was resisting the urge to take off my own mask. The mask was so hot and uncomfortable and I am very sensitive to anything touching my skin.

Once I boarded the plane, the structure and controlled atmosphere allowed me to somewhat relax for the first half of the flight. I chatted with the girls and enjoyed their company while we headed to our destination. We talked about our year in lockdown and laughed about the shared commonalities. The second part of the flight was not as fun. In general, because of my sensory issues, I have difficulty sitting for long periods of time. I wanted to stand up on the plane, but I forced myself to stay in my seat because I was afraid of walking past individuals who might have COVID-19. Sitting the entire time was excruciating. The only thing I could think about by the end was moving. I was relieved when we landed in Cancun. I could finally stand up. We had arrived!

The social rules related to COVID-19 were different than I expected in Mexico. There were requests for people to stand five feet apart to maintain social distancing. Immediately I became concerned. The rule was to stand six feet apart in California. Why was it dif-

ferent here? My friends reassured me that we would be okay. They explained there would be a lot of differences throughout the trip. Some of the new things I experienced included temperature checks on my arms and a fog disinfectant that was required before entering or leaving most buildings or areas. My friends were always there to explain the rules and demonstrate the actions to quell my fears. Some of the precautions just overwhelmed my senses, such as the frequent smell of disinfectant that gave me a headache. Occasionally I would choose to stay at the resort to recover from some of the additional sensory stressors while they went out.

Before leaving the country we had to get tested for COVID. I stayed home most of the pandemic so I had not needed to do the COVID-19 test before that day. I did not know what to expect and was fearful of the process. Would the swab hurt? How long would it take? Would I catch COVID while my mask was off? Questions rushed through my mind once again, but I knew I had to do it to board the plane. Upon arrival, my friends helped me fill out the forms. They once again demonstrated the process and got the test before me so I could watch the process. Their support increased my confidence. When my turn approached, I sat down, pulled down my mask, and let them swab my nasal cavity. While the test was uncomfortable, I did it. I was proud. And while I took as many precautions as possible, I've since tested two more times to verify the negative results.

Overall, our 2021 girls' trip was worth the wait and the increased stress. We even got to swim with dolphins and see the amazing Chichén Itzá Mayan ruins. While experiencing those activities was wonderful, the time I spent with my friends was extraordinary. I reconnected with them after a year of isolation and learned some of the new rules I'll need for the foreseeable future. Those things alone made it a successful trip. If I had to find the silver lining of a global pandemic, the enhanced appreciation for relationships would be at the top of the list. All individuals need connection. It's what makes us human.

More about Kelly . . .

 As we enter life after lockdown, I am most concerned about . . .
the confusion regarding constantly changing protocols and social rules.

As we enter life after lockdown, I am most excited . . .
to engage in community activities and resume a typical routine.

Kelly Londenberg, BS, COTA/L, is an autistic adult and licensed pediatric occupational therapy assistant primarily serving children on the spectrum. She has served on the boards of several autism organizations and speaks educating others on topics related to sensory processing and living on the spectrum.

COMPUTER GAMING AND COVID

TONY ATTWOOD

The past year has marked us as one of the only generations to experience a global pandemic. The pandemic kept people at home, something that suited many autistic individuals. But it also limited the opportunities for social and emotional growth for autistic teens and young adults, and one of the obvious outlets became computer games. These games were already intensely important to many autistic youth, but now they became more so, as there was little else to occupy their minds and their time. Computer games can be beneficial, but they can also be addictive. This is a story that needs to be told, because nobody else is talking about it.

COVID's impact on the autistic teen or young adult

Many individuals have begun displaying an increase in routines and rituals, heightened sensory sensitivity, and more engagement with special interests. These are all ways of coping with anxiety. People have been cooped up together for the past year, which can be difficult for a person with autism who craves solitude. There may even be anxiety about what will happen when we begin to have more face-to-face contact and are forced to endure crowds again.

There is a misconception that people with autism lack empathy. The opposite is actually true: Autistic individuals are often acutely aware of other people's mental states. The news speaks of a killer virus and the rising numbers of dead; children worry about their family members' health. There has been more free time at home this year for the anxiety to percolate and one way to alleviate that anxiety is the computer game.

Computer gaming—a perfect fit for autism

There are a number of factors that make computer games extremely popular with people on the spectrum. Gaming provides a sense of achievement and identity. It allows you to show your capabilities independent of autism. The main issues of autism are social-conversational, but in gaming you have no real socialization and you have no conversation, so you have basically bypassed autism. Gaming is a natural talent because it suits the autistic cognition. However, it also involves considerable practice. A person can become a master of a skill that requires great ability but also practice. It is the same for a child with computer games. They are talented at computer games, and are motivated to practice. If you want to measure the intelligence of an autistic child, watch them play computer games. The game bypasses their autism, they are highly motivated, and you can see how quickly and effectively their brain works.

66 With gaming you have a sense of achievement that is truly gratifying, especially as it is valuable to your peer group. 99

If you are not good socially and you are not good at sports, your intellect is very important to you, and you want to prove how smart you are. You want to demonstrate your intelligence and you want other people to appreciate that intelligence. With gaming you have a sense of achievement that is truly gratifying, especially as it is valuable to your peer group.

Autistic teens are searching for identity. *Who am I? Why am I here? What is the meaning of life? Where do I fit in? I know I'm supposed to be like everyone else, but I'm not. I want a sense of identity and self-worth that is defined by something that is valued by my peers.* The computer game does that. It gives a sense of identity to someone who is searching. The computer game becomes a way of fitting in. It becomes your identity when you have few ways to define that identity. And autism can make a person very lonely. Without social skills, it is sometimes hard to fit in to most same-age groups. Bullying and being excluded can leave autistic teens feeling isolated, while gaming provides a connection with fellow gamers who actually seek you out, rather than shun you.

Computer games give you immediate feedback. As many as 75% of those with ASD also display characteristics of ADD and ADHD. Computer gaming suits those characteristics, as it is based on immediate feedback on one's performance without any waiting, which autistic people often dislike. Unlike school, where you may be waiting on feedback from a teacher, the game provides immediate feedback.

People are excited to see you online and that kind of genuine, deep welcome is intoxicating to someone with autism. Someone in your peer group actually wants to know you, and is pleased that you are there. Rather than the students who sometimes bully and tease and reject and humiliate, these gamers want to know you and are proud to be your friend. They give you compliments and admiration. But more than that, with your gaming skills, you also become a teacher to some, a mentor to others. You advise them. You are wise. You are talented. You are someone special.

In e-sports, a subgroup of gaming, there are leagues with teams and supporters; logos and colors; managers and favorite players. Players are bought and sold. There are e-sport competitions held in convention centers with thousands of people watching gamers. And in this world, you, the autistic individual, are the person the team wants to recruit. You are a hero in that world. Finally, you have a social network where you shine.

Gaming as a coping mechanism

During COVID, anxiety and depression increased for many people, including people on the spectrum. A computer game is a thought blocker for anxiety and depression. When you are engaged in the game, you don't feel anxious and you don't feel depressed. Instead, you suppress and compress your thoughts and feelings. Computer games are more powerful than medications or cognitive behavioral therapy because they encourage the classic autistic characteristics of avoidance and suppression. When you are playing the game, you are in a bubble. Your problems disappear and you don't care about anything else, but when you switch off the game, those feelings come back. Parents become frightened to see how angry their child becomes when asked to turn off the computer. What is actually happening isn't really anger: It is the fact that their powerful feelings have not been dissolved or resolved. Once the game is gone—boom! The feelings are back, and they flood you with fear and despair.

> **❝ Computer games are more powerful than medications or cognitive behavioral therapy because they encourage the classic autistic characteristics of avoidance and suppression. ❞**

A substitute for social interaction

In autism, social emotional reciprocity is a core issue. In a computer game, you don't have a real conversation going on. You don't have to worry about reciprocity, you don't have to read body language, and you don't have to be involved in social chit-chat. One of the interesting things is that there are often chat lines in computer games, and they provide a means to communicate through typing, rather than talking. Clinically, that can be very valuable. When a client sends me an email, I may receive far more information and insight into the individual's world than I do in person, because it involves typing, not talking. There is a greater fluency and disclosure of thoughts, feelings, and revelations of the self through typing, rather than talking.

The games have very clear and simple rules that aren't like social rules. Social rules are inconsistent and complex, and there are always exceptions. Neurotypical kids do things that that are against the rules and get away with it, even though you're not supposed to get away with it! But in gaming, there are simple rules that are always enforced. There is no inconsistency and no uncertainty, so you are secure in the rules of the game.

A sense of pleasure and enjoyment

If you ask a neurotypical about the greatest moments of excitement and joy in their life, it usually involves another person—giving birth, getting married, falling in love. But with autism, other people can be a source of confusion, so pleasurable memories rarely involve them. Computer gaming, on the other hand, gives you experiences of pleasure and enjoyment when there are very few in your life. This is incredibly intoxicating. Gaming is addictive because it feeds into pleasure-seeking and enjoyment. For someone who may have few pleasures in life, experiencing such a high level of excitement—perhaps the greatest enjoyment you have ever received—is euphoric.

Creating an alternative world

In the real world of daily life, the teen with autism is often not respected or included. But here in the computer game, you are in a world where you are both respected and included. The special interests of people on the spectrum are often an attempt to find a world in which to belong. Anime, Pokémon, Manga—another culture, another country, another time in history where you fit in. Science fiction—you go to another planet where you are recognized and valued. The game creates an alternative world where you have a sense of belonging. The real world may not value you or respect you, but in this world you are remarkable, and that's why you want to stay.

Avatars are virtual selves that you can create in a computer game. An avatar allows you to experiment with personality, analyzing the interests and people who are important in your life. This is what most teenagers do in the real world. *I'm going to be an adult, so what kind of adult am I going to be? Who do I value, who are my heroes, and can I borrow some of their characteristics?* In a computer game you can experiment with that even further. If you're concerned about your weight, your avatar is slim; if you're concerned that you're not smart enough, then your avatar is a genius. It is very powerful.

The dangers of computer gaming

Immersion into computer gaming can mean that individuals are not learning to cope with emotions. Instead, they're learning to avoid them. They are compressing and suppressing, and are not processing their feelings appropriately. This means that when they start playing the games in earnest, their emotional maturity freezes and levels off. Emotional regulation is stunted. Individuals learn to rely on the game rather than the actual social skills which will serve them in the real world.

When we look at the long-term effects of gaming, we see medical issues. Individuals become overweight, with poor eating habits. Junk food is quick and easy while you are on the computer. Some individuals will spend enormous amounts of time online—from 10- 16 hours per day. There is a lack of exercise and exposure to sunlight, so health effects arise.

It is also very disruptive to sleep patterns. One of the effects of extended screen time is that a person's thoughts increasingly spiral once the game is turned off. Thoughts become incoherent and cha- otic, and sleep becomes more and more elusive. That's why there should be no screen time for one to two hours before bed. In autism, sleep has always been a prob- lem, from infancy on through senior adulthood. Sleep is important for processing intellec- tual information and processing emotions. When you have a good night's sleep, inappropriate behaviors diminish. With too lit- tle sleep, the opposite is true.

> 66 One of the effects of extended screen time is that a person's thoughts increasingly spiral once the game is turned off. 99

One of the inherent dangers in gaming is a potential tie-in to gambling. In computer games there are commodities called loot boxes. These loot boxes pop up during a game, offering the opportunity to purchase something that may or may not contain useful items. Most boxes have ordinary items, but the gamer will continue to buy them, lured by the possibility of scoring something big. The odds of it having what it advertises are very rare, but the possibility keeps gamers buying more, and so gambling becomes embedded in games. Parents should be aware of this connection, as it is one more avenue to addiction.

When gaming becomes an addiction

The computer gaming industry has the potential to rob us of some very bright minds, who may get caught up in the addictive side of gaming. When teens begin to avoid things that were recently part of their routine, there may be a problem. If you tell your teen to get off the computer for lunch and they become incredibly agitated, avoiding lunch in order to play the game—that's a worry. If they become upset when a legitimate request interferes with access to the game, then the depth of engagement is now of considerable clinical concern. Their world revolves around the number of hours they spend on the game, and they become agitated when other activities interfere. For example, you used to have evening meals as a family, spending time together. Now the teen arrives at the table at the last moment, bolts down food, and then, boom. Gone. No conversation. No engagement. The individual withdraws from a variety of activities that used to be important for the family and enjoyable for themselves. The game is taking control. This is common in addiction: Instead of the person controlling the game, the game is controlling the person.

One of the first casualties of any addiction is truth. The individual will hide their actual time online, like an alcoholic hides their alcohol. They will also have access to games on their phones. Gaming should absolutely be included in the same category as alcohol and drugs for individuals with autism. These individuals struggle, not with autism, but with emotional regulation. Because the game is so good at moderating intense emotions, they are reluctant to switch to anything else.

Dealing with the addiction

One thing that parents should not do is take away the game as punishment. The games provide the teen or young adult with an identity, coping strategies, a social network—what they live for. If adults remove this without providing the child with other coping mechanisms or alternative activities, this ends up being not punishment but revenge. Parents will end up escalating the punishment from a day to a week to the threat of totally removing the computer, and the teen will respond with defiance and anger. It can quickly escalate into a civil war that no one wins.

If we want to address the behavior constructively, it is important to carefully identify the issues of behavior management or encouragement of chores or other commitments. There must absolutely be consequences, but they must be appropriate. For example, if a teen does something that upsets his sister, an appropriate response might be to have him take responsibility for one of her chores for a week. The time that is spent on that chore would have been spent on the computer, so it is a means of restricting access through teaching an appropriate replacement. It is possible to use the computer as a reward. For example, if the child does their homework, they can have an extra half hour on the computer. This uses the computer as a reward or an encouragement, rather than as punishment. It also teaches a part of growing up. You want more time on the game, but you've got to do your chores. That's life.

When a parent suspects addiction, they can use logic to deal with it. Get a big piece of paper and list the positives and negatives of computer games with the individual. The positives are that it helps manage emotions and it makes the child popular. So how can we help the individual achieve these things outside the game? We can find more conventional and diverse ways of achieving those things, initially in addition to the computer game and eventually as alternatives. Next list the negatives: Being overweight, spending huge amounts of time on the game and nothing else, the lack of honesty, and the lack of constructive ways in their lives to learn to deal with emotions. Help the individual compare these lists and set goals.

In terms of strategy, first get an accurate accounting of the amount of time spent gaming. Instead of aiming for an unrealistic goal, like an entire game-free day, try for something more reasonable. For example, start with reducing time by 15 minutes every day for three weeks. If successful, then decrease by 15 more minutes for three more weeks. Use small steps. Parents must provide alternatives that bring pleasure to the child, like being outdoors or spending time with pets. Families must also try to help the individual increase their social network through constructive means so the individual is actually learning to relate and manage conflict.

There are currently few treatment options for addiction in autistic individuals. Therapy for addiction needs to develop expertise, theoretical models, and a whole range of strategies for gaming addiction, especially for autistic individuals. We need psychiatrists and psychologists who are aware of this and work to modify therapy to accommodate the autistic way of thinking.

Final thoughts

As we continue to deal with the effects of the current pandemic, it's important to realize that many of our brightest autistic individuals are going into the medical and research fields. These individuals, with their logical brains and skill at analyzing systems, have the ability to understand the behavior of a virus and can use their intellect to help develop cures. The intense focus of which they are capable allows them to tolerate 18-hour days in a lab. Instead of looking at a computer screen, they are looking into a microscope. Let's hope that we can guide them to those labs, and show them that their brilliance is not only appreciated, but desperately needed, and that they are indeed invaluable members of society.

More about Tony . . .

 As we enter life after lockdown, I am most concerned about . . .
an increase in autistic teenagers engaging in computer gaming compared to pre-pandemic levels.

As we enter life after lockdown, I am most excited about . . .
reconnecting with autistic friends and family members in Europe and America.

Tony is a clinical psychologist who has specialized in autism spectrum disorders since he qualified as a clinical psychologist in England in 1975. He currently works in his own private practice, and is also adjunct professor at Griffith University, Queensland and senior consultant at the Minds and Hearts clinic in Brisbane.

Tony has been invited to be a keynote speaker at many Australasian and International Conferences. He presents workshops and runs training courses for parents, professionals and individuals with Asperger's syndrome all over the world. However, COVID has temporarily ended international travel and his presentations are now available via web cast with more information at www.attwoodandgarnettevents.com

Books

- Asperger's Syndrome—A Guide for Parents and Professionals
- The Complete Guide to Asperger's Syndrome
- Exploring Depression, and Beating the Blues, with co-author Michelle Garnett
- Been There. Done That. Try This! Tony Attwood, Craig R. Evans, and Anita Lesko (Eds)
- CBT to Help Young People with Asperger's Syndrome to Understand and Express Affection, with co-author Michelle Garnett

COLLEGE: BACK TO CAMPUS

LINDA MURDOCK

Very soon, most college campuses will be welcoming students back to more traditional living and learning environments. Over the past year, universities have offered a variety of options to students. You may have been learning in a remote model, in a physical classroom but with masks and social distancing, or perhaps in a hybrid model using a combination of the two. Some campuses closed residence halls and only allowed take-out style dining options. As we transition back to campus this fall, some of these options may still be in place, but universities will be eager to make things as normal as possible for students.

Masks

The key to having a successful transition back to campus will be flexibility. Let's start with masks. Your campus may have a policy to require masks or it may not. If the policy indicates you should wear masks in certain settings, it's important to follow that policy. Once a policy has been set, students are expected to follow it without argument. Arguing with an individual professor will only frustrate both parties and leave a bad impression on the professor. This part is pretty straightforward; if there is a policy, follow it. Let's consider some cases where the rules are not clear. You may encounter the following scenarios:

1. The university may indicate that vaccinated people do not have to wear masks; however, university personnel are not responsible or potentially even allowed to verify vaccinations. Individuals are expected to comply based on the honor system.

2. The university may leave it up to individual professors to set the rules in each class. In this case, you may have some classes, labs, or offices where you are expected to wear a mask and others where you are not.

3. Professors and other authority figures may indicate masks are technically required but then give tacit approval to ignore the rule. In this setting some may be following the rule and others may not.

4. The university may say that masks are not required but an individual professor might indicate that they require them to be worn in their class or office.

These gray or unclear areas may cause you to feel anxious, uncomfortable, or even angry. If this happens, remember that you can only control your own behavior. There have been many altercations over masks during this pandemic year and the first goal is to prevent a disagreement or combative situation. First, remind yourself what the official or stated policy is. If the requirement is to wear a mask, do so, even if others do not comply. If you feel uncomfortable that others are not complying, speak to the authority figure (professor, director, or manager) in private at a later time. Speaking out to the crowd may cause you to be singled out, adding to your discomfort in the environment. Second, if there is not a mask policy but an individual asks you to wear one, it would be polite and kind to comply. Another person in the environment may have a serious health condition or extreme fear of the virus. As members of a shared campus community, looking out for others and taking their needs into consideration is the kind thing to do. If you feel a professor is openly disregarding the policy of the university, I would recommend sending a nicely worded email to the professor, like the example provided here:

Dear Professor Smith,

I would be more comfortable in your Economics 101 course if you would require the class members to wear masks in accordance with the university policy.

Thank you for your consideration.

If the professor does not comply with the policy after you have communicated directly to them, it is acceptable to speak with the department chair.

In another scenario, the official policy might indicate masks are not required, but you would prefer that everyone wear one. While it is acceptable to tell a small group of peers that you would appreciate it if they would wear a mask, you cannot require or demand that they do so. Additionally, it would not be acceptable to ask an entire class to wear a mask if they are not required. If you find yourself in this situation, try to find a seat that is socially distanced and wear your mask. Remember, you can only control your own behavior.

Awkward Conversations

I think we can all anticipate awkward conversations this year about vaccines, COVID testing, and positive cases. Some individuals may openly announce that they had COVID and may describe what it was like for them; others may not wish to share this information. Some individuals will announce that they have been vaccinated and then ask you if you have been or if you plan to receive a vaccination. You also may encounter individuals who do not take the virus seriously or who may believe it to be a hoax. One thing is for certain: People have strong opinions on these issues. As with the mask issue, we want to avoid confrontation. Even the most socially adept among us have trouble navigating conversations with those holding opposing beliefs related to this pandemic and the importance of vaccinations. I offer the following suggestions.

1. You have a reasonable *need to know* the vaccination status of your roommates and romantic partners. These are the individuals with whom you are in close contact and who pose the most risk to you. It is acceptable to politely ask whether these individuals have been vaccinated.

2. You do not have a reasonable *need to know* the vaccination status of your professors, classmates, and acquaintances. Some individuals will talk openly about vaccines and you can engage in this discussion if the other person brings it up. If the discussion gets confrontational or individuals seem uncomfortable, it's best to drop the issue.

3. If another person openly expresses viewpoints that are in opposition with yours, remember that no amount of arguing is likely to change either person's mind. If asked, you can simply state your belief and then suggest you change the topic of conversation. Continuing to share data, articles, or video clips will only serve to escalate an argument. We have to accept that other people are allowed to come to different conclusions and hold their beliefs just as strongly as we do. Sometimes this seems completely illogical or

incomprehensible, but it is true. Name calling or belittling another person will not change their mind and will only lead to anger and hurt feelings.

4. It is not reasonable to expect roommates or friends to continually be tested for COVID in order to make you feel more comfortable. We are responsible for our own comfort. If you are uncomfortable attending classes in person, check to see if there are online options available at your university. You can also get take-out meals rather than eating with a group in the cafeteria. If it makes you uncomfortable to attend sporting events or social events on campus, you have the choice not to attend. You cannot control how others behave at these events. You cannot impose extra guidelines above those required by the university, nor can you ignore the requirements. If masks and social distancing are required, and you do not wish to comply with those rules, the only option is not to attend.

Course Flexibility

During 2020 and the first part of 2021, most universities offered more flexibility to students in terms of absences, making up work, and providing the option to attend classes and meetings virtually. Professors and students embraced some of these changes and appreciated the added flexibility. But some of the policies made it harder for professors to teach and assess to their normal standards. Some forms of instruction made it more difficult for students to pay attention, ask questions, or remember assignments.

Going forward, some of the flexibility students were afforded during the pandemic may no longer be allowed. The syllabus for each class will describe the rules for attendance, the expectations for excused and unexcused absences, and the mode of delivery for the class (in person or virtual). Over the last year, students may have been allowed to attend virtually at their discretion. Some professors were required to teach simultaneously in two platforms, with some students in the classroom and others attending through internet platforms like Zoom. Although the intention was to provide this flexibility so that students could stay home if they were not feeling well or had been exposed to COVID-19, some individuals used this added flexibility to attend class from a vacation spot or simply to stay in bed. Be mindful this may not be allowed going forward. In order to teach in both platforms, changes to the course expectations, materials, and activities had to be made. Professors may not wish to make those changes going forward.

Professors may expect students to attend in person unless they can provide an approved excuse. Students may not be allowed to make up work, particularly tests, without an approved excuse. Students no doubt enjoyed the extra accommodations provided by professors and it may be hard to transition away from the expectation of flexibility.

It may be an adjustment to give up the flexibility we have all come to enjoy, but remember these decisions are made by the professor. Do not ask for an explanation as to why the professor cannot simply allow you to Zoom in to the class. Do not expect to be able to take vacations on days when the class is scheduled to meet. It is important to read the syllabus and adhere to the rules for attendance and make-up work.

Transitioning Our Appearance Back

This last year many of us spent our days in yoga pants or sweat pants. We may have skipped a few showers and worn our hair in a messy bun more than we should have. As the world comes back to normal, so must our appearance. While college students typically are not expected to dress up for class, there are some minimum expectations. Please shower daily and after exercise. Expectations for hair washing differ based on hair texture. However, if you wash your hair as frequently as your parents expected you to when you were living with them, that ought to do it! Please do not wear pajamas, the clothes you slept in, or dirty clothes to class. Do not attend class barefoot. Professors shouldn't wear yoga pants to class but it's probably ok for students to do so unless you attend a college with a dress code. Also, it is important to know and comply with the dress code for certain courses like practicums, internships, or lab experiences. Professional dress is typically expected in graduate-level courses.

Are Some Changes Here to Stay?

As we emerge from this unprecedented time in our history, some are questioning if aspects of our culture are changed forever. The answer to this is probably yes: For some people, certain behaviors or preferences may be different going forward. So, how will you know what the rules or expectations are? Expectations will be fluid and variable. We will all have to be vigilant about picking up on both social cues and clues in the environment. One example of this is hand-shaking. Shaking hands was expected in professional situations and some social situations. Going forward, some have suggested that we do away with this custom. Previously it might have been seen as offensive if an individual offered their hand and the other person declined to shake it. Now, it is to be expected that some individuals prefer not to shake hands, opting instead for a fist or elbow bump or even a small wave or slight head-bow. When a person offers any of these greeting gestures, if you are comfortable, reciprocate in kind. If you are not comfortable, simply state something like, "I don't really shake hands anymore" and offer an alternative such as an elbow. There is no need for a lengthy explanation. The same rules apply to hugs. You should not feel pressured to hug someone. One way to handle this is to offer a small wave and a smile before the other person has the opportunity to lean in for a hug. If you end up feeling awkward in any of these scenarios, it's ok to just say that you feel like the rules have

> " . . . simply state something like, "I don't really shake hands anymore." "

changed since the pandemic and people have different levels of comfort with hugs or handshakes. Most people are aware of this and have had similar awkward moments.

Additionally, we can expect people to have a stronger appreciation for hand-washing and the use of hand sanitizer. If you go into an office and notice a bottle of hand sanitizer positioned so that visitors can easily access it, it is polite to use it. You may also go to a doctor or dentist office where the receptionist may ask you to wash your hands before taking a seat. Parents may ask friends to wash their hands before holding their baby. That being said, it would be considered rude to ask someone to wash their hands in most other situations. You should not ask your classmates if they have washed their hands. Similarly, if you go into a student dining facility on campus, it would not be appropriate to ask everyone at a communal table if they have washed their hands. In general, we should all take every opportunity to wash our hands when in public, especially before meals and after sneezing or blowing our noses. We just have to trust that others will do the same.

You may observe that some individuals are more hesitant to share food or drinks than before the pandemic. If someone offers to share with you and you do not wish to taste what they are offering, you can say "No, thank you" in a formal setting or among friends, "Nah, I'm good" will also suffice. If pressed, it's fine to just state that you are really trying not to eat or drink after people any more. People should not take offense as this has always been a matter of individual choice. Nor should you take offense if someone prefers not to eat or drink after you.

> 66 Going forward, it's best to give others a little extra personal space. 99

After over a year of social distancing, the idea of being in a crowd, standing close to others in a line, or dining next to strangers can seem unfamiliar and may take some getting used to. Going forward, it's best to give others, especially strangers, a little extra personal space. Look for signs that others are uncomfortable, such as stepping or leaning backwards during conversations. If you are in line behind someone, and as the line moves forward, they look back to see where you are, this is a clue that you might be standing too close and should give them a bit more space. A good rule of thumb is to stay 2-3 feet behind someone in a line and about 3 feet away when speaking to a stranger or acquaintance. Close friends or roommates generally interact in closer contact. When entering an office, stand back away from the desk. If the seated person scoots their chair back or reacts with surprise as you advance, it's best to back up a bit. Some quick conversations can be had from the office doorway in lieu of entering the office.

Final Thoughts

This last year has been hard on all of us. We have had to be flexible and accept changes that were often unwelcome or disappointing. Other changes weren't so bad and we have probably all learned some new skills and proved our resiliency. As we transition back to a more normal version of our lives, the most important things are to continue to be flexible, be courteous of others, and to remember that we can't control other people's behavior, only our own. When in doubt, strive to follow and respect policies and attempt to be sensitive to other people's perspectives. I wish you a successful college experience!

More about Linda . . .

As we enter life after lockdown, I am most concerned about . . .
   being in large crowds with people who may not be vaccinated.

As we enter life after lockdown, I am most excited about . . .
   traveling again.

Dr. Murdock is a Professor and Chair of the Communication Sciences and Disorders department at the University of Montevallo. She teaches courses in research methodology, clinical methodology, literacy, special education, language disorders, and autism. She is the author of *Improving your College Experience: A Workbook for Students on the Autism Spectrum.*

ADULTING IN THE TIME OF COVID

AMANDA BACKER

For a minute, try to remember a time in your life when you felt completely sick with panic. Think about the way your stomach churned or the way you shook with fear, as you walked into the first day at a new school or your first job interview. Was it hard for you to get out of your car? Did you wish you could just run away? Do you remember how tempting it was to just stay where it was comfortable?

Have you ever tried to concentrate on something really important while you were feeling overwhelmed, uncomfortable, or while you were experiencing physical pain? Maybe you were in an incredibly noisy room, surrounded by a smell that was making you nauseous, or maybe you had a pounding headache. How well could you concentrate? Even if you knew exactly what needed to be done, were you able to do it well?

Lastly, I want you to think of a day when you were trying your very hardest to reach a goal and just kept getting held back. Do you remember how frustrating that was, and how badly you just wanted to give up? Imagine how it would feel to experience all of these types of feelings at once, every single day, and to know that you must overcome them all to reach your goals. These are the types of barriers that many people on the autism spectrum were already struggling with on a daily basis *before* the pandemic hit.

The coronavirus pandemic turned the world upside down overnight. Feelings of anxiety, the loss of confidence in social skills, increased attention to sensory sensitivities, and the widespread experience of unemployment (regardless of qualifications) have become all too familiar to everyone. For those on the spectrum, the pandemic just made it worse.

The California Autism Network was created specifically to support adults on the autism spectrum to overcome barriers to success in their educational, employment, and social goals. Entering back into society after this pandemic presents many new challenges and obstacles that our clients must face and overcome. However, we are beginning to see that there is light at the end of the tunnel for them and that things may work out better than originally expected.

Matthew's Experience

When Matthew contacted our center before the pandemic, he was a freshman at a local college. He was having an extremely difficult time passing his classes and explained that he was feeling completely overwhelmed with the whole college experience. The academic and social expectations of college were more than he could take on at once. Matthew struggles with extreme social anxiety and he found himself "freezing up" when asked a question during class, or during presentations and group projects. He didn't know anyone on campus and desperately wanted friends, but he didn't know how to initiate conversations with others. He was even surrounded by campus security one day because he appeared to be "stalking" a girl on campus. He explained that he was following her and staring at her, but was just trying to think of something to say. Matthew's anxiety towards college life was at an all-time high, which made him feel like giving up. Although he had heard of on-campus disability support, he did not seek help because he "didn't know what to ask for." This is when he discovered our program.

> 66 . . . he did not seek help because he didn't know what to ask for. 99

Matthew participated in an assessment to determine the exact support he needed and began targeting his individualized goals. Just as he was beginning to improve in his self-management, self-regulation, self-advocacy skills, and his social skills, the pandemic hit. Matthew was terrified to transition to a completely new set of expectations, and he completely shut down.

We worked diligently with Matthew to get him adjusted to this "new version" of school and familiarized him with the differing expectations and responsibilities involving virtual interaction. To his surprise, he realized that it was much easier for him to stay organized, ask questions (via the chat box), follow instructions, and learn new concepts when he participated in classes this way. With the social pressure removed, it was easier for him to focus and learn. Eventually, he found that he even felt more socially confident on camera than he usually does during face-to-face interaction. He explained that during virtual interactions, he could just turn off the camera or say he was having technical difficulties if he needed to take a break. In addition, it was much easier for our program to monitor Matthew's progress during virtual instruction. We were able to assist him as needed to get appropriate tutoring and services from the disability program, communicate with professors and peers, and learn to manage his time and priorities effectively.

Matthew's grades improved dramatically and he even began to form acquaintances through his virtual classes. We found ways to observe these social interactions and coached him through them from the sidelines, so he was able to practice his social skills in a very real way. Matthew has now established relationships with his peers (because of his beaming online personality) and feels prepared to meet them in person now that most of his anxiety about interacting with them has subsided. Matthew also chose to participate in our center's group meetings, where he was paired with adults with autism who share similar goals. This helped him to blossom and begin forming deeper connections with people who share common struggles and interests.

In-person instruction will resume at Matthew's school in the fall, and Matthew is actually excited to go back! We will ensure that Matthew is prepared to handle sudden anxiety with coping strategies, in-the-moment "escape" plans, and scripted responses to common conversation topics. Matthew was given a second chance at college life, and with the added practice and slower-paced transition to college during the pandemic, he is sure to succeed this time around.

Chelsea's Experience

Chelsea came to us to improve her communication skills and to receive assistance in finding employment. She has a large personality and is skilled in conversation, but she had a difficult time monitoring her facial expressions and often offended people with her comments. Chelsea wanted to find a job in a "social atmosphere," but knew that she needed support to be successful with this. After her assessment, which determined a need for training involving self-monitoring, perspective-taking, and professionalism, she was hired to work at a local grocery store.

> 66 She has a large personality and is skilled in conversation, but . . . often offended people with her comments. 99

Things were going well for Chelsea until the pandemic. She was working in the epicenter of the chaos and, in addition, was required to wear a mask the entire time. Although Chelsea was aware that she had sensory sensitivities related to smell and heat, she was not prepared for how difficult it would be for her to work under these conditions while tolerating a mask. She explained that the mask trapped the smell of her breath, which when mixed with the scent of the material of the mask, made her feel incredibly nauseous. Wearing a mask also caused Chelsea to become over-heated, which fogged up her glasses and sometimes caused panic attacks. This, combined with the absolute madness of the grocery store, triggered several rude comments to customers and Chelsea was written up twice.

After searching for a mask that was more tolerable, we worked closely with Chelsea's manager to temporarily place her in a posi-tion that didn't involve high-pressure situations. We also worked diligently with Chelsea to target her ability to handle stressful cus-tomer service scenarios appropriately through role-playing practices.

Once Chelsea adapted to wearing her mask, she began to recognize a different issue. Since Chelsea has always had to actively think about her facial expressions during in-person interactions, the fact that her mouth had been hidden by a mask for so long caused her to lose her ability to monitor the facial expressions she was making; even a simple smile began to feel forced. Chelsea has been working intensively to improve her facial expressions in front of the mirror to make sure she can still make herself look "happy and comfortable" while she is speaking.

Now that masks are no longer required and the grocery store chaos has died down, Chelsea has begun to work as a grocery bagger again. She enjoys customer service and can smile and interact with customers appropriately. She even says that people seem nicer now than they were before the pandemic. She is proud that she was able to keep her job through those stressful times and feels that the experience made her stronger than ever. She commented, "If I could get through that, I can get through anything."

Adrian's Experience

Adrian needed assistance in improving his confidence and his interview skills. Although he has a degree in computer science and has applied to countless positions over the years, he had never been hired. He explained that he "looks good on paper" and was called in for many interviews, but his anxiety was so high that he never performed well or received any offers. Adrian admitted that he couldn't even bring himself to walk into a few of the interviews and that he stopped talking during one of them because he was being asked too many questions at once and his "brain froze up like a computer does."

We decided to target Adrian's interview skills through 1:1 practice and were also able to address this issue through group role-playing practices with peers. Since many of our clients struggle with interview skills, we were able to pair Adrian with a group of young adults who were all trying to improve in these specific areas. Once Adrian saw that he was not alone in these struggles and that many other adults with autism who were qualified (or

> 66 Once Adrian saw that he was not alone in these struggles . . . he didn't feel as discouraged and began to improve rapidly. 99

even over-qualified) for positions couldn't get past the interview process, he didn't feel as discouraged and began to improve rapidly. Sometimes clients don't like to refer to our group sessions as "support groups," but in many ways, that is exactly what they are. As a team, this group of young adults was able to participate confidently and successfully through mock interviews with multiple volunteers from their specific career fields.

Things were looking up until the pandemic began, and then there were absolutely no companies hiring new employees. The 1:1 and group meetings continued; however, they were moved to virtual platforms. After the initial adjustment to online meetings, something interesting began to happen. We noticed that many of our clients seemed much more confident virtually than in person, and began performing beautifully during mock interviews. Since the pandemic, there have been multiple "work from home" positions that have opened up.

Adrian began participating in virtual interviews, which he performed extremely well on. He was hired for a customer service tech support position right away! Since the position is 100% virtual, it allows him to troubleshoot customer issues from his personal computer in the comfort of his own home. Adrian explains that he is a completely different person when he can work virtually because all of the social pressure is taken away and he can just focus on what he knows best.

Although he continues to attend the individual and group meetings through our program, his goals for improvement have changed from finding employment to maintaining employment, and are also more focused on personal improvement in social skills and self-regulation. In addition, he has developed many meaningful relationships within the peer group and enjoys having his "social time" separate from his "work time." This allows him to focus on these situations individually since he explains that, "It's just too hard to do both at the same time."

A New Beginning

While the pandemic was a dramatic hardship for all of society, it made us all stronger in so many ways. We have experienced a level of stress throughout the past year that makes our struggles *before* the pandemic seem like child's play. Through hardships comes self-knowledge, and we have all realized things about ourselves and others that we may not have seen without the giant magnifying glass of the pandemic. In a way, it forced society to pause and "smell the flowers." Through shared struggles, empathy and kindness grew. Everyone was pushed to their limits and will hopefully enter back into society feeling stronger than they were before.

In addition, the pandemic forced society to think outside of the box and to get more creative in its approach to success. It sparked new and more flexible ways of thinking and operating, specifically for education and businesses trying to stay afloat. As everyone moved solely to virtual interaction, an entirely new dimension of education and available job opportunities have presented themselves. This has been extremely beneficial to our young adults with autism.

Although the coronavirus pandemic was detrimental in so many ways, it developed a society with more compassion, empathy, and understanding of individual barriers and hardships. In many ways, it drew people together and created so many exciting opportunities that wouldn't have existed otherwise. As the country reopens and heals, a fresh perspective and open-mindedness may be exactly what society needs so that our adults on the spectrum can succeed.

More about Amanda . . .

As we enter life after lockdown, I am most concerned that . . .
things may never be the same again.

As we enter into life after lockdown, I am most excited about . . .
how change presents many new opportunities.

Amanda Backer has worked in the field of autism for 17 years, and has served this community as a special education teacher and intensive behavior intervention specialist. She is the founder of the California Autism Network, which focuses primarily on supporting adults with autism to form connections within the autism community, successfully pursue post-secondary education, and find meaningful employment.

Website

https://californiaautismnetwork.com/

REBOOTING AFTER LIVING VIRTUALLY (AND VIRTUALLY NOT LIVING)

SANDY PETROVIC & DAVID PETROVIC

Sandy's Story

I am the mother of a young-adult son who is on the autism spectrum. The product of early special education and years of multiple interdisciplinary therapies, David is now a master's-prepared middle school teacher, national speaker, and author. As a college instructional advisor and tutor, I have witnessed the various effects of coronavirus-induced restrictions on our special-needs students, in addition to its effects on my own son. I have also conversed with both these groups regarding their concerns, actual and anticipated, in returning to life as we once knew it. David and I have separate perspectives on the associated personal, social, school, and work considerations. We hope that sharing our experiences will assist you with adaptation during these unprecedented times.

Personal COVID Challenges and Reevaluation

I suspect that the "unknown" elements of COVID-19 were the basis of society's monumental challenges and stress: loss of control of our lives, change in every aspect, and not knowing *when* or *how* the pandemic would end. As if fear of disease or death for self or loved ones was not enough, the loss of relationships, physical contact, and milestone celebrations compounded dismay, anxiety, and at times, hopelessness. Difficult for neurotypicals, these challenges and those posed by reacclimating to "normalcy" are amplified for individuals on the spectrum—and moving forward, even "normal" will likely be different.

Initially, our nuclear family unit provided each other emotional support. Most importantly, my husband and I encouraged David's sharing of problems and fears to decrease his burden. We could then clarify information, reassure David, and discuss concerns. We brainstormed suggestions for novel emerging dilemmas. I could also explain and ensure his competence with COVID-19 safety measures. But as time went on and losses compounded, I occasionally saw David pass through the Kubler-Ross stages of grief. He returned to periods of quiet and solitude in his room. As he began to confide in us, I was stunned that his concerns were not only about what was aborted but also for what he anticipated. Would he remember how to socialize when it was time? Would he lose some of the headway he had made professionally? David spoke of his fears for reentry long before it became a topic in the media, and it was only months later that I realized he was not alone with these internal struggles. Despite all his progress and all that he had achieved, I feared his regression to darker times.

In contrast to the many young adults who came back to the nest during this crisis, we jointly decided that David would move out into

his own apartment mid-pandemic. This exciting milestone was to have already occurred following months of preparation, but it was then postponed due to lockdown. We initially did not want him alone and further isolated as the pandemic took hold. But as David settled into the new norm and practiced safety measures to the letter, he demonstrated renewed readiness. With more free time born from the cancellation of social activities, we speculated that adding domestic responsibilities to work obligations would not overwhelm David. Rather, we hoped the long-sought independence would add to his confidence, self-esteem, and optimism, thereby using this turbulent time to his advantage. We also hoped it would give him something new and exciting to focus on and help distract him from despondency. Frequent communications to guide unknowns and provide support completed our transitioning efforts. David will later address the questionable wisdom of this decision and how lockdown impacted the outcome.

In a new twist, this milestone venture was a tradeoff for meeting other needs we were always central in providing. Once he moved out, David was no longer in our inner circle. When visiting, we now needed to socially distance and wear masks, limiting exposure to each other. Physical contact was no longer safe, further decreasing David's needed sensory input and human connection. Though not equivalent or optimal, occasional use of a weighted vest helped replace firm pressure for loving hugs, and squeeze balls or exercise helped alleviate David's stress. But the best intervention for resumption of touch and peace of mind was vaccination for each of us.

COVID-19 has been beneficial in prompting self-evaluation of personal sanitation practices and displays of affection. I have always been a hugger, but I doubt that I will ever be so free with casual greeting hugs again. I may even place them in the invasive category in some situations, and I have renewed respect for others' "personal space." Smiles and warm words can go a long way in communicating affection, for even if coronavirus becomes controlled, there will always be pathogens that cause illness. Frequent hand cleansing, staying home when sick, and sanitizing phones, keyboards, and shared surfaces or equipment are all smart practices that we should continue moving forward. The emerging philosophy that people bear social responsibility to protect others, as well as themselves, will always be relevant. Masking may be individually desired for particular situations even after mandates are lifted—and chosen for assorted reasons besides not being vaccinated—so assumptions should not be made about that masked person. The above practices may also help to reduce anxiety as we learn to gather in groups once more.

As we resume work and school on official grounds, it may be comforting to realize that anxieties and concerns are shared by most *everyone*, including our

> **"** As we resume work and school on official grounds, it may be comforting to realize that anxieties and concerns are shared by most everyone . . . . **"**

teachers, professors, colleagues, and management. We are *still* all in this together. And we will learn helpful strategies as we go, just like we did on our journey through the pandemic. Remember that you acclimated back in the past after every summer off or each extended leave of absence. If this takes a little longer because of these unique circumstances, then it takes longer, and it may need some tweaks. There is no posted expiration or due date. And you do not need to go it alone.

Back to Campus

I work at the Thrive Learning Center at Notre Dame College which serves students with diverse special needs, including individuals with autism. Shifting to a virtual learning platform in 2020, we later expanded to a hybrid model of mixed in-person and remote learning. New methods of teaching, learning, tutoring, and testing were immediately instituted, along with the bumps and bruises that accompany large-scale training and learning curves for all parties involved. It was a stressful and herculean undertaking. While not ideal, goals were met, and learning was achieved. People are incredibly adaptable and resourceful, but we are now asking our student body and personnel to adjust once again.

This fall, we plan a complete return to campus with all associated activities. Within our department, preparations are underway to transition students back to classroom learning and college experiences. Representatives from the college counseling office have on-site presence in our center via a private satellite office. Collaboration with mental health professionals is wonderful to help meet the holistic needs of our students. Throughout the pandemic, these professionals counseled students who sought their services, and they will continue this individualized effort to ease stress and anxiety as pupils return to campus. Workshops and a video presentation are also planned additions to increase general student access and address common issues.

A newly-built sensory room has been constructed within the Thrive center for its members' exclusive use. Complete with a massage chair, soothing music, soft lighting, and aromatherapy, it is a convenient retreat from the stress of daily life. An innovative option to allay anxiety, we welcome its introduction during campus reintegration.

Thrive's Freshman Seminar Class aims to assist with college integration even in "normal" times. The instructor has extensive experience serving students with learning disabilities, and she will be joined this fall by a licensed clinical counselor. Together they will address the added challenges of adjustment to college life following the uncertainties of an unusual high school senior year.

Additionally, first-year and transfer students enrolled in our learning center attend *our* specialized orientation program in addition to that required by the college proper. Questions and concerns can thus be addressed early for students and their accompanying parents, and communication will continue thereafter. Besides on-site tutoring, Thrive students attend weekly progress meetings with our instructional advisors to keep academic priorities and coursework on track. These meetings will give extra opportunities to assist students' executive functioning and assess for stress and needed assistance.

Intentional social events, especially at the onset of the semester, will ease the students back into group interactions and allow for practice of appropriate social skills. The goals are improved acclimation, increased camaraderie with peers, and feelings of safety and belonging.

According to Mary Jo Levand, Director of the Thrive Learning Center, students may also need to acclimate to rigorous course loads if volumes and expectations exceed that which they experienced with remote learning. She further suggests that despite the excitement associated with being back on campus, anxiety may still exist regarding safety from contracting COVID-19 despite vaccinations. She suggests a "no judgement" campaign to increase the comfort of students and personnel who opt to wear masks. Perhaps parents and educators can adapt some of the above ideas for use in their schools or programs.

Jumpstarting Reintegration

Proactive preparation is better than passive worry, so I suggest informal home activities (*see below*) that can jumpstart reintegration for students. Some may also be applicable and helpful for returning to work settings. I utilized most of these with David throughout his summer recesses regardless of grade level, and they served him well to keep him intellectually sharp, ready to learn, and confident in his abilities:

Home Activities

- Read for an hour a day and practice relevant math calculations.
  - Consider critical thinking or comprehension drills.
- Review study skills or take a course on this topic.
  - Focus on study techniques, test-taking strategies, and paper writing.
- Take advantage of offered open houses and orientations.
- Begin waking earlier two weeks prior to the start of the school year to reset your inner clock and gradually increase productivity in preparation for increased demands.
- Wake earlier on school days than remote learning required—extra time for personal grooming, attention to appearance, and commuting is once again necessary.
- Utilize all the help and programs offered to assist with reacclimating.
  - Do not let pride or self-consciousness make the transition more difficult than necessary.
- Verbalize your needs to those who can help address them; share your feelings and concerns.

Finding the Balance

Reentry will be challenging for *everyone*. Faculty will need to revamp coursework. Office personnel and those who share common work areas will need to reestablish personal workspaces and boundaries. This includes readjusting to the noise and the distractions of adjacent colleagues. Likewise, students will again need to think, learn, and study in group settings. Though remote school and work formats forced isolation and limited interactions, there were some advantages besides access. Productivity may have increased for activities requiring concentration and freedom from interruptions.

Despite the value of peer comradery for team building, working relationships, and social satisfaction, it would be interesting to note how many hours of one's workday are spent in activities that are unrelated to the job agenda. Readjusting to sensory bombardment and developing the self-discipline necessary to work efficiently will be difficult. The use of earplugs or headphones can help tune out undesired stimuli and send others outward signals that you are engaged in cognitive activities. It is important not to interrupt persons with closed doors and other signs that they are not free to talk. These signs may include their active engagement on computers or screen devices, speaking on phones, reading or writing, using tools to tune out others (headphones/earplugs), or nonverbal signals. Examples of behaviors that discourage interruption can be obvious, such as the person holding up their hand or index finger, or may be more subtle, such as the person avoiding eye contact or not turning away from the task to face you. It may be worthwhile to display comical signs or develop other creative symbols to indicate periods of unavailability. This could prevent frustration and achieve the necessary balance between productivity and socialization.

David's Story

It has been a very long fifteen months, but I am feeling much more hopeful since I became fully vaccinated. COVID-19 magnified many long-standing challenges caused by my autism, and it presented some new ones, as well. But I am emerging stronger from what I experienced and learned.

Changes and Challenges

The move to my own apartment had plusses and minuses, and I do not regret my decision to take that leap during the pandemic. It felt good that I was living on my own and no longer needed to communicate or coordinate daily activities with my parents. I was not nervous about the financial or domestic needs, and I was initially able to keep up with the cleaning, grocery shopping, and other new demands while staying on top of things at work. Using the CDC's recommendations, I was not nervous about going on errands.

However, with everything shut down, it soon became all work and no play. Even for the months when we were still on school grounds, I felt  like I was in survival mode and unable to do my job justice with all our imposed limitations. I could not be the teacher I wanted to be. That wore me down. In addition, it was winter, and the shorter days and long periods indoors further isolated me. I was deprived of all theatre involvement, which is my passion and balancer. Life had lost its excitement. Frequent communications and weekly visits with my parents helped clear up some of my mental fog, but I found myself getting into bad habits and I lost interest in things that used to bring me joy. I spent a third of my life in various therapies learning how to be social, get off screens, and leave my room, and I was suddenly thrown back into that existence. All the things I fought so hard to achieve were being stripped away.

Beyond LIKING my hard-won social life, I NEEDED to engage in relationships and theatre to ground me and give me balance. Without them, I succumbed to laziness; everything shut down and there was nothing I valued to do. Giving in to the pessimism, there were days that I would binge on food, social media, or sleep. Or on the other extreme, sometimes I did not eat. I feared that I might develop an eating disorder if I didn't break toxic habits. I was meeting my responsibilities, but just barely so. And I still have lingering negative thoughts about selfish or prideful people ruining it for everyone else due to not complying with health mandates.

Bouncing Back

When vaccines were finally being offered and I could see light at the end of the tunnel, it just hit me that I needed to stop using COVID-19 as an excuse for being lazy. As things started opening up and I got vaccinated, I realized that my current choices were no longer acceptable. I realized I had no one to rely on besides myself. If I wanted to live on my own and be an adult, I needed to stop making excuses. If I slept in, I inevitably wasted the day. It's all about putting in the effort. I began to regain the drive to have a well-kept, highly ordered way of life. To balance me out, I was finally cast in an outdoor socially distanced live theatre production. The camaraderie of the cast reignited my aspirations to do well in all aspects of my life, rather than to just passively survive.

My work week was dedicated to teaching and rehearsals. I then used my weekends to the max as I intended to do when I first moved out. I now had the drive. I began setting my alarm on days off to get myself in the right frame of mind. I used Saturdays for errands, shopping, and cleaning or decluttering. Sundays were dedicated to church, laundry, seeing my family, and planning

> 66 I started to feel that I had a role in society coming back, and I was once again optimistic 99

for the work week ahead. Putting forth the effort to set up and execute a tight schedule gave me satisfaction and validated that I DID have it within me to be independent. I started to feel that I had a role in society coming back, and I was once again optimistic in my personal and professional lives.

I'm glad I moved out when I did, difficult though the isolation was. I feel as if otherwise, I would never have had this realization and turning point. At home, I may have easily been "cared for." But on my own, if I didn't do it, it wouldn't get done. I was at a stage where my parents should be helpers, not doers, for situations and things that I could do on my own. Life isn't about excuses. I figured out the strategies necessary to live a fulfilled life, and I now acknowledge that I can keep things going even in the most difficult of circumstances. I learned from what I did and did not do. I learned how to take care of myself.

Sensory Challenges

Sensory issues highly impact my life, and they affected my COVID-19 experiences as well. I hugely missed the friendly sentiment behind hugs when contact was restricted. But with my autism, I also desperately craved the associated physical compression that alleviated tension from my anxiety. I mentally and physically NEED hugs! A firm embrace provides me with therapeutic relief. Besides the reopening of all social opportunities, my greatest excitement in being fully vaccinated now lies in being able to hug my equally vaccinated family members and friends.

From the start of this COVID-19 challenge, my biggest fear was potentially regressing in my sensory tolerance. I was accustomed to my get-up-and-go lifestyle that I had worked so hard to achieve. It took me years of therapy to get comfortable in social situations. To have it snatched away from me for more than a year left me with lingering doubts as to how I would react when everything started up again simultaneously.

That fear became a reality when I found myself going through a panic attack in my apartment after a socially hectic day of a socially hectic week (meaning social interactions, not recreational activities). I HAD regressed in my sensory tolerance. Before COVID-19, I had learned, with great effort, to embrace and thrive in highly stimulating environments. I now had to start over. Truthfully, I also think my reaction resulted from the build-up of everything the year 2020 threw at me which I had never allowed myself to emotionally let out. Getting through that week allowed for a clean slate and it was all uphill from there. But could my extreme reactions have been prevented?

Learn from my mistakes: Implement your sensory accommodations EVEN IF YOU DON'T THINK YOU NEED THEM. If I could do it over, I would not have assumed that I still "had it." From the start, I would have utilized my prior strategies to build up tolerance (earplugs, weighted vest, squeeze balls . . .) BEFORE experiencing distress. I would have more gradually increased my activities. Going from a nonexistent social life to full throttle activities without a bridge caused me panic attacks and angst.

Social Consciousness

Although it was difficult to teach or easily breathe while wearing a mask, I grew accustomed to it and gladly accepted it for the greater good. While others are up in arms to relinquish masks because of the suffocation they may feel physically, mentally, or emotionally, I myself have gained a liberation. It is much more beneficial to me to embrace my mask and be able to hug loved ones and move on with life rather than to keep my face bare.

I have a fear that shutdown will happen again, whether from a coronavirus variant or from reckless or inconsiderate people who are not following recommendations. All of this is out of my control, except for what I choose to do personally. I am choosing to continue wearing a mask in close contact situations (such as air travel) for my own peace of mind and to feel that I am contributing to the prevention of another shutdown. And if we *did* backslide as a country, then I at least have the assurance that I was not a part of that. You cannot control other people, but you can control what you do. My advice? Do whatever is comfortable for you in compliance with mandates. Always take steps to make sure that you have a healthy body, mind, and spirit so that those around you can also have a healthy body, mind, and spirit.

> ❝ You cannot control other people, but you can control what you do. ❞

Strategies for School and Work Reacclimation

Shifting to my COVID-19 work life, regardless of onsite or online, I could not be the teacher that I knew I was. I could not create a dynamic work environment with the social distancing, masking, or remote means required. I had limitations on my creativity. All the additives that make school fun were also taken away, such as field trips, parties, or assemblies. So even when our school resumed complete in-person learning in January, it still was not the ideal learning environment, which was frustrating for everyone.

Restrictions will be largely lifted at school this upcoming fall. However, returning to pre-COVID ways will be gradual, pending the development of safety strategies. There will likely be stress and barriers during this time of transition. I plan to keep lines of communication open with my students to help them reintegrate. I want them to feel supported and comfortable in expressing their concerns. Alleviating angst can hopefully free up their minds to learn. No longer held back by CDC restrictions, I look forward to once again implementing diverse forms of teaching that bring fun back into learning. I hope enjoyment can squelch students' unease. I will keep my expectations and standards high but will initially be more flexible as they acclimate. The year will be a testament that in times of adversity, they can find ways around obstacles and come out stronger.

In the workplace, employers should provide a haven to help employees thrive. Keeping lines of communication open can make all the difference, as it has for me at my job. Encouraging comments and concerns, made anonymously if desired, can clarify issues that need to be addressed. It helps employees feel seen and heard. Collaboration and engagement can help morale and cohesiveness. It also highlights key issues and concerns.

Employees need the proper tools to help them achieve their maximum potentials, which would have mutual benefits. Accommodations when returning to work might be needed for many individuals, but I will focus on people with autism. I have already addressed sensory concerns and strategies that can assist. For me, pacing not only helps with my thought processes, but it keeps my mind organized and enables me to handle input from stimuli. Allow opportunities for employees (or students) to move around in socially acceptable ways, especially during socially escalated situations. For example, permit employees to take walking breaks or to work while standing. Take stairs instead of using elevators to work off tension.

To prevent being overwhelmed by tasks, list everything that needs to be accomplished. Determine the varying degrees of importance that each task holds and then make a schedule. Seeing it in writing alleviates the stress of forgetting and frees up your mind. It seems less daunting when you realize that you do have the time to get the jobs done. If you have questions or concerns, seek out clarifications immediately. Do not let uncertainty fester. If there are changes in the new work routine, enact strategies to help remember them, such as leaving yourself phone reminders, sticky notes, or posting schedules or lists of changes in your workspace.

> " To prevent being overwhelmed by tasks, list everything that needs to be accomplished. "

When you get home from work, allow yourself downtime to rejuvenate and regain your sensory composure. For me, that may even involve a power nap on an overstimulating day. Later that evening, I find it helpful to map out what I need to attend to the following day. That next day seems to go smoother if I prepare ahead of time. The weekend should be a balance of work and play to restore vitality and get in the right frame of mind for the upcoming work week.

If you have unfortunately lost a job due to COVID-19 circumstances, give yourself time to grieve and then start taking steps to find a new job. Even if the job is not ideal, remind yourself that it doesn't need to be permanent. Reach out to connections and research job postings. Use this time to improve yourself and maximize your potential to be hired. This may include taking an online course or watching videos on interview strategies and/or building your resume.

Final Thoughts

Through my COVID experiences, I learned that I must put forth an effort to uphold my quality of life. I learned that relaxation needs to be of positive quality. I needed to break bad habits and not give in to laziness, which is different from relaxing in a healthy way. For me, waking early on days off increased my productivity and gave me extra time in my day once life reopened.

Don't allow yourself to become stuck, settled, or even sloth. If you stay on top of even the most minute tasks, that is transferrable to the bigger tasks. When everything was stripped away, it was more important than ever to put one foot in front of the other. If we lose our drive, then we lose our sense of self, and that could affect cleanliness and health. Staying on top of basic human needs makes difficult circumstances bearable enough to maintain our dignity while going through them. If people around us see that we are still holding up our personal standards, it might rub off on them too. The takeaway: It's important to put wellness above everything else. Material and societal things can be stripped away, and all we have left is our wellness.

As a social studies teacher, let me remind you that there have been major calamitous hardships in every decade of our history: influenza, world wars, the great depression, polio, the AIDS epidemic, 9/11, terrorism, and so on. There were many apocalyptic notions that each would be "the end." But with every problem, a solution was found or the issue receded. We *will* have more crises, so extract and build upon what we learned through COVID-19 to make future hardships more bearable. Don't dwell on what was lost. Purpose can come from what we went through to find solutions for future hardships. As the saying goes, those who don't learn from history are doomed to repeat it. It is important to educate autistic people and family members to develop strategies to use in trying situations.

It might give them peace of mind that they are taking steps to be proactive and endure. This past year has changed me, and for the first time, I'm starting to see how it changed me for the better.

More about Sandy . . .

🏠 As we enter life after lockdown, I am most concerned about . . .
people relinquishing caution and consideration of others.

🌐 As we enter life after lockdown, I am most excited about . . .
embracing my grandchildren, as well as how creative and resourceful our world has become.

Sandy Petrovic, RN, BSN, is an instructional advisor and tutor in a college support center for students with learning differences at Notre Dame College, Thrive Learning Center. She is also the mother of an autistic young adult, David, with whom she co-authored *Expect a Miracle: Understanding and Living with Autism* (www.aspergermiracles.com).

More about David . . .

🏠 As we enter life after lockdown, I am most concerned about . . .
going into another lockdown.

🔗 As we enter life after lockdown, I am most excited about . . .
hugging my family, friends, and loved ones again.

David Petrovic, BA, MAT, is a master's-prepared middle school/junior high teacher, a national speaker (including a TEDx presentation), and a man who embraces his autism. He is the co-author of *Expect a Miracle: Understanding and Living with Autism*, as well as many magazine articles and blog posts (www.aspergermiracles.com).

Website and Blog

https://aspergermiracles.com/

OUR FAMILY WAS MADE FOR QUARANTINE

LESLEY CLARK

People often ask us, "How was quarantine with Jalon?" We always answer that we have been quarantining long before the pandemic. Our family often turned down invites, we don't go on vacation, and we never do anything on a whim. Everything in our lives revolves around keeping peace, harmony, and sanity while trying to raise two young men; one of whom has autism and Fragile X syndrome.

Jalon is a nonverbal, very strong, routine-based, warm, loving, and kind man. Jalon has always been kind to others, but when younger he was not so kind to himself. When frustrated as a young boy, he would become self-injurious. He would scratch himself to the point of drawing blood and bite his hand. That was the first thought I had when I found out the schools were closing. *God, please don't let him be self-injurious again.*

I have anxiety and every time a long break comes up, I break down. Jason (my husband, our rock, and dad to the boys) always talks me through it. He will take a few days off work to help me care for Jalon. Just imagine the heartache and confusion we experienced when thinking how we were going to explain quarantine to Jalon, and that his whole routine was about to change.

I had just lost my mother in December of 2019. In February, we started hearing about this deadly virus. In March, we were locked down and schools were closed. My husband, God bless him, was already working from home most of December as we were all grieving. Now he had to help me cope with Jalon being home for an undisclosed amount of time. We had no idea how we would get him to wear a mask. Jalon has sensory issues and does not even wear a regular t-shirt. We

Jalon–looking so grown up

thought, he can't get COVID—he's nonverbal and he wouldn't even be able to tell us he needs help.

Lucky for us, receptive language is a strong ability of Jalon's. We would explain to him that there's no school for the first two weeks. Then we started a new routine. We would think of ways to keep him busy without letting him get bored. We would take car rides, go for walks, go in the yard and garden. Then after the summer of 2020, the school year started. Virtual school was an absolute nightmare. Jalon has a basic understanding of his routine concepts such as school, eating, riding the bus,

Clark Family–Branden, Lesley, Jalon, Jason (L–R)

and routine tasks around the home. What he doesn't understand are things like social distancing, time, illness, and critical thinking situations. He didn't understand why we had to do school on a computer.

He absolutely hated it. I would not force him to get on because life was hard enough. Since he doesn't have a voice, we are his voice. If we see he's struggling with something, we don't force it. That's what parents with typical children sometimes overlook.

We just want both of our boys to be happy and live life to the best of their ability without us forcing our ideals on them, what we think they should be, and what they should be doing in life. Now comes the hard part, getting back to "normal." We don't know what that will look like with Jalon. He doesn't social distance, he doesn't wash his hands without help, he puts things in his mouth, and he can't wear a mask. We were very, very terrified but also extremely excited that they closed schools. We still feel school is not a safe place for

Jason–proud of the shirt I made for him

Jalon. We will have to wait and see what the schools have in place for the fall, but we have a feeling that nothing will be good enough and Jalon will be safer with us. He is already almost aged out of school. He is now 20 years old and has gotten about all he can get from school.

My life as a mother and wife hasn't changed much since COVID. I have been very grateful and thankful that we have done pretty well. We have all been home since March of 2020. We have been here to help each other. I understand that some kids need to get back to the classroom and that some parents work out of the home. Luckily, Jason and I were unknowingly preparing for this our entire adult lives.

In closing, I would like to say, we as parents, guardians, and care-givers always make sure our loved ones' needs are met. In the process, we often neglect our own needs. I take time before I get up with Jalon to do yoga five days a week. I also take 15 minutes to meditate a few times a week in the evening. You must take care of your mental and physical state to be able to give the care your loved one deserves. May everyone stay safe!

More about Lesley . . .

As we enter life after lockdown, I am most concerned about . . .
life not ever being or feeling "normal." I know that Jalon's life will not even come close to resembling what it was pre-pandemic. That gives me a lot of worry and uncertainty about his near future.

As we enter life after lockdown, I am most excited about . . .
Branden being able to go back to school. He was half way through his freshman year of high school when lockdown started. He has spent his entire 10th grade year distance learning. I want him to experience high school like his dad and I did with school dances, football games, group activities, etc.

I am a 42-year-old, stay-at-home mother of two amazing boys ages 20 and 16. I have been married to Jason, an amazing man, father, and role model to our boys for 20 years.

OLDER AUTISTIC ADULTS EMERGING FROM QUARANTINE

WILMA WAKE

My hands shook as I started the ignition in my car. This was it. The end of my isolation.

For over a year I had avoided being in the company of others. I was strict in my quarantine, as I'm 74 with some health susceptibilities. I had cut off all in-person contact. My social work practice was now through Zoom, Doxy.me, or telephone. For groceries, I shopped online at Walmart or New Morning, our local health food store. I ordered online, paid with a credit card, and then drove to the store where groceries were put in my trunk.

I've maintained contact with my autistic adult support group on Zoom. We've been meeting twice a month online and still have not met again in person in more than a year. We used to have monthly outings, but none of those happened during lockdown. Today is our first. Our groups' first post-pandemic outing. It was also my first personal outing.

I started the car with shaky hands.

Was I ready? Not at all. Not even close. I'm an older autistic woman. Eight years ago, my autism diagnosis turned my world—my entire life—upside down.

The diagnosis helped me realize how unsafe I've always felt in a world I don't understand. The pandemic lockdown was the first time I had been able to live a life that felt safe—living alone without personal human contact.

I didn't have to coax my aging brain to remember directions to an unfamiliar place. I didn't worry about where I had left my cell phone or my coat or my purse.

I harbored a deep, shameful secret. I loved the lockdown. Never had I felt so certain of my environment or so safe in it. No more getting lost trying to find a new location for a meeting. No more racing out of my house late, again, for a meeting that I still had to drive to.

But this day would break that habit. I would meet other autistic friends for a walk and lunch out.

As I drove there, I kept wondering if I was making the right decision to attend and if our autism group was making the right decision to hold an in-person activity. I reviewed the safety measures. We decided that anyone attending would have to be fully vaccinated.

> 66 I took a deep breath and started my engine. It was time. 99

We would be outdoors in a large, open area. That did feel reassuring. I wasn't sure about lunch. I'd wait to see how I felt later.

I took a deep breath and started my engine. It was time.

I love the drive along coastal Maine to the Rachel Carson Nature Preserve. It is a natural treasure and always a thrill to visit. Yet I hadn't been here since before the pandemic—too nervous about running into other people.

It was refreshing and breathtaking to again drive along coastal Maine. My eyes and heart took in the beauty as I drove.

It lifted my spirits to be back on the road again. It was great to arrive at the preserve and see my autistic friends waiting there. I had a frustrating job trying to find a parking spot—the post-pandemic crowd was there!

The walk was breathtaking, as usual.

It was good to be walking with three autistic friends in the woods, chatting about the things in our lives that only other autistics understand. It had been so long since we had seen each other in person. The beauty of the scenery helped to heal my qualms. It was good to be with autistic friends again.

Afterward, Rob, Nate, and I decided to go out to eat. For each of us, it was the first time since the pandemic that we had been to a restaurant. We chose the Maine Diner in Wells, as it had a large tent outside with tables. They did have picnic tables where we could eat take-out. But the tables in the tent had table service. After over a year of no restaurants, we wanted to be served at the table.

As we ate, we talked. Rob is also an older autistic adult. We discussed our difficulty getting out after the pandemic. Rob had occasionally been to a café or picked up carry-out.

Rob expressed some of what I was also feeling. He said, "It does feel strange to be with people again. There was so much about the pandemic that was comfortable—knowing I didn't I have to go to social events or talk in person with people."

As I drove back home that afternoon, I realized that I had taken a major step. I had seen friends in person and had dined with them. I breathed a sigh of relief. That had been the hardest step—just to begin.

> 66 That had been the hardest step—just to begin. 99

When I got home, I noticed the clutter in my house and decided I wanted to start spring cleaning. It was time to open my home and my life to other human life again. I started to cry when I realized it was over. The total isolation was over. As much as it had felt safe, it had also felt lonely. I had isolated not just from people, but from many of the outdoor adventures that I usually did with other people. It was now time for life to begin again. I dug into spring cleaning with new hope in my heart.

The following weekend, our Zoom support group for autistic adults met and we discussed the end of the pandemic. A number of folks—especially the older ones—noted that they had found the pandemic relieving and comfortable. Social events were canceled and many events were online. Most of us had found relief from our unrelenting social pressures.

I acknowledged my guilt that there was much I liked about the social isolation of the pandemic. Our older autistic adults also acknowledged that change was hard. First, we had adapted to being at home; something that was easy and natural. Now we had to get used to being in the world again with our autistic anxieties.

As we talked, it became clear that our support of each other was an important element in making that change to go back into the world. Social interactions are hard for all of us, and we've had a year of minimal interactions. We tend to feel uncomfortable in the company of others, and it's hard to keep up with all the neurotypical conversations taking place around us. Being in our own support groups—where it's the norm for attention to wander and to need information often repeated and explained—is a safe haven. As we move back into the world, we take our safe harbor of other autistics with us.

> **66** My most important resource during the pandemic . . . is other older autistic adults in my life. **99**

I was diagnosed eight years ago and my most significant healing has come from autistic adult support groups. My most important resource during the pandemic, and its ending, is other older autistic adults in my life.

From my own experiences and talking with older adults in my autistic support community, I have some suggestions for other older autistic adults emerging from lockdown.

Be gentle with yourself, and take the time you need to re-emerge. This is especially true if you are looking to return to the job market.

Older autistic adults have a much harder time in the world than older neurotypical adults

I worked with two other autistics to survey older autistic adults around the world. One survey question was: "Do you believe you have been discriminated against due to being on the spectrum?" The result? "Nearly two-thirds of the respondents indicated they have been discriminated against in some way. For those who answered 'yes' to this question, the next question was 'How have you been discriminated against?' 83% said they had found discrimination in jobs" (Wake, Endlich, and Lagos 2021, 92-93).

If you are getting back to work, keep in mind that a lot of people are returning to the job market, and younger people (including younger autistics) have an advantage over older autistics. A number of the survey respondents said that they had a hard time finding employment, and were often turned down for jobs they were qualified for.

The reality is that younger, neurotypical people do significantly better in the job market than older, autistic adults. This is not your fault; you are going into a job market where, due to your autism and your age, you are at a disadvantage. Don't blame yourself for that.

Acknowledge any depression and low self-esteem.

In our survey, 58% of the older autistics said they were feeling depressed and 52% had low self-esteem (Wake, Endlich, and Lagos 2021, 112). Forty-four percent had tried therapy, but there were numerous comments on how ineffective the therapy was. Most said their therapist knew nothing about autistic adults and was not helpful.

Most of us have or have had problems with low self-esteem. Almost all of us older autistics grew up without a diagnosis. (A rare exception is Temple Grandin.) We grew up thinking there was something wrong with us, and that we had to hide it (many of us call it "masking").

If these things are true for you, then you will probably need more time to find a job or resources, and you may get depressed and conclude it is your fault.

Recognize the social factors that make it hard for you to function as easily as most neurotypicals. Don't blame yourself.

So, we older autistic adults need to recognize our age AND our autism. We need to be gentle with ourselves, especially with a major undertaking like re-emerging after a pandemic.

Find support for yourself.

One of the hardest aspects of being an older autistic adult is that we have so few support resources. Here are a few to consider:

1. AANE: Asperger/Autism Network (https://www.aane.org/). They offer tremendous resources for autistics, their family members, and professionals. Their website contains a huge array of resources including books, groups, and professionals. They offer a significant number of support groups online—including for older autistic adults. Their groups are either free or low-cost. They may also be able to refer you to supports in your own community.

2. There are several Facebook Community Groups, such as Autistic Older Adults (https://www.facebook.com/groups/oldsteraspieshfas/about). This group is designed to bring older adults on the spectrum together to discuss common interests or share ideas.

3. Another resource is Autistic Self Advocacy Network (https://autisticadvocacy.org/). ASAC not only provides information about disability rights, they also develop autistic cultural activities and leadership trainings.

4. Research possible resources for older autistic adults in your area. There are more groups, more trained therapists, and more older adults getting diagnosed. If you can't find one, consider starting an informal peer support group.

Be kind to yourself and find support—especially from other older autistic adults. It will help you let go of guilt and blame for things that aren't your fault. As you re-emerge into the world, you can reassess which aspects of your life you valued and want to reconnect with. You can also think about changes you want to make now—in a job, in support resources, in your self-esteem.

See the opportunities for growth and change that await us as we re-emerge from lockdown!

More about Wilma . . .

 As we enter life after lockdown, I am most concerned about . . .
remembering how to interact with people in person.

 As we enter life after lockdown, I am most excited about . . .
being able to walk around anywhere and celebrate our beautiful world.

I am an autistic adult in my 70s. I am a social worker and love working with other autistic people. I am assisted in my work by therapy dog Coco-Puff. Because of a weak leg she can't walk much, so during the pandemic I spent hours pushing her around the neighborhood in her car.

Books

o   *Older Autistic Adults in Their Own Words: The Lost Generation,* with co-authors Eric Endlich and Rob Lagos
o   *Crystals, Crosses, and Chakras: A Woman's Mystical Emergence*
o   *Wings and Roots: the New Age and Emanuel Swedenborg in Dialog*

Website

Awakeningswithwake.com

Reference

Wake, Wilma, Eric Endlich, and Robert Lagos. 2021. *Older Autistic Adults in Their Own Words: The Lost Generation.* Shawnee, KS: AAPC.

SECTION 4
INTO THE COMMUNITY

The community has long been a challenging environment for many individuals on the spectrum, as it is full of unpredictable noises, sights, and physical contact. It is also a source of confusing but necessary social interactions with unfamiliar people. However, as the chapters reveal, people on the spectrum often revel in the opportunities the community offers. From food to the arts to travel, the community offers a smorgasbord of activities that are not only necessary—like doctor appointments or stores—but fun and exciting.

Sydney Edmond, Larry Bissonnette, and the Dalusong family share insights on how the community provides depth to their lives, while Jill Hudson, Sheri Wilkins, René DeLoss, and Jek Barrozo offer suggestions for how to mitigate the unpredictability, the social challenges, and the sensory overload. While returning to the community provides unique health and safety challenges, it also provides a new appreciation for the fact that all individuals deserve access to the joys of community life, as well as the accommodations necessary to feel successful and confident. We all can provide the support and advocacy needed to ensure that such access is achieved.

What are you most looking forward to as we start going back out into the world?

> 66 Now that I don't have to stay home anymore, I want to help take care of the animals so they can help other people. 99

Bret Gaon, age 24

> 66 People are better. Go to Santa Cruz. 99

Josh Pope, age 27

> 66 Now that I don't have to stay home anymore, I want to go to the Orange Empire Railway Museum. 99

Kravin K, age 12

> 66 I want to go to Disneyland. 99

Ryan D, age 18

> 66 I want to go on a trip to New York after COVID. 99

Kaitlyn Revell, age 24

ARTS AND AUDIENCES AND AUTISM, OH MY!

SYDNEY EDMOND

I was particularly anxious when COVID struck. The news reports were frightening. I was paralyzed with fear and wanted to stay indoors and away from all people. I was even scared to be around family and I insisted that they all wear masks around me. It was horrifying. Like a scary book or movie. I held myself back from all exercise other than the treadmill and a bit of ballet practice because I was too frightened to go outdoors. I think that because my disability sprung from out of nowhere, I knew deep inside that one little virus can destroy your life. It can cripple you with symptoms you have no control over. And in this case, it could kill you or someone you love or someone you depend on for support. It was frightening. Well, being a painter, I was fortunate to have my art; it was terrifically therapeutic for me to lose myself in my work. And I worked a lot. I completed some of my best paintings during the quarantine.

I want to begin by saying that reintegrating will require that I tackle my fears of becoming infected with a virus that may harm me. This

will be an overriding source of anxiety all the time. I will wear a mask in crowds for a long time to address this. I will also stand away from people whenever I can and instruct my support person to honor my worries. Wellness is a precious thing and I long to keep possession of it.

I will find many things challenging as I reintegrate back into normal society. As an artist, I am called upon to present and discuss my work with customers. This was difficult for me initially because I type to

Self Portrait
March 29, 2020

communicate and require a calmness in order to collect my thoughts and then gather enough control over my body to type. It took quite a while and loads of practice to finally accomplish this skill. I was a regular at our local monthly *Art Off the Walls* exhibit that our city freely holds for artists in this area.

Attending so often allowed me to practice almost every month. But this treasured opportunity was canceled during the pandemic. Also, other special events where I was to present my paintings were canceled. And so, my skills have also been canceled and I will have to develop those abilities all over again.

The environmental sensory overload at these and other events will also be a high hurdle to challenge me. I have an

Maiko's First Dance
July 19, 2020

intolerance of the sound of people yacking on and on, and it's way worse when there is a whole room full of them. I become all prickly and agitated and begin screaming. This is not particularly pleasing to people nearby. I eagerly try to stop but I cannot. Once begun, my scream takes over and I often will collapse in agony over the horror of my actions. Actions that have reduced my reputation severely in the eyes of everyone present. I wonder if you realize how difficult it is to live under the control of such a wayward body? It weighs heavily on me every moment. However, I did find ways to keep it at bay and was able to blend in with my fellow artists. Now I must face the challenge anew and pray that I put all of the difficulties behind me again.

One With the Music
May 23, 2020

I am certain that I will need many practices to be able to tolerate art exhibits now that reintegration has begun. I will need to practice my calming techniques in order to handle being in such an overwhelming situation after having spent a year quietly at home. I will probably need to wear headphones and listen to music in the beginning. I prefer not to depend on my music to stay calm because it interferes with my ability to interact with customers and other artists. I will need to wean myself off of the headphones gradually. I also think that I will need to interact and type with my support person or text with family members when I begin exhibiting again to warm up my ability to communicate with my customers. This will also distract me from my anxieties because I must focus particularly intently when I type. I look forward to testing myself in this arena.

I am inspired to paint by beautiful things. I was first inspired by going to an art museum and surrounding myself with all the beautiful, thrilling, enchanting paintings of artists throughout history. I felt I must try it and began my career as a painter that day. I was particularly engaged by paintings of ballerinas. I love ballet for many reasons. The music, the graceful movements, the colorful stages, and the costumes of the dancers. I love it so much, particularly when I attend live performances. But I am sad to say that the thrill of it can overwhelm me and I make a spectacle of myself. My first experience attending a major ballet company's performance was cut short when I was asked to leave. So I began then working on controlling my excitement. After a great many practices, attending smaller local ballet performances and sitting in the back so I could make a quick escape when needed, I was successful in bringing myself up to form. It was a challenge. I had to leave early on my own accord sometimes. Well, it was just too good. Too exciting. Too wonderful to tolerate for long. But, after a few years of practice, I attended a major ballet company's performance again and was able, with a few minor outbursts, to stay for and enjoy the entire performance. I was so very happy! I began attending them regularly. Of course, when the pandemic came along all performances were canceled. Both professional and local performances were no longer an option. I will now need to walk that path of training myself to sit quietly in a theater to watch performances again.

Palomino
March 8, 2020

I have already begun preparing myself to attend ballets. I recently went to a local student performance in a small setting with a sparse audience. It was attended by people, some of whom wore masks and others who didn't. I am unable to control others, unfortunately, or they all would have been wearing masks and keeping distant from one another. I have to protect myself. So I sat in the very back away from others and wore my mask. I must be prepared during reintegration to do what is right when others fail to, in order to address my anxiety over possible infection. I did wrestle with my excitement over attending a live ballet however and did scream or squeal sometimes. I made it through the first half and partway into the second before I popped out for a break to calm myself. It felt too overwhelming to go back inside so I decided to leave. Next time

I will bravely go back in and test myself a little longer. I may tuck my music and headphones into my bag so that the excitement will become overruled by the peacefulness of the music. I will prevail!

Since I was a young girl of twelve, I have often had the great honor of being asked to speak in front of a live audience. Sometimes I speak alone and sometimes on a panel. It was terrifying as a young girl and only slightly less so as a woman. I would look around the sea of faces, the multitude of eyes, and worry about what they thought of me. I would sense their eager listening and hope that they heard the loud longing for acceptance and respect in my words. But it is strangely enough more difficult speaking on a panel. When I speak on a panel, I must take my turn and experience the anxiety that comes with waiting, over and over. In spite of my affection for my fellow panelists, in spite of my interest and respect for what they

Little Dancer
May 8, 2020

have to say, I become more and more anxious each time I must wait my turn. I wonder if they feel the same? If so, it doesn't show. I, however, used to get overwhelmed at times and scream. Or hit my support person. It took a while for me to learn that people were listening to me with interest and that I was also respected. I was pleased and calmed a bit knowing this. I love public speaking and educating people about what it is like to live in an uncooperative body, to not be able to speak as they do. It is my mission in life to encourage everyone to offer alternative communication methods like typing or using a letterboard to people who cannot speak. I hope to continue speaking out for all those who haven't a voice. However, apparently, I will have to once again develop the ability to lower my anxiety levels while in the process of doing my mission.

I have concerns about once again speaking in front of a live audience because I have been tucked away at home for so long. I have had the opportunity to speak on Zoom pleasingly about both my art and autism. It was a lovely opportunity to hone my writing and presentation skills. I was, even then, sitting at home in my art studio,

RBG
June, 2021

nervous knowing people were watching and listening to me. However, being at home, it was particularly pleasing to be able to pop into bed right afterward to calm myself with a blanket and soft music. But being on Zoom, as difficult as it was, didn't compare to speaking to a crowd of people seated before me. There is no way to practice this other than by doing it. At first, I think I might wear my headphones when it is not my turn to speak in order to keep calm. Once again, I must face my fears and be a lovely speaker.

In closing, I would like to speak about parents, support staff, and co-workers of people who are neurodiverse like me. Redeveloping our skills will be exhausting for those of us on the spectrum. I hope that parents, support staff, and co-workers will allow us to take as many breaks or naps as we require in order to build up our energy levels and sense of calm. People need to be prepared, to expect that we will become emotional or lose control now and then because

'Maiko and the Bluebird' and me, June 26, 2020

we are tired and out of practice. When this happens, parents, support staff, or co-workers need to remain calm and encouraging. They need to be understanding. To see the sorrow and frustration we are feeling behind our behaviors. Let us have some time alone to gain control over our impulsive body and allow us access to whatever calms us. For example, as you know by now, I listen to music as a lovely, relaxing way to calm myself. Some other people might play video games, do a puzzle, or go for a walk. Whatever it is, it is precious to us, and I hope we will all be able to have our calming influences handy when necessary during this challenging time of reintegration.

More about Sydney . . .

I am a 28-year-old woman with autism and apraxia. I have learned to type to communicate because apraxia makes it impossible to speak. I am a painter and a poet and a public speaker. As we enter life after lockdown, I am still most concerned about contracting the virus, but I am very excited about attending a ballet again.

Artwork

o   Facebook: www.facebook.com/SydneysArtWithAnAutisticTwist
o   Redbubble: https://www.redbubble.com/people/SydneyEdmond/explore

Book

o   *The Purple Tree and Other Poems*

ENCOURAGING POSITIVE BEHAVIOR OUTSIDE THE HOME

SHERI WILKINS

As communities begin to open, and there are more opportunities to venture out and about, parents will want to fine-tune their behavioral techniques to ensure that family outings are fun and not frenzied!

The first thing to remember is that venturing out and coming in contact with others in new situations is bound to be somewhat stress-inducing for everyone. For children who lack mental flexibility or who find sensory input challenging, the reality of engaging in novel activities in new and different places, and with new people, may result in undesirable behavior.

When planning for excursions outside the home, it can be helpful for parents to remember to BREATHE! Of course, you'll want to actually, physically breathe, but for our purposes, BREATHE stands for:

B: Begin by clarifying expectations.

R: Reinforce positive behavior.

E: Expect the best.

A: Anticipate challenges.

T: Take breaks, if needed.

H: Have a sense of humor.

E: Enact an escape plan.

Begin by Clarifying Expectations

Before venturing out and engaging in a new activity, clarify behavioral expectations in advance. If you've already identified a set of three to five behavioral expectations for activities at home – great job! You can simply spend some time discussing what those expectations look and sound like in the new environment.

If you have not yet identified a set of expectations to guide behavior across a variety of contexts, now is a great time to take that step. Many families find that three general expectations that work across situations and time are: Be safe, be responsible, be respectful. These expectations are general enough to be adaptable to any situation and they can be further defined to clarify behaviors appropriate to a specific environment or activity.

> 66 Be safe, be responsible, be respectful. 99

To clarify and further define these expectations, ask "What would it look like to be safe in this place or engaging in this activity?" Think about what safety would look like or sound like in the new context. Capture three to five ideas that provide clarity about the expectation in the context. For example, being safe at the dentist might be clarified as "Wear your mask while waiting in the dentist waiting room." Next, clarify the other expectations, again asking the questions and describing the behaviors you want to see. Make sure you are stating the behaviors positively! It's much more effective to let your child know exactly what *to do* in a specific situation, rather than identifying what not to do. This is a terrific activity to do with your child as you can discuss together what the expectations are, as well as what they look like in context.

Reinforce Positive Behavior

Before you engage in the new activity or go to a new environment, think through how you can reinforce your child's positive behavior. It is tempting at times to think that our children should engage in desired behaviors just because it is the right thing to do. However, we know from research (and from our own experiences) that providing reinforcement for doing the right thing increases the likelihood of the desired behavior occurring. For instance, how many of us would continue to go to work and work hard if we were told that we would no longer get paid for our efforts? It's likely that we would decide that we don't really need to do our best if we are not getting any reward at all for our efforts.

In thinking about providing reinforcement when away from home, think about ways to provide encouragement that are portable, can be used easily, and that your child finds fun. One idea that many parents and educators have found effective is to adapt the idea of a store customer reward punch card for use with a child. This method of reinforcement involves a small card, often the size of a business card, that has boxes that can be checked

PUNCH CARD

- ❑ Check-in 1
- ❑ Check-in 2
- ❑ Check-in 3
- ❑ Check-in 4
- ❑ Check-in 5
- ❑ **REWARD**

off, leading to a bigger reward. Discuss what reward your child would like to earn and how many intermediate positive check-ins they will need before earning that reward. When you go out, make sure that you have a card available, that the big reward is clearly defined, and that your child knows that they will be reinforced when they follow the expectations.

One thing to keep in mind about reinforcement is that it can be a very effective way to teach desirable behavior. For reinforcement to work in this way, it is important to remember to tell your child why they are being reinforced. Instead of saying "Good girl," and checking off a box on the reinforcement punch card, tell your child why they are receiving the reinforcement by stating, "Thank you for being responsible by picking up your trash and throwing it away in the trash can." Linking the reinforcement with the desired behavior increases the probability that you will see more of the positive behavior in the future.

Finally, when your child has earned their reward, make a big deal out of it! Let your child know that you are proud of them for their efforts and that you are excited that they earned their reward. To make your reinforcement even more effective, consider keeping some activities contingent upon positive behavior. If the reward for filling a positive behavior punch card is 15 minutes on a tablet, but the child knows that they will be allowed to spend an hour on a tablet regardless of behavior, the reward will lose its effectiveness. Make the reward something that is unique and highly preferred to increase the desirability.

Expect the Best

Before going out, reiterate the expectations and the reinforcement system and let your child know that you have confidence in their ability to meet the expectations. Be positive and encouraging and let your child know that you are committed to helping them have a good time and be successful. Initially, it may be wise to plan short outings that are limited in scope. Perhaps returning to a favorite play area or going to a familiar store or restaurant for a short period of time will allow for some practice, along with reinforcement, for a successful experience. Plan to start small, experience success, and build on the positives!

Anticipate Challenges

Before you start, think through possible problems that could arise. Think about what might go wrong and how you can prepare ahead for those contingencies. If the new environment might be loud and the noise might result in dysregulation for your child, what are some tools you might have available? Perhaps you could pack some noise-reducing headphones to have on hand if needed. If your child might have to wait and could become bored, leading to undesired behavior, are there some activities that you can have on hand that would be appropriate in that environment?

Tools

By thinking through what challenges might occur and planning ahead for how you will respond, you'll feel much less stressed and will have a greater likelihood of success. Even if you fail to anticipate a particular problem and experience challenges, take it as a learning experience and an opportunity to do a more thorough job of planning ahead in the future.

Take Breaks, If Needed

Understand that returning to the community and pre-pandemic activities may require learning new behaviors and coping strategies. In situations where masks are required and social distancing is expected, it is normal to feel an urge to get away to take a breath and regroup. Before leaving for an activity, discuss with your child that it is ok to need to take a break, how to signal the need for a break, and what the break might look like.

Ideally, the need to take a break will be identified prior to your child becoming dysregulated due to the environment. Talk with your child about how they might identify that they are in need of a break. What will they pay attention to so that they know that it is time for a break? What will you be watching for that would indicate that it might be time for your child to step out and self-regulate?

It might be a good idea to plan for short "step out and breathe" breaks during a longer activity. Identify how often breaks might be needed and where a break might be taken. Identify a quiet and safe location to step away and provide a calming activity, such as looking at a book, using a fidget, doing calming exercises, or listening to relaxing music. Use a timer (a great one is the Time Timer® App) to signal a stopping time and reinforce your child for participating in the break-time activity.

Have a Sense of Humor

Understand that even your best planning may not prevent a behavior incident from occurring. Have fun defining and describing your expectations and developing your reinforcement system. Enjoy reinforcing your child's appropriate behavior and make sure to let them know that you're appreciative of their efforts. Even if things don't go exactly as planned, choose to see and celebrate the positives! Realize that entering back into pre-pandemic activities is going to be stressful for most people. Try not to take things too seriously. Give yourself and your child a pat on the back for doing something new and resolve to try again.

Enact an Escape Plan

Finally, take some time to plan out how you will respond if your child becomes dysregulated and needs to leave the activity. Think through how you might exit as easily as possible. It might be helpful to enlist the help of family or friends to support you in exiting the location or activity if needed. Don't look at a need to leave as a failure. Instead, focus on what went right, what you learned, and what you might do differently the next time. Understand that a variety of factors may influence the success of a particular outing or activity and take one step at a time.

Conclusion

Getting back to pre-lockdown activities is extremely exciting for some people, whereas it is being met with some trepidation by others. As you begin engaging in activities that you and your child enjoyed pre-lockdown, realize that new patterns of behavior may have emerged and that some behaviors may need to be re-learned. Don't stress, and remind yourself that if you BREATHE you will be far more likely to enjoy a return to activities in life after lockdown!

More about Sheri . . .

 As we enter life after lockdown, I am most concerned about . . .
staying healthy as communities open up and people are gathered together more often.

✈ As we enter life after lockdown, I am most excited about . . .
being able to travel and see family overseas again.

Dr. Sheri has been a special educator for over 35 years. She is the mother of four grown up sons, two of whom have required special education and related services in the past. She is also the proud grandmother of five grandchildren. Dr. Sheri and her husband live in California and Central France and enjoy spending time with family, eating good food, and gardening.

Books

○   *FLIPP the Switch: Strengthen Executive Function Skills*, with co-author Carol Burmeister
○   *FLIPP the Switch 2.0: Mastering Executive Function Skills from School to Adult Life for Students with Autism*, with co-authors Carol Burmeister and Rebecca Silva

SENSORY STRATEGIES FOR SUCCESS

JEK BARROZO

COVID-19 emerged as a novel virus, often leaving healthcare professionals and scientists with little knowledge of what to expect. Many of the protocols changed over the course of the pandemic, causing confusion for some individuals with autism, making it particularly hard for them to learn the new social norms and rules and leaving them with feelings of anxiety and bewilderment. In addition, there are sensory factors that may cause challenges for individuals with autism when it comes to returning to "normal" life. This chapter will give guidance and tips on navigating challenging COVID protocols for reintegrating into the community successfully, including returning to school or work, washing hands, using hand sanitizer, wearing a mask, dealing with plexiglass, and vaccinations.

Why is it difficult to return to school and work?

For over a year, COVID restrictions and rules altered our daily routines, habits, and rituals. Schools were either closed or taught online and businesses have shut their doors or moved their employees to a virtual platform. In general, most of us altered our participation in school and work environments, creating new routines, but those newly established routines are now changing once again as restrictions are being lifted and community life is returning to a pre-pandemic state.

Establishing routines usually promotes increased independence, provides structure and stability, and allows people to predict activities, but changing routines multiple times can disrupt the predictability autistic individuals thrive on. Furthermore, the new routines have increased demands by adding activities such as wearing a mask and washing hands more frequently. Some routines have changed the social rules expected in community situations; now it is no longer expected to shake someone's hand or to share food or drink. Frequent changes in routines may frustrate or confuse some individuals, making it more difficult to function independently when new rules and routines are established.

Individuals may experience frustration not only from the increased changes and expectations in routine, but also from the overwhelming sensory world that is waiting outside of the home. Because of the stress of the past year—caused by additional social rules and safety guidelines for masks, social distancing, and plexiglass placed around the community—many individuals on the spectrum are increasingly sensitive to sensory stimuli in the environment. Exercise, heavy work activities, and consistent schedules may help increase tolerance to sensory stimulation. But during lockdown, individuals were in their homes with decreased physical activities. Once they begin reentering the community, their lack of physical activity may increase their sensitivity to stimuli they once tolerated. They may not tolerate wearing shoes for as long, have become more sensitive to sounds in stores, or have become overwhelmed with lighting in the office and classroom faster than before. It may take days or months before they can tolerate the same stimuli they could before the pandemic.

TIPS for self-regulation:

- Engage in exercise routines to increase tolerance to challenging situations by calming the nervous system (e.g., walk, yoga, sit-ups, push-ups, sports).
- Use mindfulness activities, such as body scanning, to increase body awareness.
- Prime the individual for new expectations from schools, stores, and other community outings by providing visual schedules and written COVID-19 guidelines (with photos, if necessary).
- Provide social narratives on what to expect in the community.
- Teach tools and strategies to use when confronted with challenging situations, e.g., breathing, providing safe space to go to deescalate, asking for help, etc.
- Use self-monitoring strategies to maintain awareness of emotional state and possible solutions/tools to utilize for regulation.

Why is it difficult to tolerate plexiglass?

Plexiglass has been placed in multiple settings to help prevent the spread and transmission of COVID or other viruses. It may be located in front of a cashier at the store or between a ticket taker and a fan at a baseball game. There may be plexiglass around desks in the classroom or between cubicles in an office. Many environments are using this clear plastic to assist with safety; however, it may pose a challenge to some individuals with autism.

Visual sensitivity experienced by some on the spectrum may cause difficulty when encountering plexiglass. Individuals may become extremely distracted by the visual glare and reflections of the glass, making it difficult to concentrate. It may also distort the images behind the plexiglass, bending the images, making them bigger, smaller, or irregular-shaped. Some individuals may become scared or confused by this visual misinformation and have difficulty approaching areas with plexiglass.

Plexiglass can also distort auditory information. Some people on the spectrum already have difficulty with auditory processing, and adding plexiglass may increase their difficulties with hearing information clearly. In addition, the plexiglass itself may refract sounds or cause echoing, which will also increase auditory sensitivities.

Physically navigating environments such as a classroom, restaurant, or workplace can be difficult for most individuals on the spectrum. Adding another object, such as plexiglass, in the room changes the layout and increases the difficulty of navigating the space. Individuals may pause or need additional cues to figure out how to complete tasks they once knew how to do.

TIPS for tolerating plexiglass:

- Place plexiglass away from direct lighting to reduce reflections.
- Place plexiglass in less trafficked areas.
- Add stickers or icons to plexiglass as a visual cue.
- Provide sunglasses or hats to reduce visual input.
- Provide headphones to reduce noise.
- Increase visual cues, e.g., use written words and pictures to increase receptive understanding of auditory information.
- Orient the individuals to the new set-up of the environment by priming them, e.g., taking them on a tour or showing them pictures.

Why is it difficult to tolerate hand sanitizer?

Hand sanitizer is an excellent alternative when a sink is not immediately available for hand washing. Since the start of the pandemic, an increasing number of community settings have it available for customer use, and some individuals may keep a small bottle in their bag or purse for instant access. While hand sanitizer may be helpful for killing viruses and germs, some autistic individuals may protest its use it in their day-to-day routines.

The strong odor of hand sanitizer may be overwhelming for individuals with smell sensitivity. The high alcohol content makes it a powerful smell even if scented. In fact, scented products could make it worse for some individuals because of the combination of scent and alcohol.

Individuals with touch sensitivity might become uncomfortable or overwhelmed by using hand sanitizer. Some brands may leave a sticky sensation and overwhelm a person's nervous system, causing a fight or flight reaction. Additionally, if the individual has small cuts or abrasions, it could leave a stinging sensation and become painful. This stinging sensation may be more intense than for neurotypical people, as some individuals with autism have a heightened sensitivity to pain.

Planning motor actions can also affect the ability of the individual to apply and use the hand sanitizer. First, they need to figure out how to open or access the hand sanitizer from the pump and then how to rub it until it disappears. It can be difficult for individuals with body awareness issues to figure out where to apply the hand sanitizer. An individual may automatically put sanitizer in their hair or mouth when it is given to them. The more times an individual must apply sanitizer in the day, the more stress they will experience.

TIPS for tolerating hand sanitizer:

- Complete deep pressure and hand warm-up exercises (e.g.,squeezing hands, clapping, rubbing hands together, etc.) prior to using hand sanitizer to increase tolerance.
- Allow the individual to choose which scent they prefer.
- Provide task analysis and visual supports showing each step of the application process.
- Try different brands that may have different textures.
- Offer a paper towel or wipe once application is completed to reduce residual textures and smells.
- Check for cuts and abrasions before application.
- Provide social narratives to explain the importance of sanitation.
- Allow the individual to wash their hands instead.

Why is it difficult to complete hand washing?

Washing our hands is critical to maintaining health and safety throughout our lifetime and it is also a very complex skill. Some individuals with autism may have difficulty with hand washing due to a variety of factors, including sensory and motor difficulties.

Touch sensitivity may make several steps of the hand washing process difficult to tolerate. The individual may have difficulty with the sensation of soap and suds and may fear their clothing becoming wet. They might also avoid handwashing due to difficulty with tolerating the texture of a hand towel when drying their hands. Touch sensitivity also includes intolerance to water temperature. It may be painful or uncomfortable for the individual if the water is too hot or too cold. What complicates things is the combination of multiple temperatures and textures, such as cold sticky soap with warm water, causing the nervous system to become overwhelmed.

For individuals with sound sensitivity, handwashing can be a nightmare. The bathroom itself often echoes with sounds of water coming out from the faucet, water hitting the stainless-steel sink, hand blowers, paper towel dispensers, flushing toilets, and manual or automatic soap dispensers, causing the individual to become overwhelmed with painful stimuli.

While sensory information can overwhelm the system, hand washing also requires many more steps than using hand sanitizer. Turning the faucet on and off, getting a paper towel, throwing the paper towel away, and even wiping hands require increased planning for motor actions, increasing the demand. Individuals may have difficulty knowing which steps to complete while washing their hands and may skip certain steps within the sequence, causing frustration.

TIPS for hand washing:

- Provide social narratives to explain the importance of sanitation.
- Complete hand warm-up and deep pressure exercises (e.g., squeezing hands, clapping, rubbing hands together, etc.) to increase tolerance.
- Provide task analysis and visual supports showing each step of the application process.
- Provide headphones to reduce auditory stimuli.
- Roll up sleeves and remove excess clothing to avoid it becoming wet.
- Use other settings to wash hands, if possible, e.g., a portable handwashing station or a kitchen sink.
- Provide a choice between using hand sanitizer and washing hands.
- Place a rubber mat or wash cloth in the bottom of the sink to reduce sound.
- Provide choice of textured towels to use.

Why is it difficult to wear a mask?

As we begin venturing into the community, masks may be required to enter businesses, events, school, or work. This poses a problem, as some autistic individuals may have difficulty tolerating, wearing, or observing the rules of mask-wearing. Some individuals may avoid going into the community because they do not want to wear a mask. Other individuals may not be allowed into schools or businesses if they do not put the mask on. Being able to wear a mask is a critical skill to address to reduce isolation.

One challenge to wearing a mask may include sensitivity to touch or smell. This experience is a common phenomenon for individuals with autism. It may be painful or uncomfortable for them to tolerate light touch, particularly in the facial area, which has an abundance of nerve endings. In addition, the smell of chemicals, detergent, or breath while wearing a mask may be off-putting and cause nausea or discomfort.

Autistic individuals have also described increased difficulty with mobility when wearing a mask. Many individuals with autism have difficulty with body awareness, which is the sense of what different parts of their body are doing at any given time. Because body awareness is a challenge for many people with autism, some individuals compensate by using their vision to watch what their body is doing. When wearing a mask, the individual's peripheral vision is blocked, causing the autistic individual to rely more on their body awareness. Because body awareness is challenging for some autistic individuals, they may become clumsy, tripping more frequently while wearing a mask.

Finally, individuals with autism often have difficulty with novel tasks due to the sensory, motor, and cognitive challenges involved. Masks are a relatively new addition to our society, and we have little exposure to wearing them in a variety of settings. Additionally, unpredictable circumstances such as needing to wear a mask in a classroom but not in a restaurant can be confusing.

TIPS for tolerating a mask:

- Use social narratives explaining when and why we wear masks to provide predictability and understanding of rules.
- Provide choices or different mask types including different patterns, designs, and textures to allow the individual to find what is most comfortable for them.
- Offer tighter fitting shoes or clothing to provide comfort to individuals who have poor body awareness when their peripheral vision is blocked by a mask.
- Use a transparent mask to decrease obstruction of peripheral vision.
- Attach buttons to a hat to hold mask loops if the individual can't tolerate loops behind their ears.
- Have the individual brush their teeth before wearing the mask if they are sensitive to smells.
- Let the individual choose a detergent or fragrance that is pleasant-smelling to them.
- Complete heavy work activities or exercise, e.g., sit-ups, push-ups, or pulling a wagon, before putting the mask on. Heavy work calms the sensory system making it more comfortable and tolerable when the individual puts the mask on.

Why is it difficult to receive a vaccination?

Some individuals may want to receive a COVID-19 vaccination from their healthcare provider but find it challenging. Several factors may increase the challenge, including new situations, unpredictability, and overwhelming sensory information. There are multiple settings where an individual may receive a vaccine, including clinics, hospitals, pharmacies, drive-thru clinics, or home settings. The individual may be initially overwhelmed by the process of checking-in, waiting in the waiting room, and understanding the role of the multiple healthcare professionals they encounter. Additionally, the sensory information of the environment –including multiple sounds, lighting and smells—can be painful to the individual. Although receiving the vaccine is reassuring, it may still be painful, and pain may be amplified in someone with autism.

TIPS for receiving a vaccine:

- Complete heavy work activities to calm the nervous system before leaving for the clinic, e.g., sit-ups, wall or chair push-ups, carrying grocery items, laundry baskets, or pulling a wagon.
- Take headphones, sunglasses, fidgets, baseball caps, or weighted blankets to help reduce sensory overload while waiting.
- Provide a visual schedule of expected activities and procedures to provide predictability.
- Develop a social narrative describing what is to be expected during the vaccination process.
- Bring a preferred item to use to help distract the individual from the vaccine.
- Talk to the healthcare provider before the appointment to discuss concerns.
- Ask to wait outside and be called in when appointment is ready.
- Ask the vaccination center or clinic to create a calming room with low sensory stimulation in the facility or clinic.

What comes next?

COVID-19 has vastly changed the lives of individuals across the globe in the past year. The alteration of routines, expectations, and new social rules caused stress for most individuals. Individuals with autism, however, may have even more difficulty adjusting to the changes, due to the increased sensory and motor demands. Supporting the new sensory and motor challenges needed to follow COVID-19 protocols is vitally important in helping autistic individuals reintegrate into community, work, and school settings comfortably, safely, and successfully.

More about Jek . . .

 As we enter life after lockdown, I am most concerned about . . .
how the new COVID-19 protocols will impact students we serve in the school setting.

As we enter life after lockdown, I am most excited about . . .
working in person, and providing more supports to our students as they integrate back to school and community.

Jek Barrozo, M.A., OTR/L, ATP, is a pediatric occupational therapist and assistive technology specialist. Jek is active in parent and teacher trainings, conducting national, international, and local presentations on topics related to autism; self-regulation; sensory processing disorder; and assistive technology, including augmentative and alternative communication (AAC).

PAYING FOR COFFEE IS PAYING FOR INCLUSION IN SOCIETY

LARRY BISSONNETTE

The use of spaces in the community was locked down for me for most of the last year. Most places let me order takeout but lots of places required you to use a preventing-hand-touch method of payment like a credit card, which I don't have and lack the precision in my fingers to put into card reading machines. This meant that I had to depend on others to pay my bill.

It is important to me to have control over my money and I may not be able to unless I learn to use a card. Looking into the future, people like me will handle money less and lose lots of opportunities to meet people in restaurants, especially coffee shops. Places to meet people are hard to find in the community and coffee shops may let a greater diversity of people participate in doing something together because more people drink coffee than any other beverage.

Practically, looking at the plentiful availability of cards, it shouldn't be difficult to get a card but the opportunity to ease into the use of one may be limited not by the ability of people like me to learn skills in money management but by the attitudes of society about our potential to learn these skills.

So the issue of adjusting to life in the community is less about autistic people changing and more about people in society making shifts in the accessibility of technology so that all people can order and pay for their coffee independently.

More about Larry . . .

Larry Bissonnette is a disability rights advocate and artist who lives in Williston, Vermont. He has been painting and drawing since he was a young child and exhibits his art both locally and nationally. Over the past 20 years, he has been a featured presenter at many national educational conferences and has written and spoken on the topics of autism, communication, and art.

Larry is both the subject and writer of a film about his art and life called, "My Classic Life as an Artist: A Portrait of Larry Bissonnette" (2005) and starred in the documentary, "Wretches and Jabberers" (2010). He also is a contributing author to, "Communication Alternatives in Autism: Perspectives on Typing and Spelling for the Nonspeaking" (2019), a book edited by California Lutheran University professor, Dr. Edlyn Peña.

IT'S FINALLY TIME TO GO OUT AGAIN!

JILL HUDSON

Now that the world is starting to open back up, there are many things that you will be able to do out in your community that may not have been as routine this past year as they once were. These might include going back into your favorite store, going out to a park, participating in an activity with others, or catching up on doctor appointments. We will explore the subject of doctor and dentist appointments more in-depth, addressing specific supports for these somewhat new and changing environments. But first, let's look at a few supports that will need to be considered as the post-pandemic world slowly, and often not uniformly, adjusts.

Social Distancing

In many places, you will continue to hear about the need for social distancing. This can be a somewhat abstract concept to interpret. Or it may be confusing without knowing or easily interpreting the nuance of the markings being used in the location, such as if some chairs have a tag or X on them, are those the ones allowed to be used or does that mean they are the ones that are off-limits? How much space equals six feet? Why are some places allowing tables or chairs to be seemingly closer together? It could even be somewhat confusing to sort all of the subtle rules, such as initially being asked to stand far apart from others shopping in the same store as you, but being able to stand closer than six feet to the person ringing you up, or to the doctor who is examining you. Consider introducing the Distance Ring for proximity.

The Distance Ring shows a series of concentric circles in different colors (represented here in shades of gray, but labeled with the color). Each ring of the circle represents different groups of people or environments and can be used to show how close people can safely stand in proximity to the individual. For example, the individual is in the center while the closest circle is red (closest), representing family, hugging your mom, etc. The next circle, yellow, might represent people to whom you can get a little closer, such as a cashier at a store. The next circle, green, could be for desks at school or tables at a restaurant. All of the circles are good; they just represent people and distances as needed at different times and places. Introducing the scale in advance and practicing the different amounts of space before going into public environments will help the individual better adjust and approximate how close or far to stand. It gives predictability and also establishes a rule that has built-in flexibility that can be followed and scaled as needed.

Distance Ring

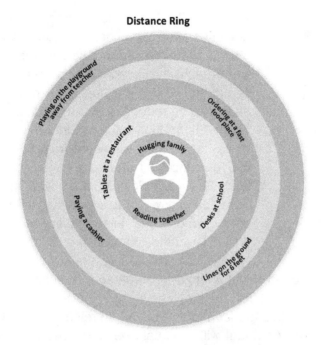

Limiting Capacity

Some places will continue to limit the number of people allowed inside at one time, so there may be a need to make an appointment or reservation in advance or to wait in line once you arrive. Making a reservation eliminates or lessens the amount of time you would wait out front at a restaurant, in the lobby before getting your hair cut, or in the waiting room at the doctor's office. Some places may have a line, such as at your favorite store or the grocery. Overall, the goal of limiting the capacity is to reduce the number of people inside at any one time and to reduce your wait time when you arrive. But even with an appointment or a reservation, sometimes a location, like a veterinarian or doctor's office, may ask you to wait in your car when you arrive. You might need to stand in a line outside at specific socially-distanced markers on the ground until others exit the location, allowing you to move forward in line and eventually have your turn inside. Consider using a waiting plan or a transition cue to help make the time more predictable.

Countdown

5
4
3
2
1

Use a 5-4-3-2-1 countdown instead of a certain amount of time or number of minutes, which may change or not be known. The countdown allows you to remove a number at your own discretion or increment of time based on how the line seems to be moving or your best guess based on the information you have. Introduce the idea by saying that you will count from five down to one, and once you get to one it will be their turn. It is as easy as holding up five fingers and slowly taking each down, or quickly typing the numbers on your phone and deleting them as you count down. The time between the removal of each number can vary: Maybe the five to four is long because the individual is engaged in an activity while waiting and not really noticing the length of time or the removal of the numbers, or maybe the five to four happens quickly to reinforce that the time is being reduced and it will eventually be your turn. If you are still on three and it is your turn, you can quickly reduce to two and then to one! This makes the experience more predictable for the individual, as the number one represents the end of waiting, yet gives you flexibility to adjust the countdown to meet the situation, as the time may change.

Mask Guidelines

Although a state or a county may be considered open again, most offices and local establishments have been given the opportunity to decide their own specific guidelines when it comes to masks. Many have posted a sign on or near the front door as you enter that specifies the guidelines for needing to wear a mask or not for that location. These guidelines vary from place to place. It will be important to add a step to your thinking to stop as you approach a front door to look for the sign, read it, and then know to put your mask on or not before you enter. For example, if a store does not have a sign posted, it is ok to walk inside without a mask on or to ask someone about the rules once you walk inside. When it comes to your mask, did you get one that is your favorite color or that has your favorite character on it? What makes wearing your mask more fun? Consider using a Power Card to establish the importance of following the guidelines and as a reinforcement for a favorite motivator (Gagnon and Myles 2016). Power Cards pair a positive statement about a situation with a picture of a character from an individual's favorite video or a preferred celebrity or other significant person in the person's life.

Just Like Superhero Hal

Superhero Hal says to wear your mask:

1. At school

2. At the store

3. At the restaurant

4. At the movies

Foundational Supports

As you begin to venture back out, consider the supports and strategies that have been beneficial in the past and how they might be adjusted for this new reentry into the community. What will best address the needs or be most beneficial in the specific environment to which you are going? How can you create an opportunity to engage more fully and successfully? The Blueprint below provides an outline of ten areas to consider when building comprehensive supports. How could utilizing these in conjunction with one another provide a strong foundation and wrap around perspective as you venture out into the community?

SUPPORT	STRATEGY	DESIRED OUTCOME
Waiting plan		
Communication		
Social		
Visual		
Hidden Curriculum		
Sensory		
Motivation		
Behavior		
Transition		
For sibling or other students		
Additional activities for school:		
Additional activities for home:		
REWIND		

The Blueprint gives you a big picture plan that can be created and shared with others—family members, coaches, medical personnel, teachers, group leaders, etc.—to help communicate needs and plan supports for the individual in each situation or location (Hudson and Coffin 2007). It is a tool that could be written out or eventually used as a thought process or mental checklist across activities and settings.

Many have found that some strategies or supports can be used in multiple environments, others being slightly adapted or modified as the location changes. Some may be very specific to just one setting. But the hope is to set up each individual for success—for those adventures that are planned out in advance as well as when a spontaneous opportunity arises, and even for a sudden change of plans.

Now let's get more specific and talk about someplace many of us haven't visited for the past year—the doctor or dentist office. The doctor and dentist can be anxiety-producing and intimidating places in the best of times, but right now they are also unfamiliar, due to the time that has passed, as well as the change in protocols and new expectations. Read on for suggestions to make these visits successful experiences.

Going To the Doctor and Dentist

Seeing the Doctor

Prior to your appointment, call to inquire about any new steps or processes they have put into place. Will you wait in your car? Will you park and enter through the same door as before? Perhaps there will be more people you see throughout, or possibly you might engage with less than the usual number of people during your appointment.

Identifying People With Their Mask On

When you first walk in, you may be given a new mask to wear. You can take off the mask you were wearing to put on the new one that they give you. Or you may be able to put their mask on top of your mask if you prefer. The mask they give you is especially protective and designed to wear in the medical environment. Some offices will have you wear your own mask. Every office may be different. The majority of people  that work at the doctor's office or at the hospital will be wearing a mask and may also have on additional protective coverings. Either in advance of the appointment or as you meet people who will be caring for you, take a photo of their face with their mask on and another photo of them without any coverings. Print or make a collage of the photos, placing them side by side with their name so you will be able to know who is coming in to see you.

Communication and Visual Supports

Since the doctors and nurses will be wearing masks throughout your appointment, this may lead to muffled conversations or not fully understanding or hearing everything that is being said. It might help to create a written list, a visual schedule, or a graphic depiction of the steps involved with the appointment, so they can be pointed to when talked about to better ensure everyone knows what will happen next.

Doctor's Appointment List

- ❑ Drive to office
- ❑ Wait
- ❑ Go with nurse
- ❑ Get weighed
- ❑ Sit on bed in exam room
- ❑ Check temperature
- ❑ Doctor checks my ears
- ❑ Doctor checks my throat
- ❑ Go home

Going to the Doctor Schedule

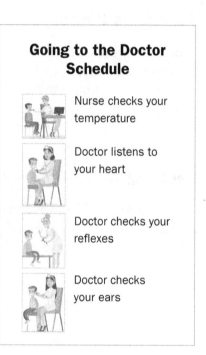

Nurse checks your temperature

Doctor listens to your heart

Doctor checks your reflexes

Doctor checks your ears

Adding Reinforcement

These items can also be crossed off or removed as they are completed to indicate the lessening number of steps or tasks left in the appointment. This provides predictability to the individual about what is occurring and what comes next as well as helps them know how many items remain to be completed before you are done. In addition to the communication support, reinforcers could be placed throughout the list to give the individual a break in between steps.

Reinforcements could also be used incrementally throughout all of the steps, for example, by giving a teen who loves space and astronauts a themed sticker to cover each item as it is completed.

Not only are each of the needed medical requests/task being covered over and no longer able to be seen, but the page is now filling with a more desired visual. Once the appointment is complete, the individual can be reinforced with time to look at a space book or play a space game.

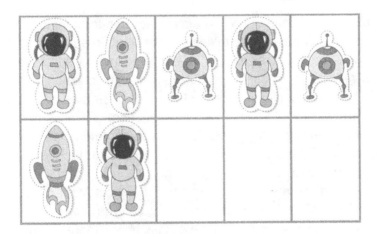

Adding an Object or Movement

Another way to support communication and the transition of one step to the next step is to use visual turn-taking. As the nurse points to the next item on the list, they also hold a brightly-colored squish ball. The nurse points to the step on the page, explains what will occur and demonstrates how the equipment will be used. The nurse then places the squish ball near the individual, indicating it is their turn to complete the step. This again provides some predictability for the individual that the next step is occurring and allows them to visually orient to the nurse giving the explanation, and then to recognize it is their turn. Once the step is complete, the squish ball returns to the nurse, who repeats the sequence again, pointing to the next step on the list, explains what will occur, demonstrates how the equipment will be used, and then places the squish ball by the individual. Any reinforcing object could be used—taking turns wearing a crazy hat or simply bouncing a tennis ball back and forth, a fire truck driving between them, or even using a stuffed animal and creating the story that the stuffed animal wants to get a good look as the nurse explains and demonstrates the step, and then moves to sit near the individual as they complete the step.

Extra Preparation—Planning Ahead

The medical environment was often anxiety-producing for individuals even prior to pandemic, so taking special consideration for sensory regulation and reducing anxiety for the new masking and social distancing measures could be helpful. You know the cues of your child, so help to communicate those to the medical staff as you all work to create an environment, provide information, and build in strategies and supports to use throughout the appointment. You might go in advance of the appointment to take a video of the steps—from exiting your car in the parking lot to walking in the doors, checking in, walking down the hallway, and into the appointment room. Take photos of the medical staff who may greet you along the way or provide care during the appointment. Take photographs that you can place into a flip book to talk through a step-by-step process before arriving on the day of the appointment. You might even practice for a few days with your child, driving into the parking lot, walking into the building, putting on the new medical mask, checking in by saying hello at the front desk, and then leave. Revisiting this environment in increments and in a manner that is reinforcing to your child could lower the anxiety and increasing the predictability and familiarity of arriving on the day of the appointment.

Seeing the Dentist

All of these ideas can also be incorporated when you go to the dentist office. One thing that makes these two environments different is that at the dentist office you will eventually be asked to take your mask off so the dentist can see and clean your teeth. The dentist might wear an extra mask or even a face shield. Just like when you go to see the doctor, you can also ask the dentist for a photo of their face without their mask on and put it next to the one with their mask on.

Become Familiar With the Environment

In addition to the ideas above for going to a doctor's office, here are a few suggestions to help with some of the sensory sensations at the dentist's office. When you first walk in, ask if you can look at the tools and instruments that the dentist will use. You can even ask to smell the toothpaste and pick out a new toothbrush. You can watch to see how the chair moves, and when you are ready, have a seat and ask the dentist to move you up and down a few times before they get started with your cleaning.

Wiggle, Freeze

As you get comfortable with the chair, ask the dentist to lay you back where you will be once the cleaning begins. Practice laying as still as a statue! Then wiggle, wiggle, wiggle, and when the dentist says "freeze," you freeze back to a statue. And again, wiggle, wiggle, wiggle, then freeze! See if you can stay as still as a statue the whole time the dentist is cleaning your teeth. Create a signal to ask for wiggle breaks throughout as needed. Or talk about predetermined times during the cleaning when the dentist can give you a wiggle break, and then freeze again as the dentist gets back to work. For additional support, you could create a visual to accompany the actions of wiggle and freeze, flipping them over or alternating which is being held up.

Additional Sensory Supports

To help you stay relaxed during your appointment, you can ask to wear the x-ray apron the whole time. It is like a heavy blanket and can be very calming to your body while you sit or lay back in the chair. After you have had a good look around the room and at the special tools the dentist will use, try putting on sunglasses to help shield your eyes from the overhead lights as you lay back. If you want to reduce the noise coming from around the dentist's office and the other patients, wearing headphones lets you choose what you listen to while you get your teeth cleaned. You might pick your favorite music or even listen to a story being read. This will help to pass the time during your appointment.

Final Thoughts

The supports listed in this chapter can be used for a variety of settings and can be tailored to an individual's interests and needs. Be creative! You can pull images off of the internet or you can draw your own, add in pictures cut from a magazine, or have your child help you create an image. The sky is the limit, so grab your visual supports and get back out there!

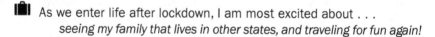

More about Jill . . .

 As we enter life after lockdown, I am most concerned . . .
that we may still go back and forth with masks and guidelines for a while until it really is under control or goes away.

As we enter life after lockdown, I am most excited about . . .
seeing my family that lives in other states, and traveling for fun again!

During this extra time at home, I have enjoyed sitting in my hammock, as well as reading a lot more books than usual. In my everyday job, I work with professionals from across the nation and around the world to consider supports and services for individuals with autism and their families. Previously I worked in a children's hospital and I continue to provide trainings internationally in the healthcare field as well as across a variety of other community, home, and school settings about providing supports for individuals with ASD and their families. I believe all individuals and their families can and should be a vibrant part of their community!

PARENTS ARE EXPERTS, TOO!

RENÉ DELOSS

Rushing, rushing, rushing to get out the door. You can't be late this time! You grab the snack, the favorite fidget, a backup fidget (just in case)—it's time to hit the road. Okay, we're making good time. Who said that going back into the community would be hard? This outing will be a piece of cake!

The thought of going into the community can sometimes be nerve-racking, especially after being at home for over a year without opportunities for practice, and *especially* for those on the autism spectrum. As a parent or caregiver of a child with ASD, you might feel overwhelmed returning to do things in the community, like going to the grocery store, the library, or a restaurant. But there are simple things you can use to help your child communicate, deal with confusion or frustration, learn to wait, and more. You may have seen them at school or are already using them at home. These tools are especially useful in the community. But what happens when you and your child with autism go run errands or go visit friends and you don't have these very useful tools with you? This chapter will not only describe how to use supports to help your child have successful community outings, it will also show you how to make them on the spot, and all you'll need is a pen and paper.

Helpful Things to Have When You Go Out

There are a variety of things that are useful for when your child needs support out in the community. These supports are meant to provide structure and clarity to the parts of an outing that may be abstract and cause anxiety for your child. The following are examples of supports that can be utilized during your next excursion.

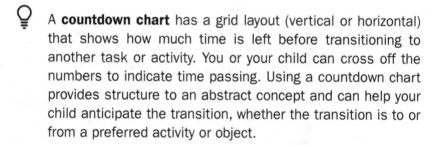

A **countdown chart** has a grid layout (vertical or horizontal) that shows how much time is left before transitioning to another task or activity. You or your child can cross off the numbers to indicate time passing. Using a countdown chart provides structure to an abstract concept and can help your child anticipate the transition, whether the transition is to or from a preferred activity or object.

A **choice board** is a grid or table with pictures and/or written words of the choices offered. They help by providing visual support and a sense of control when your child is asked to make a choice. Choice boards provide a visual representation of items/activities and are organized in a way that helps make choices easy to understand.

A **first/then card** shows the first item or activity on the left (labeled "first") and the second item or activity on the right (labeled "then"). This is used to support a transition from a less preferred activity to a more preferred one. It can be written out or use simple pictures.

A **token system** is a grid that depicts how many "tokens" your child must earn before receiving a preferred item or activity. It's a way to reward your child for a particular behavior. For example, say your child wants to play a game on your phone, but you need them to go to the grocery store with you first. They can earn "tokens" (stars or stickers) for staying with you as you shop, for following directions, etc. Once they earn all of the predetermined number of tokens, they earn the game.

A **wait card** helps by providing a visual cue for the abstract concept of waiting. The card usually has the word "wait," but can say other things (e.g., "It's time to wait." "I need to wait." etc.) You or your child can hold the card while they are waiting for their turn or waiting in line—this can help give structure to the time spent waiting.

Emotion cards have a visual depiction of an emotion on one side and strategies for how to manage that emotion on the other side. For example, an "angry" emotion card would have an angry face on one side, then on the other side it could have things like, "Take deep breaths," "Count to 10," or "Time alone." These strategies can be written out and/or have pictures, depending on the needs of your child.

While you may have these types of supports at home or have some from your child's school, you are absolutely capable of making and using them whenever they are needed. So, what happens when you find yourself away from home and in need of supports for your child?

Getting Out the Door

You arrive at your destination in one piece, and not even late. Just as you're congratulating yourself on being an amazing and completely together adult, your child starts to have a meltdown. They're screeching and start to pull away from you. Uh-oh, what triggered it? Maybe they're wearing the wrong socks, the ones with the extra-itchy seam?

Maybe when you rushed them out the door, they became dysregu-lated? Maybe they just don't feel like being here? Whatever the cause, you realize . . . you forgot the supports you would normally use and you're not sure how to get through this meltdown without them. This is now your cue to panic. Obviously, this will be the most disastrous outing in the history of outings.

Except, hope is not lost! You actually have the tools you need to conquer this excursion: You and your expertise.

> 66 But first things first: The most important thing is to stay calm. 99

In the moment that your child becomes dysregulated and acts out, you might feel helpless or out of control, especially if the tools and supports that you normally use are not readily available. But first things first: The most important thing is to stay calm. If you're stressed, your child will sense it. Model calm, controlled behavior. Lower the volume of your voice, use clear concise language, and stop talking altogether if possible. (Don't worry, you can freak out on your own later.) Right now, it's all about showing your child what "calm" looks like, even if you don't feel it yourself.

When your child starts to have a meltdown, tools like the ones men-tioned above can provide the structure needed to help your child feel heard and supported while they find their way back to being regulated. At the first signs of dysregulation (screeching and pulling away from you, in this case), your child is telling you through their behavior that they need support. This is the right time to try figuring out what would help them. But before you decide which tools to use, there are some simple techniques you can try to help your child find control. So, think of what *you* would need to handle things better and apply that to your child. Some quiet time? Find an isolated area and take a few minutes to get away from the situation. A big hug? Wrap your child in your arms and give them a squeeze. More structure? Fewer demands? A good cry? If it's not clear right away what they need, try something you would find calming.

Don't forget that no matter how much language your child usually has (verbal or nonverbal, as both are equally valuable), when they are upset, it all goes out the window. Think about when you've been upset. Maybe after a heated conversation with your partner in which you both argued in circles without coming to a resolution, and left the situation frustrated with each other. Or after a confrontation with a coworker who accused you of intentionally leaving them out of an important meeting. How articulate were you in that moment? Our kids are just like us, whether they have verbal language or not. Just because they can't say how they feel doesn't mean that they don't have the same feelings.

Your Child Has Calmed Down: Now What?

Now that your child has regained some control and is more regulated, they are more receptive to any tools you can use to help them. Depending on what caused the initial meltdown, you may need to provide more structure to the situation. For example, if your child is having difficulty waiting in line or for their turn, using a countdown, a first/then visual, or a wait card might be helpful. If your child needs more support or motivation for following an instruction, you might use a token system. If your child is having difficulty completing a task or series of instructions, drafting a quick visual or written schedule or checklist might help.

Something to remember: These behavioral supports are meant to be quick, DIY replacements for *existing* supports. They are not meant to be introduced and taught while out in the community, and definitely not while your child is still dysregulated.

Running through the list of supports you would normally use in this situation, you fish around in your bag until you find a pen and a scrap of paper. No problem, you can make exactly what you need to support your child as you navigate this outing.

How to Make Useful Supports on the Spot

With your trusty pen and paper, you can make the tools your child needs! It doesn't have to be complicated; there are simple fixes that require nothing more than your pen and paper. It doesn't have to be fancy either, just useful. Using supports is not only for experts who work in education or in a clinic—remember that you are the expert when it comes to your child and you are just as capable of providing valuable and effective supports.

To make a quick **choice board**, draw a grid with four to six squares, then draw simple pictures and/or write out items or activities your child can choose from. The following example is something you might use at a restaurant when your child needs to choose something from the menu to order.

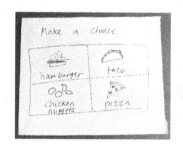

For a DIY **token system**, draw a grid (three to ten squares, depending on your child's needs). Add something like, "I need 10 stars before I earn..." then draw a simple picture of an item or activity of your child's choosing.

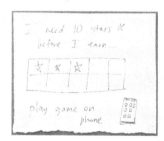

To make your own **first/then card**, draw two squares, side by side. In the left one write "first" and draw a picture of the item or activity your child will do first. On the right side, write "then" and draw a picture of the item or activity your child will do after the first is completed.

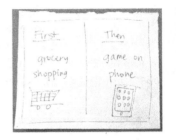

For an on-the-spot **countdown chart**, write numbers five through one, starting at the top and going down. Below one, you can write the next activity or draw a picture of what comes next. Then cross off numbers as time passes.

To make a **wait card**, write the word "wait" on the top and draw something depicting waiting (a clock, in this case). This can vary depending on your child's needs—whether they need more pictures and fewer written words, or no pictures and only written words.

For a DIY **emotion card**, write out the feeling sentence ("I feel ___."), then draw a face depicting that emotion. On the back of the card, write out and/or draw some things your child can do to feel better. Try to include things that have been helpful in the past, and that can be done when away from home.

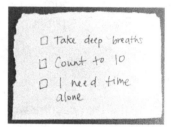

YOU Are an Expert

We have all been through a lot this past year and a half. Whether you're neurotypical or neurodivergent, whether you're extroverted or introverted, the pandemic and subsequent lockdown affected you and your loved ones in a significant way. Some individuals found the lockdown oppressing or tedious, while others found that it provided a welcome sense of relief from societal pressures. Regardless of your personal experience, it is fair to say that our world will likely never be quite the same.

Things are different now. Keep in mind that strategies and supports that worked for your child before the pandemic might not work anymore. There is heightened anxiety all around. Be flexible and creative when it comes to trying out new things when dealing with challenges in the community as society continues to open up.

It is completely normal to have doubts about yourself and about how you are doing as a parent. But one thing that you should not doubt is that you can handle this. You got through a global pandemic in (mostly) one piece, so you can get through this next part too. And remember, you are not in this alone. If you are feeling this way, chances are that other parents are feeling the same way. During the lockdown you weren't only the parent, you were also the teacher, the OT, the behavior interventionist, the speech therapist—you did it all. Things are changing again, but you can do it. You've got this!

More about René . . .

🌐 As we enter life after lockdown, I'm most concerned about . . .
backsliding as a society into what we were before the pandemic—we now have an opportunity to be more considerate and compassionate with each other; I hope we all take advantage of that.

👫 As we enter life after lockdown, I'm most excited about . . .
seeing friends and family! My husband, daughter, and I live across the country from the majority of our loved ones and the pandemic made seeing them all impossible.

I have worked with children on the autism spectrum since 2005—first as an in-home tutor, then as a classroom instructional assistant, and finally as a special education teacher. Currently, I am a stay-at-home mom for a silly and precocious toddler, and I work from home as an editor for AAPC. I live in Massachusetts with my daughter and wonderful husband, Denton, though we hope to move home to California soon.

FROM SEA TO SHINING SEA: AN AUTISM ADVENTURE

AWIT & EDWARD DALUSONG

One of the things we've always wanted to do since moving to the United States was go on a cross-country road trip. But as any autism parent would know, this is one endeavor that has disaster written all over it. Trying to go on this trip with neurotypical kids would be hard enough. One could only imagine the potential challenges and pitfalls when you include individuals with autism.

So, as we started to contemplate whether we should even attempt to do this trip, we began to assess what Ethan can and cannot do. We asked ourselves the following questions:

- Can he endure a grueling 18-day, 6000-mile road trip?
- Will he be able to tolerate riding in the car for at least 6 hours every day?

- Can we find enough stops along the way to accommodate his gluten-free and dairy-free diet?
- Will he just snap after day 4 or 12?
- What happens if he loses patience while we're in the middle of Texas or the Great Plains?
- What if it gets so bad that we must fly him home while one of us is forced to drive solo back to California?

Luckily for us, if there is one thing that Ethan enjoys most about going to school, it is riding the bus and going out to the community. When the lockdown began and he was suddenly forced to stay home for two weeks, he would often lead us to the garage to request a car ride. During the first few months of the lockdown, we were very careful not to expose Ethan to public spaces. The good thing is that he was just happy to ride in the car and wait inside the vehicle while we did our errands. Occasionally he would go in with us—he would patiently put on his mask and go into the grocery store, but for the most part, he was just happy to ride in the car.

Despite Ethan's disability, we made it a point to take him on vacation involving a plane or car ride every summer. Obviously, 2020 changed all of that. In our own way, we tried our best to explain to Ethan about all the travel restrictions and the importance of staying home. We also promised him that when this was all over, we would take him on a long car ride—the cross-country road trip that we had always dreamed about doing someday. But for our peace of mind, we knew we first had to get vaccinated before embarking on this journey.

On the first day that individuals with disabilities were cleared to get the COVID-19 vaccine, Ethan was one of the first in line to get his shot. Days before receiving his jab, we engaged him with some role-playing on how to roll up his sleeves and receive the vaccine (we would use the tip of a ballpoint pen to "poke" his arm). We were very grateful that there was a special entrance for people with disabilities at the vaccination center. When the vaccinator found out that Ethan has autism, she made sure that she used the thinnest available needle so that he "didn't feel a thing." To our great joy and relief, it worked. He sat down and even smiled as the needle entered his arm. We came back three weeks later (we did the same mock vaccination drills at home) and he behaved even better for the second shot. Having gotten that out of the way, we now were clear to move ahead and had a few weeks to prepare for our trip.

As we were getting closer to being declared fully vaccinated, the cross-country road trip plans began to take shape. We planned our route with military precision to ensure it was the best possible experience for Ethan. We began to prepare him for what was to come and what to expect. Our target destination in the east was New York City, where his sister is currently attending university. We used it as a great motivator—the idea that driving a long way to see our daughter made it easier for us to plan and endure days of driving. For our own adventurous reasons, we didn't exactly pick the fastest route. Instead, we chose a route that involved passing through cities we have never visited or seen in at least 15 years. We have a map of the United States in our living room and we patiently pointed out to Ethan each city we would need to visit. We told him where we would stop and rest each day.

We crossed 28 state lines spanning four time zones, stayed in hotel rooms in 18 different cities, drove through the punishing heat of the Arizona desert, the torrential downpours of Louisiana, and endured the unbearable humidity in New York City. Throughout it all, Ethan did not complain once. In fact, we noticed that he relished the idea of moving from one hotel to another every day. During our trip, mask mandates were lifted by the CDC for fully vaccinated individuals. For the most part, most cities did not require us to wear our masks to enter their establishments. However, when we were in NYC, the restaurants still required masks and Ethan complied with no problem. We just needed to model mask-wearing to him, and he knew right away what to do and kept it on until we told him it was safe to take it off.

We also printed out a list of restaurants or eateries where we could purchase food he would need for lunch and dinner. This meant that

we needed to be in a certain town or city at a certain time to ensure that he didn't miss his meals. We have to admit, we were very fortunate that the traffic and weather conditions were great and that we only needed minuscule adjustments to our original plan. This kind of meal planning involved a lot of luck; one freeway accident or severe weather disturbance would have immediately thrown our original meal schedule in the trash bin.

Knowing beforehand that we would be staying in different hotel rooms almost every day, we devised a way to be more efficient in handling all our clothes and personal items. We had three pieces of luggage in our car. The first contained all the clean clothes, the second served as our "hamper" for all the dirty clothes, and the third one was a small rolling suitcase which was the only one we took up to our hotel room. To give Ethan a sense of control, he picked his outfit of choice for the next destination and helped pack from the hotel parking lot every morning. During the trip, we needed to wash our laundry twice, once in Houston (we made sure our Airbnb had a washer and dryer) and the second was in New York City in our daughter's apartment building.

We downloaded Ethan's favorite *Seinfeld* episodes on his tablet to entertain him throughout the 6,000-mile trip. Once again, Ethan surprised us—during the drive we began to notice that he independently decided to lessen his screen time and devoted most of his energy to looking at the changing scenery from his window. We guessed that he was probably wondering how the desert landscapes of Arizona suddenly changed into the lush greenery of Louisiana. What happened to all that green grass in North Carolina and how were we suddenly in the middle of all these tall buildings in Manhattan? And what happened to all the trees in Pennsylvania, Ohio, and Kentucky

that all of a sudden he was in the middle of farmlands in Kansas? And why was it so chilly eating breakfast in the Colorado Rockies and, not even a few hours later, we were lamenting the heat while eating tacos for lunch in the middle of the Utah desert?

We can only hope that he was asking those questions himself. We always believed that traveling broadens the mind and hope that this was happening to Ethan as well.

Here are some tips for special needs families planning to go on a road trip:

- Plan your route ahead of time, know what restaurants to stop at along the way to ensure your child gets their meals at the same time they usually get them at home. This is especially important if your child has food allergies. Researching the restaurant's menu ahead of time is key.
- Always have water and snacks available in case of traffic or unforeseen circumstances.
- If you are driving for longer than 6 hours, plan to do several stops to give your child the opportunity to stretch and go to the restroom.
- Constantly reinforce your child for good behavior in the car.
- Show them pictures of your next destination so they know what to expect.
- Constantly update your child on the estimated time of arrival to your next destination.
- Try not to show to your child that you are stressed or frustrated. We always believe that children feed off the energy that you emit.
- Drive in the early morning so your child can enjoy the scenery and make sure that you are checked in at your hotel room a few hours before their bedtime. This gives enough time for their adrenaline from the full day of activities to wane and to prevent disrupting their usual sleeping schedule.

- Prepare for the worst-case scenario everywhere. We always sit close to the door whenever we eat in restaurants so in case Ethan gets overwhelmed, we can easily go out. If a table near the door is not available, know all the exit points and plan an emergency escape route if things get out of hand to help your child decompress.

Whether you are accustomed to traveling every year like our family, or it is something new that you would like to try with yours, following the suggestions we've laid out will hopefully result in a memorable trip. And no matter how much you prepare and plan for or agonize over an upcoming adventure, be flexible and open to the possibility that your child just might surprise you. Although we had always dreamed of this  trip, it was COVID that inspired us to try it. Life is just too short to put your dreams on hold. Although Ethan doesn't speak much, we'd like to think that traveling is part of his dreams now, too. So hit the road! Maybe we will see you out there.

More about Awit and Edward . . .

 As we enter life after lockdown, we are most concerned about . . .
the disinformation going around that can directly affect our children's health. We are especially worried about a scenario where Ethan will catch the virus and might need to be confined to a hospital where we are prevented from being by his side.

As we enter life after lockdown, we are most excited about . . .
Ethan being out in the world again because he loves going to school, being out in the community and traveling.

Awit and Edward Dalusong have been in the education sector for over 20 years, practicing both in the Philippines and in the United States. Both earned their PhD in Post-secondary Educational Administration from the University of Alberta in Canada in 2003. Soon after the autism diagnosis of their son Ethan, Awit shifted her concentration to Special Education and went on to become a Board Certified Behavior Analyst.

SECTION 5
REBOOT

The word "reboot" means to start anew, to refresh, to make a new start, or to create a new version. This pivotal moment in time—between the world of the pandemic and life after lockdown—feels exactly like that. This moment feels like an opportunity for change. As we have read the first-person accounts of living through the pandemic and seen the many suggestions for successfully adapting to the new normal, there have been underlying questions about whether or not some of the changes we experienced during the lockdown might actually be worth preserving. More services, more options—what is working, what isn't, and what is really needed.

Stephen Shore vividly recalls the moments at the lockdown's beginning, and describes how he has navigated his way through it by using simple tools and strategies. Lillian Vasquez and Bea Moise provide two powerful descriptions of how the pandemic affected their families and where they will go from here. JÂcqûeline Fede and Amy Laurent offer a provocative exploration of the most important lessons of the pandemic, delving into how this "unexpected social experiment" offered autistic individuals more control over their environment and social interactions, creating a sense of possibilities and positive options. Finally, Rebecca Silva and Ruth Prystash offer a summation of the voices in this section, pushing us to question what we know about attitudes toward the autistic community and challenging us—neurotypicals and neurodivergent individuals alike—to do whatever it takes to build a better and more just world, using the lessons of the lockdown as inspiration for moving forward.

> 66 I look forward to everything being more convenient for autistic people that came out of the pandemic, such as working from home, to stay as options and keep improving. 99
>
> Aaron Saenz, age 27

> 66 The best thing about the lockdown was all the online friends I've made, that are exactly like real friends. We play games together and we video call, and sometimes it's almost like they're actually here with me. 99
>
> Miles D, age 16

> 66 Just going forward. I will go forward as always. Just from my computer. I'm not returning. No way. There's COVID outside. 99
>
> Sean D, age 10

A PROFESSOR'S PANDEMIC TALE: LESSONS FOR COPING DURING UNCERTAIN TIMES

STEPHEN SHORE

Launch

It was approximately 11:27 am on Tuesday, March 10, 2020, and I had just finished helping a colleague set up her laptop computer so she could read emails at home. Adelphi University, where I am a professor of Special Education, announced that the campus was closing at the end of the day due to the newly declared COVID-19 pandemic. Not only did this start Spring Break early, but we would get an additional week off *after* Spring Break so that everyone could return to campus healthy. "Goodbye," I say to my colleague and I tell her I'll see her in a couple of weeks when we all return to campus. However, I didn't have a good feeling about the turn of events, so I gathered all necessary materials and supplies—just in case I ended up teaching from home for the rest of the semester. I hopped on my trusty bicycle and rode off to my nearby apartment to pack for the next day's flight to Alabama to speak at a university conference.

At about 4:30 pm my wife texted, with a follow-up panicked phone call telling me to cancel tomorrow's flight to avoid the possibility of getting stuck in Alabama. She told me to come home to Boston before possible road blockades were set up to prevent interstate travel. We had already heard of cars with New York license plates being turned back from Connecticut, as Manhattan had already been deemed a hotspot. I responded that she was being overly cautious, and that going to the conference should be fine. But bad news continued to stream in from CNN and other news outlets and I finally messaged the conference organizers that, given the situation, it would be unsafe to travel. They agreed and allowed me to give the presentation online. Besides, additional time at home with my wife is always good. Little did I know that the expected couple of weeks at home would turn into 15 months . . . and going. Fortunately, we enjoy each other's company!

> **66** Get masks, 70% isopropyl alcohol, and gloves before you drive home. **99**

It was getting close to 6:30 pm and dinner plans at the newly opened Fogo de Chão Brazilian Steakhouse that just opened nearby in Carle Place, Long Island are dashed in favor of simple take-out sushi and preparations for the return home. "Get masks, 70% isopropyl alcohol, and gloves before you drive home," says my wife. Overreaction, I think, but I scour the local pharmacies and other places only to find very limited quantities of these items. Can't hurt to have them around the house in case things really do get bad, can it?

Fold and pack, fold and pack. Rinse and repeat many times—just in case I will be away from Adelphi University for longer than expected. I am grateful that, due to my extensive autism-related travel to 51 countries across 6 continents and 48 of the United States, I am able to pack for an international trip in about 20 minutes. However, this is for an extended period, so more items must be brought with me. Fortunately, unlike airlines, my car does not mind carrying large quantities of possessions.

At approximately 10:17 pm I inform my wife that my goods are packed and I am ready to begin the 208-mile journey from Adelphi University and Long Island. "Too late," she says, suggesting that it is dangerous to drive so late when I am tired. Telling her that if the blockades as discussed earlier are true, I'd better get home sooner rather than later, and be done with it. Since the drive between my home in Boston and Adelphi University is over 95% highway, it's possible to make the trip in about 3 and a half hours on a good day—and double that if I gamble wrong on the traffic. By this time, I suspect due to concerns about COVID-19, traffic was reduced to such a degree where I made it home in a hair less than 3 hours and 15 minutes.

It's about 1:30 am and I pull into my driveway. Everything except my computer and related equipment, phone, and wallet are brought into the house with the rest of the goods to quarantine for 3 days in the basement. Drop the clothes I am wearing and off to the shower to rid myself of possible bits of virus I may have brought with me. Approximately 2:21 am and it's time for bed—at home.

At Home . . . for a Long, Long Time

It's always good to return home. As a public school music teacher, my wife was also booted from her school building, and given a week off to prepare for online teaching. Fortunately, we had purchased a laptop for her to use for a course she took last year. However, there was much work to be done getting her up to speed on using Zoom, Google Classroom, and other resources for effective online education in music. Fortunately, teaching online was easier for me as I had already been instructing in a blended model for several years to meet with my students when in far-flung locations such as Thailand, Israel, Saudi Arabia, Russia, and Australia.

Pandemic-Related Modifications

After about a week, Adelphi University announced that all instruction and other university-related functions were to transition online for the rest of the semester. In addition to making me realize that I needed to do things differently and make adjustments, there are things that those of us on the autism spectrum must be particularly mindful of in order to make it through this uncertain time of pandemic. As it turned out, I realized that these areas of mindfulness are important to everyone, autistic or otherwise. Just like in developing modifications for autistic people in education, employment, and in the community, what is good for autistic individuals often tends to be good for everyone else. Let us begin with The Big Three.

> 66 What is good for autistic individuals often tends to be good for everyone else. 99

The Big Three: Scheduling, Communication, and Self-Care

Scheduling, communication, and self-care are vital.

Scheduling leads to routines, which are important for everyone, autistic or not. We all need communication to successfully interact with others. Finally, we need to engage in self-care for good mental, physical, and spiritual health—both for ourselves, and so that we have sufficient resources to care for others.

An example of scheduling is where Temple Grandin gets up at 7:00 am (I am also up at 7:00 am) every day. Temple engages in her morning routines, has breakfast, and changes into her work clothes to be ready to work—even when she had to remain at home. I did similarly. While our morning routines stayed pretty much the same it was important to realize that changes were necessary.

For example, gone was the incidental movement from riding my bicycle between work and home, running errands, as well as walking between offices and classroom during my days on the university campus. That made me realize that I needed to substitute that morning bicycle commute with up to 90 minutes every other day on my elliptical bike to start the day. It's great when scheduling and routines can be kept the same. However, when changes are needed, they should be as small as possible and as close to what was being done in the first place. An added benefit of all that exercise on the elliptical bike was the shedding of tonnage!

Communication must be done in the way the autistic person inter-acts best. Us "talkies" can continue to speak, whereas others on the spectrum may use AAC and other means to communicate, such as visual schedules or sign language. It's vital to make sure these devices and other communication modes remain available to indi-viduals on the autism spectrum.

Finally, **self-care** for oneself so that one is available to care for others is vitally important. My exercise routine is an example of self-care. Others may seek out and use yoga, meditation, involve-ment in religion, and other activities for mental, physical, and spiritual well-being. With The Big Three as a structure, and inspired from a video posted by my friend and colleague, soon-to-be-Dr. Dena Gassner, below are ten tips that I and other autistic people have found helpful in surviving, and perhaps even thriving in the COVID-19 pandemic.

Ten Ways to Cope When Your Normal Coping Routines Are Disrupted

1. Remain connected with family, friends, support people, and others important to you. Now that we are spending more, and sometimes all, of our time at home remaining safe, gone are the days of incidental meeting with colleagues, friends, and family members whilst shopping or running other errands. All meetings must now be planned. Some options include maintaining communication by phone, instant message, email, video conferencing, and even driving to a friend's to visit at a safe *physical* distance while they may be on their lawn or driveway and you remain in your car. *Physical* rather than social distancing is emphasized because I think it better explains the actions we need to take to remain safe. My sense is that we aren't looking for people to become socially distant, as that suggestion seems to imply living more like a hermit. Especially in times like these, people need to remain socially connected, yet also remain a certain *distance* apart to remain safe.

2. Be careful about absorbing angst from others. Contrary to the myth that autistic people don't perceive others' emotions, we actually tend to connect to and sense them more strongly than the non-autistic population. We then get overwhelmed by those emotions, resulting in a shutdown, or expressing our own emotions in ways people don't look for or expect. If you are feeling unusually anxious, check to see if that emotion might be coming from others in your vicinity or perhaps from watching reruns and recaps of pandemic-based news on TV.

3. Develop and differentiate between your Plan A and Plan B. Plan A might be a quick trip to the store for groceries and other supplies. At the beginning of the pandemic, we had groceries delivered to minimize vectors of exposure to the COVID-19 pandemic. Plan A of incidental exercise and meeting with others was replaced with Plan B of scheduling time

on the elliptical bike at home and setting times to meet with others on Zoom.

4. Get outside on bright, sunny days in a safe manner. Being outside is often restorative and helps with the 3rd of "The Big Three" in taking care of yourself. Just make sure outside excursions are done safely.

5. Recognize that keeping safe during the COVID-19 pandemic requires more cognitive energy. Being fully vaccinated and with lessening threat from the virus, in-store shopping is now possible. However, the many procedures involved in managing the risk of infection—from proper protective equipment to disinfecting things brought to home to taking a shower to wash off possible contamination—all take additional effort and reduce time that can be spent on activities such as socializing with friends, work, etc.

6. Find coping strategies that work for you. This isn't regression, as we autistics are often told: It's self-regulation. Hold a teddy bear, draw, watch TV, rock, hum, and stim as needed! COVID-19 is very stressful for many of us and it's these self-regulatory activities that get us through the day!

7. Take care of yourself so that you can care for others. If taking a bubble bath with a rubber ducky floats your proverbial boat . . . then go for it! You've earned it. And feel free to reduce expectations as needed. With the additional cognitive and emotional load of dealing with the pandemic, you may not be able to do as much as before.

8. Maintain personal health, e.g., taking medication as needed, etc. Something as simple as a pillbox to organize medication can be helpful, especially when dealing with the many distractions pandemic life can bring.

9. Mask and gloves as needed when going outside. Currently, the Centers for Disease Control and Prevention (CDC)

suggests little need for gloves, except as a possible reminder not to touch your face. However, as at the beginning of the pandemic, the CDC recommends masks for indoor places and where people will be densely crowded together. If you don't have a mask, it's possible to improvise with a t-shirt, handkerchief, yarmulke, or even a bra if needed.

10. Observe protocols for returning home from being in public places.

- Less is more. Take as little as possible, as everything brought back must be disinfected and/or quarantined. In the past, I carried my computer and other items in a rucksack. When people remarked how heavy the bag was, I just told them I filled it with rocks so I didn't go too fast. Now I am a minimalist. In addition to a mask, outdoor expeditions include merely my license, a credit card, some cash, and necessary keys. Way fewer items to clean upon entering home and vectors for infection this way.
- Wipe down, leave shoes in the garage, bottom of the stairs, or other designated location to keep the virus out of your home. Many people have indoor and outdoor shoes anyway.
- Sanitize food. Some items can be placed in a sink of warm soapy water, other food such as pound cake can't be washed, however. We quarantine food for 24 hours.
- Wash up. Clothes are dropped into the washing machine and we head directly to the shower to wash up and resume indoor activities.

Conclusion: The Big Picture

With the pandemic on the way out (hopefully there won't be another wave), we have learned much that will be helpful in life in general, as well as for when the next pandemic hits, as it no doubt eventually will.

For one, we've learned that work and education can successfully be done remotely. Supervisors don't necessarily need to watch their employees work in the office to get work done. Perhaps the "new normal" will consist of blending remote and face-to-face work to minimize long and arduous commutes between work and home.

In education, some things can actually be taught better online, whereas other strategies work much better face-to-face. In cold climates, we may see snow day cancellations during inclement weather reframed as remote work or teaching days. Since many people have flourished with online learning, this will hopefully become a more common option.

As I reflect back on the past year, I can see where many of my autistic traits have served me well. Being organized and attentive to detail has kept our lives structured and helped us deal with the pandemic safely. There are things that I have missed, however, such as traveling to autism conferences and the socialization with friends that have become an important part of my life. But I feel that the most important lesson of all is that we actually accept the lessons from this year and that we use what we have learned to improve our world, rather than going back to the way things were. We can do more than survive a pandemic. Autistic people can thrive. Perhaps our lessons can lead the way for changes in the world at large so that all people may thrive.

More about Stephen . . .

 As we enter life after lockdown, I am most concerned about . . .
not learning the life lessons we have been taught during the pandemic as we transition into a "new normal."

As we enter life after lockdown, I am most excited about . . .
taking what we have learned about the efficiencies of online interaction and work we can take advantage of in our everyday lives.

Diagnosed with "Atypical Development and strong autistic tendencies" and "too sick" for outpatient treatment Dr. Shore was recommended for institutionalization. Nonspeaking until 4, and with much support from his parents, teachers, wife, and others, Stephen is now a full time professor at Adelphi University and adjunct at NYU Steinhardt School of Culture, Education, and Human Development, focusing on aligning best practice in supporting autistic people to lead fulfilling and productive lives.

In addition to working with children and talking about life on the autism spectrum, Stephen is an internationally renowned educator, consultant, and author on lifespan issues pertinent to education, relationships, employment, and self-advocacy. His most recent book, *College for Students with Disabilities,* combines personal stories and research for promoting success in higher education.

A current board member of Autism Speaks, the Organization for Autism Research (OAR), American Occupational Therapy Foundation (AOTF), president emeritus of the Asperger/Autism Network, and advisory board member of the Autism Society, Dr. Shore also serves on the advisory boards of AANE, and other autism related organizations.

Books

o   *Beyond the Wall: Personal Experiences with Autism and Asperger Syndrome*
o   *Ask & Tell: Self-advocacy and Disclosure for People on the Autism Spectrum*
o   *Understanding Autism for Dummies*
o   *College for Students with Disabilities: We Do Belong*

Website

www.drstephenshore.com

SURVIVING A PANDEMIC

LILLIAN VASQUEZ

This is one mom's story of her son's lockdown journey. Unfortunately, not all roads lead to victory. Life is hard and COVID just made it that much harder—survival mode becomes the only alternative. The ups and downs are severe. Love, determination, and the world of art may be the only avenues to survive in a world with COVID for our son who has autism. And like with Disney stories, though we are all looking for that happily ever after, sometimes we have to settle for . . . "to be continued." I hope you will see how one family living with autism worked hard to make it through the COVID tunnel. My story won't provide all the answers, but it will show how we're all in this together. Though the outcomes will vary, we must keep on trying. But during this pandemic, we were just trying to survive.

Living in a world with neurotypicals and those with autism spectrum disorder (ASD) can feel like worlds colliding. Add in a pandemic and the mental stress of this current world, and life can be a major calamity. Routine is how many on the spectrum process and function, and the rote behavior of the routine was gone. Even before the pandemic we had struggled to find an appropriate day program and services for Grant. As many families of adults with autism know, these programs are few and far between, and many will not accept individuals with additional challenges. Now the question of day programs was moot, but the need to constructively fill his time remained.

Grant is a handsome (that's how he was always described in his IEPs) 27-year-old adult male with autism. His most typical demeanor is fun and outgoing (meaning he always wants to be out and going . . . somewhere). He has some language. He can express some thoughts and desires, such as telling us what he wants to do, what he likes, what movie he wants to see, what place he would like to visit, what restaurant he would like to eat at, what freeway we should use, etc. He can talk about his surroundings and what's going on (when probed), but sharing his thoughts or feelings to express what's bothering him . . . well, that is NOT something he can do. We can probe and try to get some information out of him, but it's fragments or nothing at all. It's a guessing game and we don't usually win.

Before the pandemic, Grant had a full schedule that included going to the movies, thrift stores, restaurants for lunch, Barnes and Noble, and creating his art on paper, canvas, or business windows at several locations. And of course, spending time on his computer. Then, bam! The pandemic hit and the world as he knew it abruptly came to a halt. His greatest disappointment was not going to Disneyland on March 27, his birthday. Grant had been to Disneyland every year on his birthday since he was ten. His routines were ending and the opportunity to put them back on track was not an option.

Even before the pandemic, Grant's behaviors started to flare up. But it was decided (not by me) to end his ABA therapy. This would mean his one male therapist, Fernando, was ending his time with Grant after two years and his respite friend, Taylor, was getting ready to change his profession after working with Grant for just over two years. I could see things were going to get difficult because he just wasn't quite ready to end his ABA. With his working "friends" leaving, I was pretty sure this change in his routine meant that Grant's journey was about to get bumpy. I never could have imagined it was going to be the colossal rollercoaster it turned into. And then three months later, the pandemic hit.

His behaviors really started to escalate on a daily basis. Grant became unruly and sometimes aggressive. His meltdowns during this period didn't look the same as the ones he had on previous occasions. It was now rare when he wasn't melting down, because rage had become his "new normal." Most of the time these enormous meltdowns had no rhyme or reason, and it was a guessing game to figure out the cause. In the past, we could tell if something might trigger him, and

Momma and Baby Polar Bears

we had been at a point in this journey that we could work through it as a family. But now we struggled to figure out what was going on in his mind. We'd go down a mental checklist: Did he eat? *What* did he eat? Had he been on the computer too long? What was he watching on the computer? Did something irritate him? Was something physically bothering him?

Grant is six feet tall and weighs about 230 pounds (now 200 lbs., he lost 30 lbs. during the pandemic) and his meltdowns can really be a challenge. They are also heartbreaking. Some days and nights were truly discouraging, heartbreaking, and unequivocally hopeless. The nights were rough. The behaviors would start about 2:00 am and sometimes last until 6:00 am, when he would finally fall asleep. My husband and I would take shifts, trying to ensure he didn't hurt himself or others, or destroy the house or the things in the house. Many times, Grant would cry uncontrollably, and we had no idea what was causing it. It would hurt us deeply to see him sad and crying and not have a clue what was making him feel this way. He would say, "Grant sad." And sometimes, "Grant frustrated."

His mode of survival and way to occupy his time during the pandemic was reading and watching videos on his computer. He was

The Radio Flyer Wagon

on the computer constantly; we didn't have any other options. We would try to come up with alternatives as a way to deflect, distract, or redirect him. But it was during lockdown; there wasn't anything open and there was no place to take him that was safe. We couldn't get him to go on walks or ride his bike. On rare occasions, we could coax him into watching some TV. Some days he would be on his computer reading about animals and their habitats, or he would study the many Disney characters, even the obscure ones.

We knew things would be difficult if he started to watch three specific videos. These videos each had scenes that were a trigger for Grant. He would watch certain scenes over and over, becoming so escalated that a meltdown usually followed. If we were within earshot and we heard the videos play, we would ask him to watch something else (sometimes he would change the video), get him off the computer, or take the computer away. Sometimes we would be asleep, and he would get on the computer in the middle of the night. I know you're thinking, "Easy solution, take the computer away." But that would mean 2-5 hours of battling with him. He would request, "One *Aristocats*?" (there is a scene in Disney's *The Aristocats* where Thomas O'Malley screeches and he would want to watch this over and over), which was his way of saying, "Let me watch it once and I will be ok." And sometimes that was all he needed. His anxiety would lessen and his body would calm. But many times, he was fooling us.

An oncoming meltdown would present itself as if he was falling into a trance. His breathing pattern would change and his eyes would glaze over. I think he was feeling a lot of anxiety. He was trying to express himself about how he was feeling and was trying to process it. At that point we never knew what would work with him. I would massage his body—hands, toes, arms, back, legs, and neck. I would try weighted blankets or pillows. We would lie next to him and try to calm him down and keep him from throwing things. Sometimes he would hit himself, but only a couple of times. I guess he decided that wasn't a very good idea. He did like to throw things. We removed just about everything from his room, including items on the wall. We left pillows and blankets and many times that's what he would throw. When he threw and destroyed things, it seemed to provide some type of relief. I think he was creating his own coping mechanism. He didn't like it when he had to make his bed after tearing it apart, though. There were a couple of weeks when he just slept on the mattress with no bedding, just two pillows and a blanket to cover himself. It felt like a prison ward. He felt, and we felt, trapped.

Grant sketching

My husband endured most of the rough nights. Some nights we would only get three or four hours of sleep. I would go to bed and try to sleep, but mostly I would cry and rack my brain, trying to come up with solutions. I would lay there, anticipating the next loud screech, scream, or outburst. His daddy would take most of the "all-nighters" so I could get some sleep and go to work the next day. As an essential worker, I had to be at work every day.

Months into the pandemic, Grant's needs for regulating and calming down changed. He now would demand all the doors near his upstairs bedroom be closed and locked. He would slam the doors and lock them. For some reason, this ritual seemed to calm him. We eventually came to a compromise of just closing the doors and locking them without slamming them. Like I said, it was a compromise. It was a small win, but it was progress.

I'm just a mom, meaning I don't have a "Dr" before my name or "PhD" after my name, but I have been embedded in the autism world for over 25 years. I should've had more answers, but I was grasping at straws. I am fairly knowledgeable about autism. I have

guest lectured on the topic many times and I have produced docu-
mentaries, TV, and radio shows on the topic. I have provided advice
and support to others. But now I labored over what to do, what
solutions would improve the situation, and reached out to my autism
colleagues for ideas, thoughts, and suggestions. I didn't want to
share with too many people because I'd get tired of sharing my story,
and not having answers. I felt I was constantly in limbo.

It was like living with an alcoholic. One day at a time. Living day by
day, praying it would be a good day. And we knew he was hurting.
After most meltdowns he would apologize saying, "Sorry, mommy,"
"Sorry, daddy." Sometimes he would hold it together in public and
then fall apart once he got home. I knew I needed to get Grant back
on a routine, but I just couldn't put a routine or plan together that
would work for him during the pandemic. He would not cooperate or
show any interest. I reached out to psy-
chologists hoping for new perspectives
and insight, but nothing seemed to
help. I often wondered what our future
would hold, and if we would ever get
through this.

In the past, Grant and I would spend
time together—go to the movies, run
errands, go on long drives, wash our
car at the car wash, or go out to eat.
It was just the two of us. However, my
personal time with Grant changed out

*Grant painting windows for
Halloween*

of survival. If he was edgy in the slightest, it was frightening to go
anywhere with him by myself. I hated that I couldn't just enjoy "Grant
and Mom" time. We had always done so many things together, and
one of them included art. Grant is an artist and for years that was
our jam. I loved spending hours and hours with him, working with
him on a drawing or a painting. It brought me great joy to watch his
drawing come to life, to see the details in his art. But for seven
months Grant did not engage with any art. This too made me sad.
He would not even paint on our kitchen windows, something he had
always loved to do.

Getting vaccinated offered some hope for our world. When things started to open up in some communities, we could go some places and started to feel somewhat hopeful. We tried the movie theater, but it went so-so. I do think it made him feel like the coronavirus masking time was over. He has adjusted to wearing a mask, but he continues to look at calendars and say, "2021, coronavirus masks will be over." It is his way of trying to understand when the pandemic will end. He looks at us, hoping we will confirm that the pandemic is over. We know what he wants to hear, even if we can't say it yet. We want it to be over, too.

When outdoor eating started, it allowed us to go somewhere and do something. Having issues in our home where we could "kind of control it" was one thing, but it was very different when we were in public. One evening, when eating outdoors became an option, we were on our way to have dinner. Out of nowhere Grant fell apart—yelling, screaming, running, and crying. This one was a doozy of a meltdown, and in public. It's one thing to have a meltdown at home but if it's in public, it's really a challenge. Not because people are looking at you (we're accustomed to that, so no big deal there), but because of the safety elements (getting him in the car safely or to another safe location).

Thank goodness Grant has a daddy who loves him dearly. His dad did his very best to keep Grant safe throughout the past 16 months. He and Grant are close, and they have their own language, what I call "fun language," that Grant enjoys. It's using words and exaggerating the pronunciation or singing the words. Grant finally started doing this again. He painted on my dad's sliding glass door. He started swimming some, which helped his attitude. Anything to try and keep him engaged and to minimize his time on his computer and watching "Thomas O'Malley screech." We have started taking road trips again, and he did ok on some and not so well on others. We did attend one baseball game and he was his perfect, loving, fun Grant self. We were so thrilled to have a beautiful outing. My husband and I hope that maybe this was the beginning of our way back to "our normal," which we have missed so much.

Ours is just one story of autism and the pandemic. I prayed we would get through it without a police incident and, fortunately, we

did. My mind would race with extremely sad possibilities, always hoping for the best and scared to death of the worst. After a year and a half of lockdown, these worries never go away. I worry about Grant's regression. I worry that we might never see our fun-loving, often funny, and inspiring artist and son on a regular basis

Happy Sunshine-window art

again. I'm not sure what the future will present, and I don't have the answers that I desperately want and need. What I do know is that we are seeing more and more of the fun, engaging, sweet, and kind son we have always known. We will advocate for better services and supports for him. We will work to build better supports for families like ours. And we will continue to work to bring him back to a better place. We will never stop trying. Somehow, some way, we will do more than just survive.

More about Lillian . . .

 As we enter life after lockdown, I am most concerned about . . .
Grant being happy and reaching his social and artistic potential.

 As we enter life after lockdown, I am most excited about . . .
the prospect of Grant returning to the loving and engaging young man he was without terrors in his mind.

Lillian Vasquez works for KVCR, the public radio and television station serving the Inland Empire. Lillian is the radio host of her own show, *Lifestyles with Lillian Vasquez*. She reports, produces, and hosts a variety of programs for both radio and television. She is involved in the community with a variety of non-profit organizations and sits on the Board of Directors for Crafton Hills College and the Autism Society Inland Empire. Lillian is a wife and the mother of two, a daughter, Lindsey, 29, and a son, Grant, 28, who has autism, which she feels is her most important role. She also has two young grandsons. They bring great happiness.

HOW OUR CHILDREN THRIVED DURING COVID

BEA MOISE

January 1st, 2020 started like any other year. I have a tradition with my children to create vision boards about what we would like to achieve for the upcoming year. My daughter, Abby, enjoys this little tradition because she thinks of it as an arts and crafts project. My son Jake enjoys it, but for an entirely different reason. Jake has autism, and this activity is sensory exploration for him. He primarily plays with the glue or stickers and sometimes will sneak the materials into his mouth. He has a sensory processing disorder and is a sensory seeker; he gets his sensory needs met through art. We had no idea that this year's vision board activity would be one of many activities that would need to happen at home.

In March 2020, my husband and I started to slightly panic; we had a big trip planned for our family to go to California. We told our daughter that we had a trip coming up in March, but not our son. Jake has little to no expressive communication skills; we must guess when it comes to how much he understands. Whenever we are going somewhere, we wait until the last few days before watching videos of social narratives and explaining what we are doing. I never want to cause him additional stress and worry when things can change at the last minute, and this time was no exception. As we followed the news about COVID, we knew that this was not a trip we would have in March. With great optimism, I guessed we could reschedule it for late summer when things calmed down.

In mid-March 2020, the whole world seemed to stop. Jake is home-schooled, but my daughter is not. Jake and I have a routine with our homeschooling schedule. However, our world at home took a different turn. Without warning or preparation, both my husband and daughter were home full-time. Initially, Jake's behavior did not change because it seemed like an extended weekend or vacation. I took a step back to evaluate the situation. I was overwhelmed with work, home, and personal obligations. Whenever I am not regulated, it trickles down to Jake. I was panicked about everything; so much uncertainty and no clear plan to put in place and no explanation about what was happening or how to understand this pandemic. Oddly, Jake seemed to adjust to this new normal with an incredible amount of ease. I was taken aback by how easily he adapted from one extreme to another.

The most surprising part of this was the positive impact COVID had on Jake and Abby's relationship. The relationship that my children have with each other is a complex one. They are siblings, but Abby sometimes has the job of being the younger big sister. It's a job that we did not give to her and often take away, but one she enjoys. Pre-COVID, they spent their school days in different environments. My children were in the same school environment when Abby was in kindergarten and Jake was in 1ˢᵗ grade. At that time, they were both homeschooled, but Abby decided that she wanted to have friends and wanted to do in-person school for 1ˢᵗ grade. Now I have a 3ʳᵈ grader and 4ᵗʰ grader who have been living their academic lives separately.

The expectation for COVID at this point was nothing. I didn't expect good or bad; I just wanted to survive. I had no expectations of thriving or that my children would thrive. I made a conscious decision that if they needed to be held back another year, that is exactly what we would do. Their mental health meant more to me than academic achievement in the middle of a pandemic. To my surprise, it was not needed. They were both thriving with school and at home. Once we established a new routine of being together, Jake transitioned into COVID life quickly. Again, I was not expecting that, and I certainly was not hoping for him and his sister to become closer. The extended time together allowed for them to gain insight into a part of each other's life that was missing. In addition, they got to see each other work hard in school. Abby would help Jake with the academic aspect of his work, and he would help her with physical activities such as exercise. Jake loves P.E.; it is his favorite part of his day, while Abby dreads it; however, now they both looked forward to it.

I could not believe how well both of my kids were doing in the middle of all this. I am not sure what contributed to the positive overall experience. Looking back at it, both my husband and I made a conscious choice to keep COVID-related conversation for the evening when both children were asleep. We also did not stream the news all day from an outlet that they could view. We created a COVID-free bubble and treated this experience as an extended summer break, with added math and reading assignments. I think this was vital in keeping their minds worry-free. As for me, I felt an incredible amount of guilt. My house was anything from chaotic, but the families that I was helping through parent coaching were drowning with daily frustrations. The way Jake communicates frustration is that his sleep pattern will change. A few years ago, I noticed whenever there was a change in routine that we could not anticipate, he would go with the flow, but his sleep would be off. As a result, he would either be unable to go to sleep regularly or wake up earlier than his usual time. When you have a child who is nonverbal, behavior is all you have to understand what they are saying. Jake communicated with us like this all the time, and it took a few years for us to listen to what he was saying.

During COVID, he did not wake up early or have issues falling asleep. In fact, he and Abby started to do a "sleep camp" in the playroom that I was sure was not going to work, but to my surprise, it did. They both slept-in every single time they had sleep camp. I realized that my kids were doing well, and I also saw Jake thriving. Jake started to seek out a more reciprocal relationship with his sister. Before this, she would make him do what she was doing, or he would do his own thing. They mastered the art of parallel play but never cooperative play. The added time together created a social skills group with the two of them. For the first time, Abby had a sibling who could engage with her, not verbally, but engaging with her in his own way.

By the time we reached the summer months, realizing COVID was here to stay, we had made some adjustments to our lives and changed expectations about returning to normal. Returning to nor-

mal was no longer an option, and I was not in a rush to do so. Pre-COVID, our lives were filled with driving from one place to another. COVID gave us the ability to slow down and become more intentional in the time we spent together as a family. Focus moved away from packing our day with activities and events and we transitioned into spending time together and enjoying each other's company, but also having our own free time. Jake and Abby reached a new stage in their sibling relationship that I will continue to foster as we return to normal. Pre-COVID, they lived separate lives that came together after 3:00 pm, sometimes later due to afterschool activities and homework. Currently, they live a shared life and maintain cohesiveness in their play. Moving forward I want the engagement between my kids to endure by having them be active participants in each other's lives outside of the house. When the world fully opens, and the activities resume, they both will be there cheering each other on—whether it's a ballet recital for Abby or inclusion-football for Jake, I am going to make sure that it's not just mom or dad on the sideline or in the audience, but all of us together.

COVID wasn't what I wanted, or what I expected. There was stress and anxiety for our family, as there was for others. But for us, there was a rainbow. The new relationship between our children has helped us realize the importance of time at home. We are paying more attention to each other now and to our life as a family. We will continue to focus on these positive steps, and we will remember that while COVID was a terrible time in the world, it also allowed our family to thrive.

More about Bea . . .

 As we enter life after lockdown, I am most concerned about . . .
the increase of anxiety in neurodiverse families who are not given adequate time for a slow and gradual shift back to pre-COVID living.

As we enter life after lockdown, I am most excited about . . .
how to keep learning about opportunities to foster the positive family dynamic we have gained.

Beatrice (Bea) Moise, MS, BCCS, is a Board-Certified Cognitive Specialist, parenting coach, writer, and national speaker. Bea and her husband have two children, Jacob, who is awesomely autistic and Abby, who is simply marvelous!

Book

o   *A Child Like Mine* (Fall 2021)

Website

BeaMoiseAuthor.com

LEVELING UP!
AFTER LOCKING DOWN
JÂCQÛELYN FEDE & AMY LAURENT

This time period—the transition from "COVID-19 Pandemic Lockdown" back to "normal"—provides a unique opportunity to be reflective. Transitions often pose challenges for those that thrive in and on routine. This is known. It is often the reason cited by clinicians, educators, caregivers, and autistic people themselves for prioritizing the provision of structure, predictability, and information well in advance around transitions. Increased predictability during new and changing situations decreases stress and dysregulation. There is no doubt that supporting more predictability and structure during change and transition is necessary and that these are valid supports. There is definitely a need to plan effectively as the world transitions out of lockdown. We would also suggest, however, that in reflecting on this past year, we spend as much time considering how some aspects of lockdown life may be beneficial and perhaps should not be so readily abandoned.

What do we mean by this? We mean that it is vitally important to consider lockdown from all angles. While many experienced lockdown as a massive disruption in their day-to-day existence and struggled to maintain structure and engagement, many autistic people (and also many neurotypical people) actually thrived under lockdown conditions once the initial adjustment had taken place and a new sense of routine was established. Combing through social media posts of autistic young people and adults, recurrent themes related to this phenomenon were apparent.

Why? After the initial shock of an unexpected transition that saw the world shutting down due to the widespread threat of illness and death, as well as overwhelming uncertainty, many autistic people found that they had greater control over their day-to-day environments and interactions. Some reported that they could establish routine and predictability in ways that were comfortable for them; ways that were far more supportive of their neurologically-based processing differences. Others commented that they could turn down the "sensory intensity" of their daily environments. Several suggested that they experienced relief with the rules of social distancing in place. They also had increased access to activities and environments that had previously posed barriers due to requirements. Requirements for in-person or face-to-face attendance, driving or using public transit, and having to exist in or traverse overwhelming environments in order to engage were no longer expected. Slower, quieter, more controlled—these were a few of the words repeatedly found in the comments of posts on Facebook and Twitter.

While much of the world is excited to get back to "normal" (even this book was initially designed to focus solely on that transition), the frequency with which these positive impressions of lockdown were shared demonstrates that there are invaluable and important considerations for policies and practices to consider in our planning going forward. This is a critical time to reflect on what aspects of lockdown were effective accommodations for autistic people.

Changes to activities, environments, and interactions that supported autistic neurology were consistent with and more affirming of autistic culture. The shift to these types of accommodations and different ways of engaging increased opportunity for those that struggled because of the social and sensory demands of workplace and school environments. We would suggest that people, businesses, agencies, schools, and communities consider things differently and maintain some of the policies they implemented during COVID-19 to include accommodations and alternative ways to accomplish tasks such as remote work, online schooling for some, and the option of virtual healthcare appointments where feasible. Some autistic individuals expressed that these changes reduced demands on both energy and masking. Some commented that these alternative methods of engaging in daily activities reduced the need to plan social avoidance and made natural interaction styles more acceptable (e.g., the guarantee that any in-person contact would need to be planned and purposeful with firmer and defined parameters around touching, space, and how to interact).

Based on informal polling of the autistic community, considering a permanent extension of some "alternative ways" of doing things that emerged during the pandemic are recommended in a wide range of settings (e.g., school, work, healthcare, community and interpersonal).

Setting	Accommodations
School	• Remote instruction proactively offered as an option to all students before school begins • Continued prioritization of increasing consistent access to technology for learners
Work	• Remote access to work proactively offered as an option to all employees (where feasible) • Flexible work schedules (i.e., focus on completion of work rather than the time of day it should be worked on)
Healthcare	• Telehealth appointments consistently offered as an option where feasible • Curbside pharmacy pickup

Community	• Grocery delivery / Curbside pickup and increased local delivery from restaurants with continued "leave it at the door" policies • Offering renewal of licenses and other government forms and processes online whenever feasible • Option to meet-up and engage in social opportunities virtually
Interpersonal	• Maintain planning and predictability of family / friend visits with explicit rules for contact and interaction

As we stated before, we don't see these accommodations or alternatives as a replacement for "the old normal" ways to engage in activities, environments, or interactions. We see these as additions of possibilities to increase access for those who traditionally have encountered frequent barriers to participation in these settings.

The pandemic has provided an unexpected and unique opportunity to reflect on what is possible when we are not constricted by "normal." The information gained from this unexpected social experiment should fuel progress. Indeed, we feel that a call to action for education, public health, psychology, and other social science researchers to formally evaluate and assess this unprecedented time is warranted to supplement and further understand the qualitative and anecdotal evidence that supports the maintenance of policies like those presented above. To paraphrase Maya Angelou, when we know better, we should do better. When we further know such practices are feasible, improve well-being for some, and may very well be needed at various times in the future, we argue that it is quite logical to maintain and integrate these practices into normalcy.

More about JÂcqûelyn and Amy . . .

As we enter life after lockdown, I am most concerned about . . .
humans humaning.

As we enter life after lockdown, I am most excited about . . .
*lowered risks, lowered or eliminated death counts, lower infected
counts, and recovery for those who struggled during lockdown.*

Dr. JÂcqûelyn Fede and Dr. Amy Laurent are Co-Directors of **Autism Level UP!** A partnership of two developmental psychologists, one neurodivergent and the other neurotypical. Our philosophy is that through education, accessible resources, practical strategies and a commitment to consistently incorporating the experiences and perspectives of autistic people, we can support the leveling up of society when it comes to autism and neurodiversity.

JÂcqûelyn is a super fun, Autistic Self-Advocate. She uses her experience to help educate others about autism through lecturing, blogging and consulting on evaluation projects in school districts and communities. A full scholarship division I athlete in college, she continues to meet her sensory needs by seeking extreme physical activity. She also enjoys the use of creativity and art for expression.

Amy is passionate about neurodiversity and helping others to honor and understand the implications of «different ways of being» in relation to navigating the physical and social world. She strives to practice what she preaches and uses her love of play and movement to meet her own regulatory needs.

With respect to lockdown ending and centering our thoughts on the autistic community we will offer only JÂcqûelyn's #ActuallyAutistic perspective.

Book

o   *All The FeelZzz* (an alternative way to communicate pain, difference, and discomfort in the body), JÂcqûelyn H. Fede and Amy Laurent

Website

www.autismlevelup.com

RESET

RUTH PRYSTASH & REBECCA SILVA

Eight thousand seven hundred and sixty.

That is the number of hours in one year—each hour a chance for both love and for loss, for growth and for regression. This year seems as if it lasted a lifetime, and now that we are coming to the end of this unique moment in history, it is time to evaluate what this year meant to each of us.

This year was a catalyst for self-reflection. The question is, can it be a catalyst for change? It is clear, now more than ever before, that all of us—neurodiverse and neurotypical—have more in common than not. How can we use that understanding to create meaningful change going forward? During the past year and a half, many autistic adults enjoyed the solitude and peace of being at home. So did neurotypical people. Many people on the spectrum thrived in virtual worlds—online shopping, telemedicine appointments, and virtual school. So did neurotypical people. Conversely, many autistic adults suffered from isolation, a lack of pleasurable activities, and the change in familiar and trusted routines, just as many neurotypical people did. And more than anything else, both neurodiverse and neurotypical people seemed to mourn the social interactions that keep us all connected.

This book has presented both strategies and stories. Many of those stories contain a common thread—that in some ways the lockdown wasn't as bad as we feared, while in other ways it was much worse than we could have imagined. Before we can plan how to proceed, let's examine the impact of the lockdown on autistic individuals from both points of view.

1. Many people on the spectrum enjoyed being at home. Home is safe and it is soothing. It is more predictable than the outside world, and is generally much calmer. There are fewer people to interact with every day.
2. People enjoyed the options of curbside pickup, telemedicine appointments, remote work and school, virtual meetings. Not only were these convenient, they were far less stressful and time-consuming.
3. People enjoyed having more control over their environment. Children had fewer demands placed on them. Adults had more free time.
4. Families spent more time together and relationships thrived.
5. Because of all of the above, many individuals experienced fewer meltdowns and distressing interactions.

Now let's look at the difficult side of the lockdown.

1. Not all individuals thrived at home. Some were frustrated by the changes in routines that had been established over the course of years. Not all homes were safer or calmer.

2. The virtual and distanced options could not meet everyone's needs. Virtual schooling was challenging without interpersonal interaction, and some individuals lost skills. Important

services and therapies were nearly impossible to provide in a virtual format.

3. Some individuals were unprepared for the amount of free time they had. Their lives had depended on routine and predictability, and their education had sometimes failed to teach them appropriate leisure skills.

4. Many individuals missed the social interactions and activities they had previously enjoyed.

5. Because of the reasons above, some individuals had more meltdowns, not less.

We live in a world that is designed to support the disability, not the person. Most systems are based on financial necessities and on the ability to cause the least disruption to society. Education, commerce, medicine—all search for the lowest common denominator. Build systems that keep most of the people—neurotypical as well as neurodiverse—reasonably satisfied. Discourage complaints. Resist change. Believe on some level that neurotypical individuals, due to their greater numbers, are the priority.

> **" We live in a world that is designed to support the disability, not the person. "**

So where do we go from here, and what can we deduce from this information? It is obvious that changes are needed, and it is equally obvious that changes can be made if they appear to benefit the majority. All individuals need to have options that suit their very specific needs because looking back, it seems fairly obvious that these needs have never been fully acknowledged or addressed. Perhaps the crucial lesson here is in seeing how we all are similar, and how the changes that need to be made can be made in a way that benefits us all. To get to this point, it is helpful to reflect on the voices from this book.

There is a stereotype that people on the spectrum are anti-social and have no interest in interactions or friendships. The autistic adult contributors in this book are talented, fascinating individuals who value human connection. They speak of friendships and of mentoring others, of connecting on deeper levels. Although these relationships and connections can be exhausting, causing the authors sensory overload and social anxiety, for these individuals the trade-off is worth it. Friendship, love, affection—these are the things that COVID stole.

> **66 Friendship, love, affection— these are the things that COVID stole. 99**

One chapter describes a group of young people who long for connection so fervently that they become immersed in virtual gaming worlds, often to an addictive degree, just to find those relationships.

Second, there is a subtle assumption that people with autism have "restricted interests," as if that makes them somehow "less." Their unique fascinations are seen as quaint or peculiar, rather than what they really are—interesting and unusual hobbies. In school they are often provided with the most basic curriculum, and are not exposed to the things that many neurotypical people find fulfilling— art, sports, hobbies, travel, history, music. Sydney Edmond, despite her sensory and communication obstacles, longs to experience live performances and the visual arts. Larry Bissonnette wants the freedom to spend time drinking coffee in a café without restrictions. Grant Vasquez, though dealing with powerful sensory obstacles, wishes to paint and express himself, while also getting back into the world and the things he enjoys. Ethan Dalusong found pure joy in a cross-country road trip, staring out the window in amazement at a wide world that is often denied to those who are different.

There are also professionals and experts whose chapters are filled with brilliant advice and suggestions on how to support people on the spectrum so that they can successfully return to school and the community with a minimum amount of stress and discomfort. There are stories of adults who seek meaningful life experiences, like college or employment. These individuals can use the strategies and tools from this book to more independently and successfully manage their lives. All individuals should be able to pursue their dreams and achieve their goals, but society doesn't always make it easy. Even professionals sometimes struggle with existing systems. As some of them point out, society is not set up to support the social and sensory needs of people on the spectrum, even though the accommodations that were made during the lockdown clearly show that these supports are not only possible, but welcomed by a large segment of the neurotypical population, as well.

And then there are the parents who want what we all want for our children—for them to feel secure and loved in their homes, and to experience health and safety from a deadly virus. Like parents everywhere, they want to know that their children are understood and valued by others for their unique talents and personalities, and that as adults, their children will have meaningful and enjoyable work, balanced with a rich and fulfilling social life. Although some families thrived during the lockdown while others struggled to survive, their goals are the same—that their children's diversity is embraced, understood, supported, and accepted.

So here is our conundrum. How can society work better for people with autism when we are dealing with deeply entrenched systems that make their lives more challenging? Despite contending with obstacles of both circumstance

> 66 . . . maybe we need to see everyone for exactly who they are—caring, growing, flawed, loving, imperfectly perfect human beings. 99

and attitudes, autistic people live, love, struggle, and survive just as all people do. If there is an answer, it lies in that understanding. Instead of noticing that autistic people sometimes flap, hum, and rock; avoid or run from others; resist or lash out at attempts to help, maybe we need to see everyone for exactly who they are—caring, growing, flawed, loving, imperfectly perfect human beings. We need to value our similarities while celebrating the uniqueness of autism. And we—neurodivergents and neurotypicals—need to come together to create a world that offers accommodations instead of creating obstacles, even if it means changing this world.

Providing flexible work situations is a good example of a beneficial option that was once seen as unrealistic or impossible, but became the norm in the pandemic when it was needed for the majority of non-disabled individuals. Virtual jobs reduce obstacles for those on the spectrum, including social and sensory challenges, as in-person workplaces can be difficult to navigate and tolerate for those with extreme needs. The fact that such options have never been common before now underscores the fact that people with ASD are not always seen as important contributors to the workforce. Everyone deserves to work. It is incredibly important not only as a means of self-support, but is crucial to self-esteem and a sense of self-worth.

Telemedicine appointments and curbside pickup became a comfortable norm for many people during the pandemic, creating a cushion of physical safety from the virus. But these things also allowed individuals who struggle with crowds and interpersonal interactions with strangers to maintain their health and independence while still functioning in society. It remains to be seen if medical systems and stores will continue to provide these options.

Educators struggled with virtual learning on many levels, as the current systems of instruction and assessment are based primarily on face-to-face methodologies. Virtual learning necessitated innovative solutions by teachers and also placed great responsibility on parents and caregivers, who were expected to supervise virtual school attendance at home and to facilitate instruction for students who needed more hands-on learning. Some students had trouble attending and missed out on additional services, often falling behind in some skills. Yet many students thrived in other ways, savoring the calm home environment and lack of sensory overload so common in classrooms. If the virtual learning model were to become an option, there would need to be innovation at all levels, with support for curriculum and new technologies provided to teachers and support personnel. There would need to be an enormous investment in education and training for parents, so that they would be more prepared for the challenges of facilitating instruction, an investment that is sorely needed even without the demands of the current situation.

These virtual options for work, shopping, medical care, and school may not work for all individuals. Some people may prefer the old way of doing things, and that is ok too. But there are many reasons to provide options. This pandemic may not be over yet, and even so, another pandemic may happen in the future. Technology, innovation, climate change, and diseases may all affect our society in the not-so-distant future. It makes sense to be prepared for the next time a lockdown occurs.

What is even more important is something deeper, more profound. We live in a world where the needs of the many outweigh the needs of the few, a practical approach but not always a compassionate one. If the options described above and in other sections of this book could be offered, why shouldn't they be? Why shouldn't people with differing needs be allowed to contribute to society in a meaningful way? If we could do this for everyone during the pandemic, there is no reason we can't do it for autistic individuals, as well as other-abled individuals.

These changes may be difficult. There will need to be a shift in attitudes, something that may be challenging even for those who are committed to supporting people with autism. In many service areas for those with special needs, there is an invisible wall—a wall that divides "us" from "them." This isn't limited to the autism community; society in general tries to label and rank people; it is an uncomfortable human trait. Look at how people with autism and other disabilities have long been described: moderate/severe/

profound; high-functioning/low-functioning; levels 1, 2, 3. There are always new labels that are supposedly more accurate and more socially acceptable. The question should be, why do we need these labels at all? Most individuals on the autism spectrum do not fit in a category. Someone can be nonverbal but brilliant; be employed and successful but struggle with sensory overload and impulsive behaviors; be outwardly nonresponsive but eager to interact with others.

There needs to be a better way to support different types of individuals. This will require seeing the person, rather than the disability, and will demand a perspective that sees people defined by their abilities, not their limitations. This doesn't mean ignoring a person's autism. Rather, it means embracing them for their autism, along with every other unique and beautiful quality they possess. The attitude shift will take time and effort and advocacy. It will take people requesting, demanding, or protesting for more options, and for change. Most importantly, it will take the single most important act of all: respect.

> **❝** Respect means accepting the individual—flaws and all, not just as students or clients, but as people who can contribute, work, volunteer, give to others, enjoy their own interests, exercise their own talents. **❞**

Respect means treating autistic individuals as neighbors, coworkers, friends. Respect means providing employment opportunities and educational options. Respect means friendship without pity or condescension. Respect means never talking about a person in front of them as if they aren't there. Respect means assuming that everyone, despite any signs to the contrary, understands and seeks to be understood. Respect means accepting the individual—flaws and all, not just as students or clients, but as people who can contribute, work, volunteer, give to others, enjoy their own interests, exercise their own talents.

Respect is hard to incorporate into a system, but if it happens, it will take each one of us. Person by person, we must build respect into everything we do. Every decision we make, every choice we offer must be guided by respect, by the belief that every person deserves to live a meaningful life and to find their own unique path in the world.

In the introduction, we remembered a time when people with disabilities were buried in graves with numbers, not names. It took decades of hard work and painful growth to reshape that mentality. Just as with other civil rights battles, this one had to tackle pervasive and subtle belief systems about differently-abled people. Perhaps now, this moment in time, this frightening COVID-induced pause in the world, can be our generation's watershed moment for change. Maybe the pandemic can be more than a dark memory. Maybe, just maybe, it can be the catalyst for something more.

Eight thousand seven hundred and sixty.

Three, two, one . . . reset.

More about Ruth . . .

As we enter life after lockdown, I am most concerned with . . .
  the indifference of humans toward other humans.

As we enter life after lockdown, I am most excited about . . .
  cafes, used bookstores, and traveling. And Comic Con!

My career has been spent as a teacher, university instructor, and consultant, but what has defined me as a person are the many souls with autism and other special needs of all ages—in state institutions, non-public schools, county programs, and school districts—who have shared their lives and their stories with me. My free-spirited daughter lives in Switzerland, and I share my own nerdy home with senior dogs, books, and the injured wildlife with whom I volunteer.

More about Rebecca . . .

🏠 As we enter life after lockdown, I am most concerned that . . .
we might miss this unique opportunity to bring about positive change.

😃 As we enter life after lockdown, I am most excited about . . .
family dinners at our favorite restaurant, and going back to Comic Con.

As a college student, I volunteered in a classroom of extraordinary students with severe challenges who set the course for my career. For the last 40 years, I have dedicated my life to improving the lives of students with disabilities and their families as a teacher, administrator, professional development specialist, university instructor, and author. My husband and I are blessed with two preschool grand-littles who bring joy and laughter to our lives every day.

Books

○   *The Transitions Curriculum*, with co-author Louise Fulton
○   *SANDI-FAST Online Assessment System*, with co-author Kate Cahill
○   *FLIPP the Switch 2.0: Mastering Executive Function Skills from School to Adult Life for Students with Autism*, with co-authors Carol Burmeister and Sheri Wilkins

ABOUT THE EDITORS . . .

REBECCA SILVA has dedicated her 40-year career to improving the lives of students with disabilities and their families as a teacher, administrator, professional development specialist, and university instructor. Dr. Rebecca has authored books and other resources related to autism, assessment, and transition from school to career and adult life. As an active member of local community organizations, she is committed to supporting children and adults with autism in pursuing their dreams and realizing their potential.

RUTH PRYSTASH has been an educator for over 40 years, sharing the lives and stories of neurodiverse individuals of all ages—in state institutions, non-public schools, county programs, and district classes—as an award-winning teacher, staff development specialist, and consultant. She currently works as an editor and writer, developing and writing books about ASD. Teacher Ruth believes that all individuals deserve the chance to have a rich and meaningful life.

RENÉ DELOSS has worked with individuals with ASD for 16 years, as an ABA tutor, a paraprofessional, a research assistant, and a special education teacher. She is currently an editor, working closely with authors and publishers to ensure that high-quality, innovative books about ASD are constantly advancing our expertise and knowledge. René believes that the most important part of being an educator or editor is making sure that students and authors know they are valued and respected—no matter what.

CAROL BURMEISTER has over 40 years of experience as a paraprofessional, general education teacher, special education teacher, program specialist, university instructor, and consultant in a variety of settings. Most recently, her work has focused on the crucial topic of executive function (EF), helping students, parents, and educators understand how teaching specific skills in childhood and adolescence can have a positive impact on adulthood. Carol has been instrumental in improving the lives of individuals through involvement in a variety of organizations at the local, state, and national levels.